The visible and invisible group

The International Library of Group Psychotherapy
and Group Process

General Editors

Dr Malcolm Pines
Institute of Group Analysis (London) and the Tavistock Clinic, London

Dr Earl Hopper
Institute of Group Analysis (London) and the London School of
Economics and Political Science

The International Library of Group Psychotherapy and Group Process is
published in association with the Institute of Group Analysis (London)
and is devoted to the systematic study and exploration of group
psychotherapy

The visible and invisible group

Two perspectives on group psychotherapy and group process

Co-therapists
Yvonne Agazarian
Richard Peters

Tavistock/Routledge
London and New York

First published in 1981
by Routledge & Kegan Paul Ltd

First published in paperback in 1989
by Routledge
11 New Fetter Lane, London EC4P 4EE
29 West 35th Street, New York, NY 10001

Printed and bound in Great Britain by
Biddles Ltd, Guildford and King's Lynn

British Library Cataloguing in Publication Data

Agazarian, Yvonne

    The visible and invisible group. two perspectives on
group psychotherapy and group process
1. Medicine. Psychoanalysis. Group therapy.
I. Title   II. Peters, Richard, *1930–*
616.89'17

    ISBN 0-415-03770-0

Library of Congress Cataloging in Publication Data available

Contents

Figures

Tables

Acknowledgments and dedication

We dedicate this work with gratitude to the memory of David H. Jenkins, our teacher and mentor, whose influence we felt most strongly in the task of defining at the operational level what we 'knew' in theory.

Our thanks to the many colleagues who have influenced our thinking, to the many students who have challenged it and to the many patients who have helped us put it into practice.

Our specific thanks to Claudia Byram and Patricia White for their devotion and bravery in repeatedly confronting us with the need to clarify and edit what we had written; to Sally Cicalla and Mary Lovell for salvaging our deadlines by their weekends and evenings of flawless typing and their cheerful encouragement of *us* when so much of their work was re-typing; and to Linda and Berj for their support, encouragement and love, for their patience, for their feedback, for their contributions to the text over long hours of discussion, and most particularly for managing the impact of our authors' frustrations so that our interpersonal lives were richer, not poorer, when this work was done.

Introduction

There is a need for a book on the technique of group psychotherapy. Although this form of treatment has existed for many years now, one searches in vain for anything resembling the detailed discussion of technical problems that can be found in the literature of individual psychotherapy. The psychoanalytic literature, for example, contains numbers of excellent manuals on technique.

In the field of group, however, there is a serious need for a comprehensive volume bringing together the theory of group and the various problems of technique in a unified way. Such a volume needs to be much more than a 'cookbook' containing recipes for solving this and that technical problem.

We have just emerged from the effects of the era of the 1960s, which gave birth to a plethora of encounter group techniques and a minimum of even rudimentary theoretical considerations. The watchword of the 1960s movement was 'do your own thing', and the major criterion for leading groups was prior experience as a member; often a single experience of short duration was considered sufficient. As the outcomes of such intuitive leadership have proved to be disastrous, the need for thorough training, clear guidelines for technique and, above all, for a theoretical framework from which technical innovations can be derived, tested and revised, becomes clear once again. Psychotherapy must be a rational process from the point of view of the psychotherapist; only the patient can afford to, and should, experience it as highly emotional and intuitive.

Group psychotherapy is a rational process, a technique that can be learned by those whose personality structure and developmental histories provide the necessary prerequisites. Just as individual psychoanalytic psychotherapy is a rigorous and uncompromising discipline so, too, is group psychotherapy. As the rules of individual psychotherapy,

1

together with their theoretical bases, must be thoroughly mastered, so must those of group psychotherapy be thoroughly mastered.

Happily, the day of the group with a capital 'G' is over. Most of the gurus have turned to other, more current sources of pleasure. The devotees of instant intimacy have either found such 'intimacy' to be as lacking in quality as the other 'instants' abounding in our culture, or they have followed 'touchie-feelie' exercises to their logical and inevitable conclusion – group sex (an excellent defense against intimacy). In America, the lush funding available to various educational, defense and social welfare institutions has dried up or is differently allocated: exotic training designs are no longer spawned with a maximum of intuition and a minimum of theoretical and practical knowledge, and those in the field concerned with ethical standards have formed a voluntary accreditation association (the International Association of Applied Social Scientists, USA). With this timely departure has also passed the excess of publicity and/or notoriety which accompanied the group movement of the late 1960s and early 1970s.

So much for the group field that escaped from the medical model. For group psychotherapy that comes under the aegis of approved institutions as 'professionally respectable' there are also no clearly specified criteria for what methods are therapeutic and what are not. So pressing is this issue that, in its January 1975 newsletter, the American Group Psychotherapy Association sent out a call to the members to submit details of unusual procedures that both did and did not prove therapeutic. The professional organization of the group field itself has no clear framework for judging therapeutic structure and is still at the data collection level.

Those of us who are serious students of group psychology in general, and group psychotherapy in particular, can, once again, work in a relatively neutral atmosphere toward the further development of those more valuable concepts and techniques which have survived, most of which predated the 1960s, in any case. This book is one example of such work.

The book contains three parts. The first section is devoted to an exposition of the theoretical concepts which we think best explain the phenomena observable in psychotherapy groups. The second section discusses such problems as patient selection and initial preparation, group developmental phases, interventions and other fundamentals in the technique of group psychotherapy. The final section explores in some detail the question of co-therapy, transference and counter-transference and other more sophisticated issues in group psychotherapy. This, then, is the plan of this book. We will say more about the content of the three sections, and the reasons for our method of organizing them, below.

Perhaps the major stumbling block for theorists of group psychology is whether or not a group is entitled to be conceptualized as an independent entity. Without citing the large literature on the subject, let us simply state that the issue is between those who cannot satisfactorily explain many of the observable phenomena using theories based on the behavior of individuals, and those who find the concept that the group is different from the sum of its parts nonsensical. We take the position that this is not a simple academic difference. Rather, it is a difference that will govern how therapeutic the group can become.

The therapist must be able to recognize the manifestations of group dynamics if he is to work with them. It is the recognition, diagnosis and manipulation of these group dynamics in a deliberate manner that permits a group therapist to facilitate the development of the group into a tool of effective therapy. Without the necessary understanding and technique, the group therapist will be as subject to the resistant and fixating influences within each phase of group development as any other 'member' of the group. In individual therapy, the therapist must be able to diagnose individual dynamics and transference at a theoretical level, analyze his counter-transference, and use his interventions as a deliberate therapeutic influence. In group therapy, the group therapist must be able to diagnose, analyze and use his interventions, not only as a deliberate influence in relationship to the individual patients, but also, in a different manner, to the group as a whole. If he cannot do this, then the therapist is simply doing individual therapy in the presence of a group of people.

It is for this reason that we take the position that the group psychotherapist must understand two sets of laws, and be able to talk in two languages: the language of individual dynamics and the language of group dynamics. If this assumption is untenable to the reader, he will wish to proceed no further; if he is amenable to a discussion of the matter, we will try to make our schema as clear as possible.

We have defined a theory of group development that encompasses two sets of laws: one set of laws for understanding individual dynamics and one set of laws for understanding group dynamics. For describing and understanding the behavior of group, the authors have developed a theory of group whose building blocks are Lewin's field theory and systems analysis. Group is conceptualized as a system with two major component systems, the individual system and the group-as-a-whole system. From the perspective of the group-as-a-whole, all phenomena of group can be described without referring to the individual members who make up the group. This is the perspective which defines the *invisible group*, the group that only exists through theoretical eyes. However, as we intend to demonstrate, it is only by being able to perceive the invisible group that the group psychotherapist can make therapeutic use of the *group*. Understanding both group *and* individual dynamics permits therapeutic influence to be applied to the individual or directly to the group-as-a-whole or to both simultaneously. This dual focus increases the therapeutic potential for the individual in a complexity of ways which will be described in the first section of this book.

For describing and understanding the behavior of individuals, the authors rely on the psychoanalytic model. Since many a Tom, Dick and Harry has seen fit to call his own pet theory 'psychoanalysis', we must identify what we mean by the term. We will adhere to the mainstream or classical psychoanalytic model as represented by the works of Sigmund Freud, and modern interpreters like Edward Glover, Heinz Hartmann, Heinz Kohut, Otto Kernberg and Peter Giovacchini. While we are fully aware of what we believe is a temporary decline in the interest shown in psychoanalytic theory, we have not found any other theory that explains personality dynamics better or with more comprehensiveness. We will, therefore, use psychoanalytic theory as a base to describe the developmental and etiological bases for our patients' emotional problems, to assess their potential for change, to understand their resistances to change and to interpret their conflicts.

The authors define only the psychoanalytic constructs necessary to our argument. A number of detailed expositions of psychoanalytic theory already exist, and to repeat them is not within the practical scope or utility of this book. Where our use of psychoanalytic terms deviates from the standard explanations, we have defined them in the glossary. Where psychoanalytic terminology is used and not defined in our glossary, the definition of the terms is the same as that found in Laplanche and Pontalis (1973). Where we have modified terms to apply strictly to group psychotherapy, we have discussed and defined their meaning fully in the text.

The theoretical discussion of group dynamics is limited, in much the same manner as with psychoanalytic terms, to those variables and concepts necessary for understanding group psychotherapy. Unlike psychoanalytic theory, such information is not readily available in a form useful to psychotherapists, and the reader of a book like this one cannot be presumed to be familiar with it. A partial list of selected topics at the end of the book provides the reader with recommended reading, should he wish to pursue any subject in more detail. For those who wish to question statements made by the authors, which lie outside the authors' special field, this section will be especially useful; e.g., for those who question or are curious about the statement made in the next chapter concerning the evolutionary advantages conferred by any genetically transmitted behavioral tendencies that aid a group to breed more successfully, references to source reading are provided in the recommended reading section.

One further comment on the simultaneous use of the group-as-a-whole and psychoanalytic theoretical models. Both represent more a way of approaching and examining psychological phenomena than a hard and fast set of constructs. It is axiomatic that whenever more than one set of constructs or theoretical approaches is used to describe and analyze the same problems, e.g., atomic, sub-atomic and molecular theories, there must be no contradiction between them, and they must not yield contradictory or mutually exclusive explanations or predictions. The group-as-a-whole theory and psychoanalysis are not, in that sense, in conflict. The constructs of field theory, systems analysis and psycho-analysis yield complementary explanations of human behavior and dynamics from which predictions can be derived and tested.

Thus we have used psychoanalytic constructs and language to describe the individual patient's dynamics, and the transference phenomenon that operates between the patient and the therapist and between the patient and other members of the group; and we have used the language of group dynamics to describe the patient's role in the developmental and ongoing dynamics of the group and the patient's part in group transferential phenomena. We have used the language defined in the glossary to define group-as-a-whole. For example, the psychoanalytic model describes the unconscious displacements each group member makes of expectations and affects experienced during childhood and adolescence, and belonging to particular individuals and parental imagos, onto other group members, including the therapist. The group theoretical model, on the other hand, describes the structure that develops within an ongoing psychotherapy group, details the developmental phases of the group (including group negative and positive transference which emerges as a property of group development), and focuses on the forces that operate within the channels provided by group structure. In so doing, it provides a tool for predicting, recognizing, and dissolving the blocks and inhibitions that occur during the various developmental stages of the group in its problem-solving processes.

Even the Behaviorists are coming to see that psychotherapy is a complex process. Why then create further difficulty by adding a group dimension, if that addition entails the mastery of another dimension of technical know-how? The group situation presents attributes which are unique to itself and which can increase the power of the tools already possessed by the skilled individual psychotherapist. It is for this reason that we propose that the mastery of group theory is the only route to mastery of what is in fact another dimension of psychotherapeutic technique which yields attributes that are specific to itself.

Some of these attributes are:

1 group therapy is (or should be) less expensive and hence available to the less affluent;
2 with certain patients the one-to-one setting has a built-in resistance to feedback from the therapist; it is a 'my point of view against yours' situation. The presence of several other people removes that obstacle and may even put the patient in an 'everybody's out of step but Johnny' position in cases where his perception is particularly unrealistic;
3 data on the patient's modes of social interaction are available in a larger quantity; in the case of some patients who avoid social situations, important data are generated which would not otherwise come under therapeutic scrutiny;
4 in a further ramification of the above second and third points, the therapist has available a first-hand view of the patient's distortions of his interactions with others;
5 the patient can observe problems, behaviors and feelings similar to his own while maintaining a more comfortable psychological distance; since the behavior is not his own, he can look on it more objectively and then eventually be more ready to focus on his own version of it; the fact that the other group member is not destroyed or ostracized is particularly useful in helping the observing patient to acknowledge his own behaviors (developing and strengthening his observing ego);
6 the security provided by group support for individual members allows those individuals to ask questions of themselves or each other that might be difficult or impossible for them in a one-to-one therapy situation;
7 the patient can observe and experience different or more appropriate behaviors in others, leading to new and more desirable outcomes; this is qualitatively different from getting advice *about* new or more appropriate behaviors;
8 following from this, an established group provides a supportive

setting in which new behaviors can be tried out and, if successful, practiced;

9 patients can 'check-out' their projections with their peers; this is lower risk behavior for the patient than using a therapist for that purpose, but helps build ego strength toward that harder task;

10 there are many patients whose frustration tolerance and overall ego strength are not sufficient to permit them to work through certain issues, such as archaic or strong positive or negative transferences, in individual psychotherapy. For such patients, group psychotherapy provides the potential for exploring and working through individual transference issues via the medium of the group transference – a resource unavailable in the individual setting;

11 the problems of very strong transference which are too hard on the counter-transference of all but the most experienced and secure psychotherapists are more easily and successfully faced by therapists in a group setting when a co-therapist is present;

12 in groups employing co-therapists, a wider range of skills in diagnosis of situations and intervention is available and a far more effective check against counter-transference behavior is provided; the above only holds true where we are talking about highly trained and competent co-therapists, not where one or both are untrained or apprentice therapists.

About the authors

We, the authors, think ourselves particularly qualified to write this book for several reasons. We share a great deal of experience and training which is highly relevant for the subject matter. Both of us studied at the Psychoanalytic Studies Institute where we were trained in the discipline of psychoanalytic theory and technique. Both of us are grounded in general academic psychology and were students of group dynamics under the late eminent Lewinian scholar, David Jenkins. During the group movement of the 1960s, we took part in many training laboratories of various kinds and were, in the course of that, exposed to the best and the worst of those who were thinking about and leading groups at that time. Both of us were experienced individual psychotherapists before attempting group therapy and one of us (RP) had the valuable experience of attempting to do group psychotherapy first without, then later with, the insights provided by the group dynamics concepts. Finally, we were both heavily exposed to various eclectic and even downright 'wild' psychotherapies during the course of our training and experience as psychotherapists. This, along with the increasing sophistication of psychoanalytic theory and technique, has led to an informed choice of classical psychoanalytic thinking and technique on both of our parts, a result of increasing experience rather than religiosity or indoctrination.

We have practiced together as co-therapists since 1968, and have been working separately and together with group since the very early 1960s. Our combined group experience totals over seven thousand hours in group therapy! In our work with groups, our discussions about groups, our lecturing and supervision of group therapists, we have done considerable refining and formalizing of our ideas. Overall our approach was, and continues to be, remarkably similar. Whereas our styles of working contain some important differences, the differences come together as complementary, and provide us both with a broader scope than either of us has separately. We are pleased to find that each of us understands with ease theoretical and technical group issues which were often difficult to convey to other professionals. Each of us is able to complement the gaps in the other's conceptual schema.

Our joint endeavor in writing this book has required of us the same skills and co-operation in our work that our co-therapy endeavor has required. It is probable that we have worked together as smoothly and as well as we have in this task of writing because of the years that we have spent in learning how to work together in group. As in group, we have found that for certain tasks a joint venture paid off handsomely; for example, the chapter on special problems in group. We have also found that in certain other chapters it has made more sense for one of us to establish the direction while the other supported us in our work: for example, our division of the psychoanalysis and group dynamics aspects of this book. Thus, in our group of two, we find that our work together has permitted each of us to develop and contribute individually in ways that we doubt would have occurred had we not been members of our two-person co-therapy group! The product of this group's work represents, perhaps, more creative individuality than we could have achieved had we not experienced such close collaboration. Having spoken of our membership in our group, we will now speak of our individuality.

I, Richard Peters, first undertook to convince my co-therapist Yvonne that we should write this book. I was aware that the time had come to present what I considered our unique ways of thinking about and working with psychotherapy groups in a systematic and comprehensive way.

It became clear to both of us as we began to sketch out the contents of this book that Yvonne was the group theoretician and I was the psychoanalytic theoretician. As such I took as my second task the major responsibility for the *individual* perspective of group: that which is subsumed under the headings of the Person and Member systems.

In the process of teaching, supervising and practicing group psychotherapy, my thinking has been validated, challenged, stretched and greatly enriched by students and colleagues, but most of all by the patients who have shared their lives and their discoveries with each other and me.

As Yvonne and I viewed therapy from group and individual points of view in the course of our years of working together, constant probing of theoretical issues validating or discarding ideas in the group arena has resulted in the conviction with which our theoretical positions are held. Without the aid of Yvonne's rigorous conceptual thought, so freely shared, I would not have achieved the overview of group that I now possess. While I arrived at my psychoanalytic ideas about group independently, I find that these ideas fit very easily into those of the group analytic thinkers, and I have made use of their contributions.

The major application of my psychoanalytic thinking is reflected in the sections of this work where co-therapy, transference and countertransference are the focus. This entailed an examination of the role and person of each of us as group therapists. From a psychoanalytic point of view, next to inadequate training, counter-transference is the single major determinant of the success or failure of a group psychotherapy session, or of group psychotherapy.

The presence of each other as co-therapist affected our countertransference reactions as surely as they affected our income, and the extra time that we needed to devote to processing both the group's dynamics and our own interpersonal co-therapy dynamics. The Scylla and Charybdis of the psychotherapist are the feelings of omnipotence resulting from being greatly overvalued because of the positive transference on the one hand, and the anxiety and loss of self-esteem from the pitiless attacks of the negative transference on the other. We each experienced the other as a powerful support, a reality confronter, and an antidote both to the seduction of omnipotence and to the debilitating effects of severe hostility from patients.

I have found that counter-transference effects are strongly intensified in the group situation. I also note that there is a greater demand on our resources, caused by the necessity of paying attention to the needs of individual patients, the two-dimensions of our technique, and the requirements of co-operating with each other. It is from the never-ceasing challenge of continually developing, both as a group therapist and as a co-therapist, that I have formulated how significantly different group psychotherapy is from individual psychotherapy. It is this understanding as it applies to the psychoanalytic aspects of our theory that I hope to have shared in this book.

I, Yvonne Agazarian, took the major responsibility for formulating the theory of group dynamics, and working together with Dick in its applications to group as we knew and practiced it together.

Thus chapters 2 and 3 are the first presentations of a theory of group dynamics I first started formulating with Dave Jenkins in 1963. To the extent that these conceptualizations reflect his influence and teaching, I present them with pride. The schema of the three levels of group (chapter 6) is an expanded version of a model I developed for the group psychotherapy department of the Community Mental Health Center of the Pennsylvania Hospital between 1965 and 1970. The adaptation of the phases of group development from the Bennis and Shepard schema (chapter 5) has been an ongoing discussion between Dick and me since we first began our work together as co-therapists. In its present form, it is an expansion of a paper that was originally published in 1968. The chapter on the constructs of group (chapter 4) is the product of much discussion between Dick and me, as well as many, many hours of challenge from students in my group psycho-therapy courses. It would be impossible to separate out the many important modifications of my thinking that have come about under the influence of the ideas of you, Dick, and you, my students and colleagues. Although it is no longer possible for me to identify who gave me what, I hope that the current formulation of group dynamics constructs that are presented here provides you with a *déjà vu* experi-ence, and perhaps the pleasure in the part that your ideas have played throughout this book.

About the contents of the book

Chapter 1 provides a general picture of what goes on in psychotherapy groups. It focuses on the contributions of psychoanalysis and group theories to the understanding of the various phenomena observable or deduceable in the course of group psychotherapy. An illustrative group is manufactured in order to demonstrate the behavioral or operational data as they might, and typically do, occur in real groups. The group behavior is interpreted from several levels of both individual and group perspectives.

Chapter 2 presents the visible and invisible group. The inductive perspective from which the visible group can be observed is differentiated from the deductive perspective, from which the invisible group can be understood. Lewin's life space is adapted to systems analysis. Group is described in terms of four systems, each one of which is capable of being modified by the other three. Two of these systems, person and member, are sub-systems of the individual system and define the visible group. Two of these systems, role and group, are sub-systems of the group-as-a-whole system and define the invisible group. The relationship between the systems is explained in terms of communication channels that contain ambiguities, contradictions and redundancies in the reality and irreality information that they contain. The generalization of group development theory to group psychotherapy is explained, and the work of Bion, and Bennis and Shepard, is outlined in general terms as a basis for later chapters. A summary table presents a comparison between the dynamics of the visible and invisible group.

Chapter 3 presents the theory of the invisible group. Clinical examples of 'Ann' are given to demonstrate the usefulness to the psychotherapist of perceiving group dynamics in General Systems Theory terms, and the correspondence between this approach and psychodynamic interpretations at the individual and group level. A two-page table summarizes the theory of the invisible group in terms of the theoretical hierarchy, definitions of communication behavior and the types of theory and constructs that apply to the four conceptual systems: person, member, role and group-as-a-whole.

Chapter 4 presents the basic constructs of group dynamics: communication, role, norms, cohesiveness, goals and structure. At the end of chapter 4 is a summary table which demonstrates how each of these constructs can be defined in terms of perspectives of the person and member systems of the visible group; and the role and group systems of the invisible group.

Chapter 5 presents the phases of group development that are potential for all psychotherapy groups, together with criteria for diagnosing fixations in development. At the end of chapter 5 is a summary table which adapts the Bennis and Shepard schema (appendix 1) to the psychotherapy group. Bennis and Shepard's phase of dependent-power relations has been interpreted in relationship to Bion's basic assumption flight-fight groups, and their phase of interdependence personal relations has been interpreted in terms of the basic assumption pairing group.

Their barometric event has been related to the transference neurosis. All basic assumption groups have been displayed against the matrix of the work group, whose task varies according to the phase of development that the group is engaged in.

Chapter 6 presents three levels of group process which differentiate between three types of group based upon group goals. The summary table at the end of chapter 6 defines, for each of the three levels, the group goal; the operational objectives; membership criteria; diagnostic guides; behavioral emphasis; therapist's orientation; group achievement criteria; expected phases of group development.

In chapter 7, after a brief description of the general aims and techniques of the psychoanalytic diagnostic interview, the reader is told how to prepare a patient for group psychotherapy. This is done by discussing those issues which are likely to arise and by providing some general guidelines for handling them. The kinds of information that the patient ought to be given are presented along with the rationale for giving or withholding information.

Chapter 8 addresses specific problems in group psychotherapy at the practical level. These are: acting out and its many meanings; socializing between members; boundary behavior; group decision making; issues in members joining and leaving group; group silences; working with another therapist's group; and group size.

Chapter 9 begins by defining and examining the related phenomena of transference and counter-transference as they occur in psychoanalysis. It then extends the use of these concepts into the psychotherapy group primarily at the member level. The uses and possible dangers inherent in transference and counter-transference phenomena as they apply to group psychotherapy are discussed. The chapter provides a bridge for the individual psychotherapist to extend his skills into the realm of group at the member level and prepares him to understand in a personal way the phenomenon of the role for the group.

Chapter 10 is a brief excursion into the specific advantages or disadvantages that result from adoption of the co-therapy method of doing group psychotherapy. These are listed and discussed. The authors make no secret of their preference for the co-therapy method and present what they consider to be powerful arguments on its behalf.

Chapter 1
Two sets of laws

For reasons not always clear, there has been more rivalry and competition between applied and academic psychology than co-operation. This competitive spirit has played no small part in the development of a group dynamics versus psychoanalysis competition in group psychotherapy. Is this a meaningful difference which will some day be resolved in favor of one or the other? We think not. Here one is reminded of the bitter heredity versus environment controversy, which was resolved by interaction theory in favor of both.

The group dynamics approach stems from that branch of academic psychology which had its origin in the gestalt movement and at present is best represented by field theory (Cartwright, 1951; Lewin, 1948). The major theoretician of field theory, Kurt Lewin, believed his formulations to be in opposition to those of psychoanalysis. That was a conclusion that is not shared by many of us who are thoroughly familiar with both models, e.g., Foulkes and Anthony (1973). The psychoanalytic approach, on the other hand, originated largely in the applied field, particularly from psychiatry and clinical psychology (Fine, 1973). Both theoretical formulations have much of value to say about what goes on in groups, and both are quite sophisticated, avoiding the simplistic solutions that are so frequent nowadays in the psychotherapy world.

An interactive theory that makes use of important and relevant aspects of psychoanalysis and group dynamics is the approach we advocate in this book. The fact of the matter is that group dynamics developed as a method and a set of hypotheses about the behavior of groups and the behavior of individuals as members participating in specific groups. Hence the behavior of individuals was seen as heavily influenced by the effects of the group: the individuals were behaving as parts or components of the group, not simply as separate individuals (Lewin, 1948). This argument rests on the notion that when a group develops out of a collection of individuals, i.e. develops a recognizable and stable structure, the members are seen as *parts* of the group entity. As such they behave in matters relating to the group as interdependent members of the group, subject to the psychological laws governing the expenditure of energies within the group and to the group's aims and goals. This state of affairs is not to be viewed as antithetical to the aims and goals of the individual; he is not a slave to the group against his own interests. Nothing could be further from the truth. *He is, in fact, serving his own best interest in the way afforded by the situation in which he finds himself.* The overall aims of the group are congruent with the overall aims of the individual and represent his surest way of achieving his own aims. This is not less true because he sometimes is frustrated by his role in the group in a given situation.

The available evidence indicates that man in his present psychological and physical state evolved as a member of a small group; his existence depended upon it. The evolutionary edge was in favor of those who performed so as to achieve the group's aims, large and small; these added up to group survival and hence survival of the largest number of individuals. And children could not grow up to breed without the group's protection. Population genetics has made it clear that even a very small breeding advantage will prove decisive over relatively short evolutionary spans of time (Dobzhansky, 1962).

The degree to which the norms of a small group (of ten members or more, including children and infants) control the behavior of its members can not easily be appreciated by modern, urbanized, mass man, with his relative alienation from the extended family, neighbors, and community. In the remaining hunting-gathering groups, such as the Bushmen, this group orientation is abundantly clear; almost all behaviors and aims of the individual are congruent with the breeding survival of the group.

Psychoanalysis originally grew out of the intensive clinical study of individuals and their behavioral aberrations. It began as a theory of mental illness, but soon focused on the developmental history of behaviors, including their transformations, apparent disappearances, and later reappearances. Most of all psychoanalysis became a tool, a methodology aimed at collecting data for intense longitudinal studies of the individual. As such it gave rise to an everchanging, growing body of hypotheses, deriving from the data brought to light by the method. And, despite the religiosity of some of its proponents, it continues to be open to further theoretical growth and development; the tremendous amount of work being done on ego theory is a case in point.

It is useful here to describe the psychological elements of the small group as it is likely to be found in a psychotherapeutic setting. This description may serve to clarify where the group dynamics model is most applicable and to point out where its limitations are such as to make it more useful to resort to a second theoretical model.

The group that we observe consists of, let us say, eight patients and two psychotherapists. That this visible group has a structure (a set of established relationships of various sorts) is not clearly evident. That it has norms (unwritten rules of behavior that apply to the members) is even less evident, and it would take a number of sessions for an observer to become aware of these norms. The group has a goal (an aim shared by all members), and this would be equally unclear without careful study. All the observer would actually see is a number of people talking to one another. It might be noted that the members tended to talk one at a time, and that the topic frequently turned to the past or present relations of the members to one another. The observer might note also that two of the members (the therapists) were less active in word and gesture than the others, that the members typically performed different functions, that there were task-oriented and feelings-oriented members, that the group climate was constantly fluctuating.

To anyone familiar with individual depth psychology, it is not surprising that much goes on in interactions between people that does not announce itself to the uninitiated eye; this is true wherever the workings of scientific laws are sought for. Watching a psychoanalytic situation, one would not expect an untrained person to immediately observe the transference, see the regression, measure the fixations, tick off the defense mechanisms as they appear, and so on. Yet these phenomena would be operating, often with powerful effect upon what occurs in, and results from, the therapeutic interview.

The group likewise has phenomena operating that only a trained observer is aware of. It has *structure*: communication and relationship patterns of who will likely talk to whom, who likes whom, who dislikes whom, and who gives influence and under what conditions. It has *norms*: members are expected to do so and so at such and such a point; they are expected to be on time; not to be absent without good reason; and a number of other explicit and implicit behavioral prescriptions that affect the function, not only of the members, but also of the group-as-a-whole. It has *goals*: both the goals that the therapist is aware of, like the well-being and psychological growth of its members, and goals that emerge at the level of group-as-a-whole that can be inferred by observing the group behavior. It has *roles*: individual members can be characterized as task leaders, or maintenance leaders, or leaders of diversion, or of conflict. In addition, different members and sub-groups play different roles for the group at different times, responsive less to individual needs and more to the forces in the group-as-a-whole.

In addition to and concurrent with the above, the members as individuals are in various transference states with one another: typically the therapists are the parental imagos, and the other members are siblings, mates, relatives, teachers, or other significant figures from the past. These individual level relations between the members are determined by compromises between their conscious egos and their unconscious defense mechanisms, regressions, fixations, wishes, resistances, and conflicts.

Group dynamics can tell us what sorts of conflicts and problems to expect during the various developmental stages of the group: what problem-solving issues will arise and how to cope with them; what functional roles are necessary in order for a group to achieve specific sorts of goals. These are all group issues, whose resolution is absolutely essential to the effective functioning of the therapy group.

Psychoanalytic thinking provides to the group theorist precisely what group dynamics does not provide and what psychotherapy needs, an approach to the problem of why *one* given individual (or given part of this group) does what he does within the framework of the group's structure, norms, and goals. It is obvious that one does not create a group therapy situation in order to treat the group. Group psychotherapy is ultimately for the individual; he predated the therapy group and he will be going about his business after it no longer exists or he is no longer a member of it. It is equally obvious that in any group performing complex behaviors relevant to a group goal, everyone does something different: leadership and other roles and functions are differentially allotted. Why does A perform task functions and B perform social maintenance? If A is incapacitated or absent, why does C rather than anyone else perform A's functions and then surrender those functions when A returns, or not surrender them? Group dynamics will describe the necessary roles and functions of a group, and the pressures relevant to understanding and predicting the phenomena associated with those functions. Psychoanalysis must provide the information we need if we are to understand *who* will perform the functions and *why* those who do not, will not or cannot.

In order to help the individual to make the changes he wishes or needs to make, we must understand the individual, i.e., psychoanalytic dynamics that he brought with him into the group. In short, we need a two-theory system for understanding and performing group psycho-therapy; we need the group's dynamics and the individual's dynamics.

Let us return to our hypothetical group and observe how a two-theory psychotherapist would use theoretical models to make concrete interventions, aimed at facilitating the therapeutic process. The group's present topic is: when will the members be prepared to admit a new member to fill an existing vacancy? This subject has resulted from one therapist's remark at the close of the preceding session that she had a possible candidate for the group, which lacked one member. There is bickering over who cares and who does not care about this issue. Periodically the members try to get the therapists to say what they (the therapists) want. Tension grows over several sessions with the members increasingly voicing their sense of impotence in the matter, 'because they (the therapists) have really made the decision anyway – it doesn't matter what we say!' Patient A is somewhat detached and depressed as the process continues. Patient B feels that one of the therapists is trying to manipulate her and 'always puts me in a position where I have to do what I don't want to do.' Patient C thinks that the other therapist is no angel, either. Patient D alternates between feeling that he is 'not a person' when he 'has to accept' someone he doesn't want, and expressing rage against the female therapist for putting him in the situation. Patient E, having asked one therapist an unanswerable question, i.e., 'will this new patient make a long-term commitment to the group?' berates the therapist about her cruelty in not answering questions; she cries and says that the therapist doesn't care about her. Patient F shrinks her chubby body into her chair and looks increasingly frightened and small; she says nothing. Patient G persistently rephrases the issue by asking *whether* or not they should have a new member at all. Periodically patient H aggressively and abruptly changes the subject to today's argument with his wife: he speaks bitterly and loudly, but there is the quality of a monologue about his words, and indeed no one listens. All passively await the end of his interruptions, or seize the first opportunity to return to the topic at hand. To anyone as familiar with the individual dynamics of these people as the two therapists are, at this point, it would not be difficult to make individual interpretations based on the psychoanalytic model. These interpretations would be accurate but incomplete, and often ineffective. The psychoanalytic rule for interpretation, interpret only the level that is available to the patient's preconscious, holds also in group psychotherapy. However, as we will discuss in detail below, there is a modification of this rule that is necessary and appropriate to the group situation. The tension *at the group level* ordinarily must be resolved before individual dynamics can be looked at, otherwise the group will not 'hear', i.e., cannot make use of interpretations illuminating the individual dynamics of its members.

The group dynamics model provides the therapists with the following explanations which seem to fit the behavioral data observed: first, an established group will strongly resist an unknown new member because the whole existing structure of the group is jeopardized, and in an unknown way; this means to the members that in every significant dimension people will have to reposition themselves relative to each other in order to accommodate to the new member, and worst of all no one can tell if his or her needs will be met as well as before, or in the same way as before; second, the group will return to earlier behaviors (regress) under the high stress (frustration) resulting from such a threat; this means that it will attempt to abdicate the decision-making role it had previously achieved and try to force the therapists to make the decision for it, i.e., become authority figures. The inaction (refusal) of the therapists in regard to this demand heightens the anger and anxiety experienced by the group. Resolution is possible only when the group has generated sufficient data to indicate that perhaps the group is ready to recognize the validity of the group level interpretation. The interpretation is made that the group does not want to do the hard work of making a decision (which means facing its fears), accepting the responsibility for its consequences, and is wishing that the therapists would take away that necessity and that responsibility by making the decision for the group.

For purposes of illustration we shall assume that the interpretation was made emphatically and with proper timing, i.e., was on target and was accepted by the group. The group members then show releases of tension by sighs and by acknowledging the wish that the therapists would do the job for them; this is quickly followed by the members expressing their real fears about the consequences of accepting the new member. These expressions of fear are identified as, or followed by, associations about the past or childhood experiences of the individual members, which permit individual psychoanalytic interpretations to be made where needed. The number of such interpretations is limited only by two factors: first the overriding consideration that the group session should, in so far as is possible, *not* become an individual session performed in a group setting - an outcome that cannot be avoided whenever the therapist is not aware of, nor skilled in, the priorities of group level work; second the psychoanalytic rule that the material to be interpreted individually be already in the individual's preconscious.

In actual practice the first rule is probably violated more frequently than the second; much of what passes for group psychotherapy is simply individual psychotherapy done in a group setting, and unless the psychotherapist has been trained in the recognition and interpretation of group level phenomena it could not be otherwise.

So far it looks like a very simple thing to do group psychotherapy; one deals with group level behaviors at the group level and, following that, one uses one's psychoanalytic expertise to move into the individual members' areas of conflict as revealed during the session, making individual psychoanalytic interpretations much as one would do in an individual setting. The facts of the matter are, however, otherwise. There is the matter of *resonance* and amplification.

Laplanche and Pontalis (1973) note that 'resonance "from unconscious to unconscious" constitutes the only authentically psychoanalytic form of communication.' This is the phenomenon which is responsible for much of what is called interpretation, transference, and counter-transference, and thus lies at the very heart of the psychoanalytic method. It is clear that if resonance between their respective unconsciouses takes place in an interpersonal unit of two – the psychoanalytic dyad – it will take place in interpersonal situations where larger numbers of people interact closely. Credit for extending this notion to groups probably belongs to Foulkes (Pines, in press) and the concept is widely utilized in the group analytic literature (Foulkes, 1965; Pines, in press).

We define resonance in group psychotherapy as follows: resonance is a form of communication between group members which takes place primarily at an unconscious level, and is a function of the interdependent, affective responses of members to particular shared conflicts as stimulated in the group's working together, e.g., separation, castration, oedipal rivalry and resulting in amplification of the particular theme being resonated. This is called the 'condenser phenomena' by the group analytic therapists (Pines, in press).

As we hope it begins to be clear, we are discussing phenomena which properly belong to psychoanalytic theory but which operate on a group level and which represent a conceptual middle ground between the psychoanalysis of individuals and the analysis of the group *qua* group. It is necessary to make such conceptual distinctions in order to prevent the inappropriate use of terminology and mode, and the reification of such abstractions. Lewin (1951b) explicitly spoke of the problem of mixed models when he said that 'In the social as in the physical field the structural properties of a dynamic whole are different from the structural properties of the sub-parts.' A possible conceptual muddle can result from a failure to distinguish between group-as-a-whole and the amplified resonance-in-group of individual-level conflict. Consider the following ideas: (1) it is not conceptually useful to imagine that a group has an ego or a superego in the sense that psychoanalytical developmental psychology can conceptualize such psychic structures for individuals; (2) clearly a group has neither a penis nor a vagina and cannot as such be producing penis envy or castration anxiety; (3) it has no parents and no sex life hence there is no possibility of an oedipal triangle. It therefore makes no real conceptual sense to speak of group conflict or to describe group-as-a-whole behaviors in psychoanalytic, psychodynamic terms, all of which flow from study of the individual. It does, however, make a great deal of sense to note that such universal human issues as are described by psychoanalysis exist individually in the people who make up groups and that interaction seems to have the power to amplify such issues when they are stimulated in individuals in a group setting.

It is this particular level of 'groupness' that stands between the level of the individual as one of a collection of individuals who happen to be occupying the same physical environment, and the level of the dynamic group or group-*qua*-group with its structural properties of the dynamic whole. And this is the level upon which much of the attention of the Group Analytic Movement has so fruitfully focused. Some quotations from Pines (in press) on the contributions of Foulkes will illustrate (1) the individuals in resonance orientation of Foulkes and his followers which well justifies their use of psychoanalytic concepts to build their model, and (2) their great awareness and skillful treatment of the middle-level or resonance and amplification group phenomena. Pines notes four group specific therapeutic factors:

1 *Socialization.* Through the process of sharing, through the experience of group acceptance and belongingness, the patient is brought out of his isolation into a social situation in which he can feel adequate. 'He is a fellow being on equal terms with the others.'
2 *Mirror phenomena.* The patient can see aspects of himself reflected in the image behaviour and problems of the other members of the group. Through this he is enabled to confront various aspects of his social, psychological and body image through identification with and projection on to the other members of the group.
3 *Condenser phenomena.* Foulkes observed that even deep

unconscious material is expressed more readily and more fully in the group through the loosening and stimulating effects that the persons have upon each other. Collectively, through the pooling of associations in the group, the meanings of symbols that appear in dreams or which manifest themselves through such symptom formations as phobias can be more readily understood. It is as if what the group holds in common through their dreams and symptoms can suddenly be understood, the symbol having acted as a 'condenser'.

4 *Exchange.* Not only do the members of the group often have a lively exchange with each other of information which leads to understanding both of oneself and of the meanings of emotional interactions and problems, but this also can lead to chain phenomena and resonance. Each member of the group will reverberate to a group event according to his currently displayed level of development. Thus, for example, if a theme evolves in a group that has to do with violence, one will see how some members withdraw into silence, others display a marked interest in the behaviour of the other persons, i.e., sharing the use of projection, others can be self-revelatory about their own fantasies. Themes that arise in the group that have to do with such issues as parting, loss, grief, mourning are rich sources of information as to the current fixation and development level of the members of the group.

It now makes sense to talk about a group experiencing castration anxiety or separation anxiety, oedipal rivalry, and so on. It is because these shared experiences are the result of individual psychodynamics resonated and amplified in the collective setting that we can validly and fruitfully conceptualize them psychoanalytically. Further, as the reverberation phenomenon proceeds, the associations, dreams, and symbolic communications of the group form a meaningful and increasingly clear communication which lends itself easily to precise psychoanalytic interpretations to the group and then to the individual versions of the material stemming from each person's available level of wish, defense, or compromise formation.

An illustration follows: the group members were attempting to deal with sexual attraction to father figures in an adolescent version of the oedipal conflict. Every member responded in his or her own way to this central theme of the moment. Jane attempted to play the adult in imitation of the female co-therapist, Lois turned from flirting with the male co-therapist to pretending that she wanted to have nothing to do with either him or the subject; one male member, Joe, felt withdrawn and depressed; Hal, another male, was angry at and jealous of the male co-therapist. A third woman, Bernice, pouted and attempted to get attention through pre-adolescent behavior of the 'I'm going into the garden to eat worms' variety. All of the above was latent until interpreted to the group. The correctness of the interpretation was validated by the emergence of material about related fantasies and ideas that had occurred to individuals and been quickly dismissed by them. The interpretation itself was a typical person or resonance level one, 'there is competition for Dick's attention and people are frightened by it.'

Following a period of validation by the group's associations, further interpretations were made on the individual level, noting individual defenses utilized in defending against the threat posed by oedipal sexual material arising in the group. The specific defenses interpreted were: Jane - a well rationalized identification with a punitive female, adult imago; Lois - reaction-formation and inhibition; Joe - confusion and withdrawal into depression; Hal - isolation; and Bernice - regression into anal sadism.

The group had only five members present on this particular day: had the others been at group each would have resonated in his or her own particular fashion to the theme of sexual rivalry. To quote Foulkes and Anthony (1965), 'Each member in the group will . . . show a distinctive tendency to reverberate to any group event according to the level at which he is "set".' Set here refers to fixation at some early level of psychosexual development.

It is instructive to note that the person or resonance level interpretation brought out further material which was then used to make individual interpretations such as might be made in one-to-one psychotherapy. The sequence is rarely if ever reversed. It is also clear from the context that the usual psychoanalytic technical maxim of interpreting the defense rather than the wish was followed in this case, exactly as it would have been in individual psychoanalysis or psychoanalytic psychotherapy. Those who might object, saying that the sexual and rivalrous wishes were also expressed in the interpretation, we refer to Brenner (1976), who points out that it is impossible to make meaningful defense or resistance interpretations totally without reference to the underlying wish and threat.

All of this is gone into with the intention of making it clear that comprehensive psychoanalytic education is absolutely necessary for the understanding of some levels of group behavior and for effective interpretation. The acquired awareness of the importance of timing and of matching the interpretation to the appropriate psychodynamic level that results from the practice of psychoanalytic technique, is also valuable in developing a sense of the importance of timing and level for making interventions at the role and group levels.

For the benefit of those who do not find psychoanalysis compatible with their view of the nature of man, we wish to say that some specific comprehensive model of personality is essential for the really effective use of group psychotherapy; that interventions which only address the role or group levels are as inadequate, relative to the therapeutic potential of the group, as is the use of individual interpretations in group setting as the sole technical tool of the group therapist. It is necessary that the individual and resonance (member) level theory be congruent with role and group levels.

In summary, the many facets of behavior in a group seem to us, at this point in time, to be most usefully conceptualized at four levels, which we have termed 'individual', 'member', 'role', and 'group'. This approach we believe resolves the question of whether to pursue the individual or the group. Perloff (1967) divided group therapists into 'classicists' (intrapersonal therapy in a group setting); 'interpersonalists' (focus on dyads or subgroups); and 'integralists' (emphasis on group process). Some practitioners use more than one of these possible approaches, e.g., Manos (1979) who describes himself as an inter-personal-integralist (using Perloff's terms). We advocate all three; we subdivide the third into two categories, 'role' and 'group', and provide for the proper integration of all four conceptual levels into a theory as an explanatory framework for a comprehensive technique.

The multiple approach proposed by the present authors may be somewhat dismaying to the prospective group psychotherapist, who now finds himself advised to acquire another whole body of theory and training. Nevertheless, it appears to fit the facts as we know them, and to provide a framework for the learning of a technique of group psychotherapy which does not ignore any of the reported phenomena occurring in therapy groups. The fact that a technology is complex is not an argument against its use, nor a bar to serious students becoming proficient in it. We live in an age in which there is increasing evidence of the often tragic results of simplistic approaches to human problems and environments, however well-meaning and altruistic their proponents have been and continue to be. Thus, in fact, a formal understanding of complexity often simplifies the apparently bewilderingly complicated.

Group theory

Yvonne Agazarian with Richard Peters

Chapter 2
The visible and invisible group

People to whom the theory of group dynamics is important have done a great deal of work in an attempt to understand what group 'is' and to define it so that it can be observed, researched, written and talked about. A major problem with this task is that when different people use the word 'group' there is no way to know if they are talking about the same thing. One person's group is another person's not-group. There have been many attempts to define group in such a way that observations of the group phenomenon can be generalized, but so far in the field of group dynamics there is no generally accepted definition of 'group' *per se*. Thus, people write about group dynamics, and do research, and describe group behavior, and there is little empirical evidence that what they say is generalizable, although much of it is intuitively so.

Our own interest in defining 'group' originated in 1962, and has been an ongoing task since. During the intervening years, there have been times when group has seemed almost a mystical entity, a phenomenon as awesome and powerful as the unconscious and as difficult to comprehend and formulate. Our present formulation of group lacks the mystery and drama of the journey. In truth, once we arrived at our formulations, they seemed so obvious that we wondered why we had not seen them before.

We define group in two ways. One is related to the deductive approach and the other to the inductive approach.

From the inductive approach we define the *visible group*. From the deductive approach we define the *invisible group*. The inductive, visible group is the group that we see when we watch a group of people. It is the *people* in the visible group about which most books on group psychotherapy are written. The invisible group is the group that we cannot see because it exists only as a deductive theory. We cannot see

27

people in the invisible group because people don't exist: *ideas* about people and group do.

Failure to make clear the difference between the inductive and deductive approaches has led to much confusion in the group field. As a result, one of the most frequent discussions that we have had with our friends and colleagues is whether or not there exists an entity 'group' that is different from the sum of the individual members that make up the group. In other words, once one has finished describing the visible group and its members in terms of individual dynamics and interpersonal interactions in the group, has one then comprehensively described 'group'? Or, is there 'group' that is different from this visible group about which one can talk intelligibly without referring to the individuals who are part of it? Is there, in fact, an invisible group which one can define in terms of dynamics and structure – much the way one can define personality (also invisible!) – and about which one can make predictions, generate and test hypotheses? We answer yes: the dynamics of the group-as-a-whole are different from the dynamics of a collection of individuals. Differentiating between the two permits a way of seeing and explaining the world of group, without which the group therapist is impoverished as a therapist, much as an individual therapist is impoverished when he has not the conceptual tools to explain individual personality in terms of dynamics and structure.

Some therapists insist that it is not important to have a systematized set of constructs which define a theory of behavior. They state, in fact, that to adopt an explanatory theory explains *away* all the essential humanness which one is attempting to understand better by theorizing. Thus when we say that we deliberately influence our own behavior in a group using as our guide some group-as-a-whole theory, the implication is that not only do we dehumanize the people in the group, but that we also set up a sort of self-fulfilling prophecy by which our behavior proceeds to bring about the very dynamics that we had been predicting: in other words, that thinking makes it so. Even more vehement criticism is levelled at the idea of thinking about a group conscious – or worse – a group unconscious! To think about the unconscious, we think deductively. Therapists are quite accustomed to thinking deductively when they think about individual dynamics. However, most therapists think about group dynamics inductively, and many are resistant to any other view.

We have found it as useful to group therapists to think at the conscious and unconscious levels of *group* process as it is to the individual therapist to think at the level of conscious and unconscious *individual* process. When a therapist applies his knowledge of the general laws of personality it helps him to understand a particular individual's dynamics and behavior. When a group therapist applies his knowledge of general laws of group, it helps him to understand the dynamics and behavior of a particular group.

In the pages that follow, we outline a framework within which to collect and organize information about group. Our purpose is to explain a deductive way of thinking that will help group therapists to be deliberate and intentional about their behavior in a manner that they are not able to be if they are confined to the inductive framework. Looking through our eyes, our readers will understand why we say the things we do and interpret the group the way we do. It is not that thinking makes it so; it is that theoretical constructs are the parameters of one's ability to collect and organize data.

What is 'group'?

Aristotle said that whatever you say a thing is, it is - and upon this premise was built what we now know as Aristotelian logic (1947). Korzybski said that whatever you say a thing is, it is not (1948). Upon this premise was built the logic of General Semantics. Although these two premises appear contradictory, in fact they are *both* true. Understanding this paradox requires understanding that different levels of abstraction provide different conceptual perspectives. Thus, whatever you think a thing *is* depends less upon the thing itself than it does upon how you look at it. What a thing is *not* then becomes those aspects that are not relevant to the purpose for which you are defining your phenomena, but which may become very relevant when you need to redefine your phenomena at some other time, for some other purpose.

Understanding that different views define different realities makes it unnecessary to enter into arguments about whether or not a 'group' exists independent of individuals. If by seeing the group-as-a-whole you are able to explain things that you cannot explain by seeing it as a collection of individuals, then seeing it that way is useful. Nor does it prevent you from taking a second look and seeing group as a collection of individuals. By changing perspective it is possible to shift backwards and forwards between observing group level phenomenon that is 'not' individual, and individual level phenomenon that is 'not' group.

The visible and invisible group: inductive and deductive approaches to group dynamics

When sailors sail close to the wind, they do so because trial and error has taught them that this is how to gain speed. They have learnt to sail their boat by experience and by using their *inductive reasoning*. When fifteenth-century sailors sailed close to the shore, they did so because they believed the theory that the world was flat and they did not want to fall off. They were using their *deductive reasoning*.

By using our inductive reasoning we arrive at general principles or laws by establishing a proposition about the class of phenomenon (group) on the basis of our observations of a number of particular facts (facts about individuals). We argue from the particular to the general: from particular individuals' behavior in the group to the group. Through our 'inductive eyes' we collect as much information as we can about the way people are behaving in the group, and see if we can find ways of explaining it that make sense. Our explanations become our hypotheses, and a series of these explanations or hypotheses lead us to theories or laws of group process.

For example, a group of people may be complaining bitterly that their therapist will not help them, and at the same time refrain from either asking for help, or using any help that the therapist offers. Jack Gibb (1956) observed this kind of phenomenon in the early 1950s. He noticed that the goals people *said* they had (to get help) were significantly different from the goals they behaved 'as if' they had (to complain). Gibb called these 'as if' or 'heuristic' goals: goals that could be inferred by observing behavior. He did not state categorically that these goals existed. He did suggest that inferring this unconscious goal phenomenon explained more about members' behavior than not inferring it. For example, having induced that there is a discrepancy between what group members are 'saying' and what group members are 'doing', we can either interpret the contradiction, or we can infer that 'complaining' is goal directed, and interpret it as such. When we interpret 'complaining' as a group goal we are using our inductive reasoning about individuals' behaviour and generalizing it to 'group'. From this perspective, the label 'group' has no meaning as a separate construct independent from the members by which it is formed. A 'collection of individuals' is all we can see. The inductive approach gives us our observable, *visible* group, the group that is defined as the sum of its members. When we observe our visible group, we observe the way people are behaving in a group context. We can make observations about these people, and interpret those observations in terms of individual dynamics in ways which are generalizable to all theories of individual psychology and social psychology.

When a therapist comes to group with the knowledge of individual psychology but no training or exposure to group dynamics concepts, he can only interpret group behavior in the terms that are known to him. He sees *individuals* and calls them *members* of a group. He can only observe group inductively, because he does not have any deductive group framework. His individualized, inductive observation defines the phenomena that he observes: the *visible group*. The therapist who works with the visible group defines it as a collection of individuals. He learns his group psychotherapy skills through trial and error, in the same way that a would-be sailor can learn how to sail a boat. When he is asked to explain why he does what he does in group psychotherapy, he will talk about the individual people in the group, and their personal and their interpersonal dynamics. As a psychoanalyst, he will talk in terms of object relations theory, amplification and resonance.

When, in contrast, a therapist comes to group with the knowledge of both individual and group dynamics, he can interpret group behavior from either perspective. He can observe the visible group and interpret the personal and interpersonal dynamics. Or he can observe the group-as-a-whole, and from this *group perspective* he can interpret group and individual behavior in terms of the dynamics of the group.

The invisible group

We have defined deductive understandings of group as the *group-as-a-whole perspective* from which can be observed the *invisible group*. When the therapist who is working with the invisible group is asked to explain why he does what he does in group psychotherapy he will talk about group dynamics theory, which does not define individual member-roles but *group-roles*, independent of individual members. He learns his group psychotherapy skills by applying his theoretical knowledge. As with the fifteenth-century sailors, how much of the world of the invisible group he explores and masters will depend upon how close to the 'edge' of his mapped territory he dares to venture. How useful the theoretical map is will depend upon how well it describes and predicts what is encountered in group, and how often it is revised in the light of new discoveries.

When we start with some theory or general law (like Bion's theory of basic assumption groups) and connect it to our observations of particular facts (behavior in the group) through some intermediate construct ('as if' goals) that relates both to our theory and to our facts, we are using our deductive reasoning. We argue from the general to the particular: from group-as-a-whole to behavior in the group.

When we make deductions about our invisible group we are defining something that is dynamically different from the sum of its individual members; something that cannot even be defined as 'more than' or 'greater than' the sum of its members, but as 'different from'.

By observing our invisible group-as-a-whole through our deductive eyes, we can relate group level characteristics that are generalizable to all groups and all theories of group dynamics, and can define the components of our invisible group in any way that is useful to our own particular theory.

This kind of thinking is not intuitively obvious in ways that inductive thinking is. However, it does provide access to many other compatible constructs in the field of group dynamics that can serve to help explain, predict and guide group behavior in ways that are not available without the theory.

As we observed group as both a collection of individuals and as a group-as-a-whole, it became clear that more was happening in the group than we could easily explain and describe by confining our language to psychoanalytic and group dynamics terminology. Psychoanalysis provided an excellent language for explaining individual psychodynamics; but fell short of explaining group dynamics that were different from the phenomena of resonance and amplification. Group dynamics provided an excellent language for talking about group constructs, but not for explaining the development of the group-as-a-whole. It seemed to us that theoreticians in the field had talked about aspects of group in the way we were viewing it (e.g. Bennis and Shepard, 1956; Bion, 1962; Foulkes, 1965; Lewin, 1951a), but no unifying theoretical framework provided us with a vocabulary for describing the dynamics of group-as-a-whole in the way we saw them.

We are opposed to solving theoretical problems by inventing new terms for old constructs. For one of us, therefore, it became an ambition to formulate a theory which would describe both the individual and the group-as-a-whole phenomenon; to trace the development of a group from the state where it can no longer be adequately described in individual terms and needs to be described from the perspective of the dynamics of the group-as-a-whole without reinventing the wheel, and without solving conceptual problems by simply inventing new terms.

In order to do this, we used as our building blocks existing theoretical approaches, and combined them in ways that produced new meanings from the implications of the combination. Specifically our two major building blocks, in addition to psychoanalytic theory, have been Lewin's field theory and general systems theory.

First we turned to Lewin's field theory to describe the process by which the group-as-a-whole emerged from the interaction among individuals. The major advantage of field theory is that its constructs are compatible with psychoanalytic constructs. But whereas Freud was mainly concerned with motivation and drive, and how motivation explained a person's perception of the world and his behavior in it, Lewin was mainly concerned with behavior, and how behavior could explain a person's perception of the world (and by inference, his motivation). As most of the group-as-a-whole phenomenon is implied by group behavior, and as none of the group-as-a-whole phenomenon can be explained by individual motivation, field theory and psychoanalytic theory provided us with two different but compatible ways of describing our observations.

The background of Lewin's thinking came from gestalt theory. Kurt Lewin changed the gestalt definition of group from a 'whole *more* than the sum of its parts' to a 'whole is *different from* the sum of its parts'.

> The whole is not 'more' than the sum of its parts, but it has *different properties.* The statement should be: The whole is different from the sum of its parts. In other words, there does not exist a superiority of value of the whole. Both whole and parts are equally real . . . the whole has definitive properties of its own. (Lewin, 1951a, p. 146.)

This definitional change from quantitative sum to qualitative difference provides a conceptual link to the principle of isomorphy, which is central to general systems theory. General systems theory comprises those general principles and/or laws which are common to 'biological, behavioral, psychological and social phenomena' (von Bertalanffy, 1968).

General systems theory is the second element that contributed to the theory of the invisible group. Since systems theory and field theory have a common ancestor in gestalt psychology, systems analysis is compatible with field theory, which in turn is compatible with psychoanalytic theory. These three theories are the major conceptual foundations from which the theory of the invisible group (presented in chapter 3) has been built. In this chapter we present a simplified outline of field theory and general systems theory as a background for our later theoretical development, together with other theoretical constructs which we have adapted to our argument: Lewin's force field analysis, information theory, Festinger's theory of cognitive dissonance, Howard and Scott's theory of stress, Bennis and Shepard's theory of group development, and Bion's basic assumptions about group.

As we have said, it has been our intention, wherever possible, to use the language that exists already in the literature without inventing new terms. Therefore, when we talk of our understanding of individual psycho-dynamics in group, we use the language of the psychoanalytic literature. When we talk of the individual as a system, or as a sub-system and component of the group system, and when we talk of the group system, we use the language of field theory and general systems theory. Although both field theory and general systems theory terms are defined in the literature, there is no common dictionary for either. Therefore, to avoid misunderstandings, we refer you to the glossary for definitions.

Field theory

Lewin's field theory postulates that an individual's behavior can be predicted from knowledge of his life space. Lewin depicted life space as an egg-shaped 'map' that portrayed the individual in interaction with his perceived environment. To understand an individual's life space is to understand his goals, the tension system related to the goal, the barriers between him and his goal, and the probable next step that he will take along his path to his goal. Driving forces are the applications of energy moving him towards the goal, and restraining forces are those quantums of energy that serve to restrain him from reaching his goal. Lewin stated that to draw an accurate picture of an individual's life space was to be able to predict his next behavior.

A great value of Lewin's theory is its immense simplicity at the level of example. We illustrate the concept of the life space here in a series of maps of a donkey's dilemmas. In the first map (figure 2.1a) the donkey's goal is his supper (carrots in the next field), his 'tension system' is related directly to his goal, the barrier between him and his supper is permeable (the gate is open) and his next behavior is predictable.

Equally predictable is the second map (figure 2.1b) which shows the donkey in his 'goal' region after he has eaten his supper. No carrots, no hunger, no tension system. The donkey is satiated. (So, in Lewin's language, is the goal region 'satiated'.)

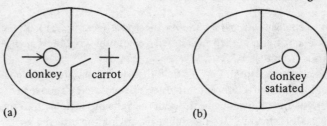

Figure 2.1 Life space before and after attainment of goal region

The third map (figure 2.2) depicts the life space of the same donkey in relationship to the carrot and the stick. There is a positive valence in the direction of the carrot, and a negative valence in relationship to the stick. It is equally easy to predict that the donkey will move away from the region of the stick and toward the region of the carrot.

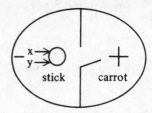

Figure 2.2 Driving forces in relationship to the carrot (region of positive valence) and the stick (region of negative valence). Force x = positive valence; force y = negative valence

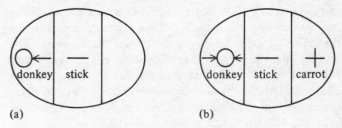

Figure 2.3 Driving and restraining forces in relationship to (a) the stick (perceived) and the carrot (unperceived); (b) the stick (perceived) and the carrot (perceived) by the hungry donkey

In the fourth and fifth maps (figure 2.3), the carrot is on the *other side* of the stick. If the donkey does not see the carrot, there will be no tension system between him and the goal region (figure 2.3a). It is as if, however hungry he is, the carrot does not exist. The fifth map shows the same territory, but the donkey's altered perception (he has seen the carrot) changes the nature of the life space (figure 2.3b). If the donkey was not hungry, then his altered perception would not change his life space from figure 2.3a.

Goal is a key concept in Lewin's field theory. The nature of the goal region defines the direction and intensity of the donkey's movement. The nature of the intervening territory defines the probable path to the donkey's goal. In figure 2.3b, the donkey's driving force to the goal is greater (the longer arrow) than the restraining force of the stick (the shorter arrow), so he will cross the region of negative valence to get to the carrot in the region of positive valence: the goal region.

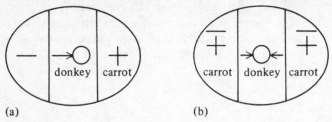

(a)   (b)

Figure 2.4 Driving and restraining forces: (a) the carrot and the stick; (b) the carrot and the carrot

In figure 2.4b, the donkey is still hungry. His goal is a carrot, and there is one to his right and one to his left, each at exactly the same distance from him. The donkey is ambivalent. If he moves toward one carrot, he moves farther away from the other. Whereas his movement toward one is helped by the nature of the driving force (the closer to the goal, the greater the attraction), he is hindered by the nature of the restraining force (the closer to the aversive goal, the greater the resistance). The donkey, to put it another way, is caught in the balance between driving and restraining forces. One way Lewin represented this balance is by a force field model (figure 2.5). Our adaptation of the force field (which makes it easier to write and read) is presented in figure 2.6. Discussion of the force field at greater length is given in appendix 2.

To summarize, Lewin postulated that the life space represented the person in interaction with his psychologically perceived environment. To know the life space is to be able to predict what the person will do next. In other words, behavior is a function of the life space; therefore, behavior is a function of the transaction between the person and his perceived environment. In the theory of the invisible group, we use Lewin's life space construct to represent both the individual and group-as-a-whole.

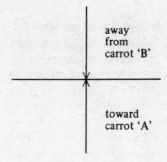

Figure 2.5 Lewin's representation of force field

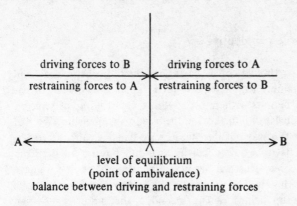

Figure 2.6 Revised representation of force field

Individual perspective

The life space definition, applied to the individual perspective, serves to illustrate some important dynamics. The individual is the member, and the environment is the group. In the group situation, the inter-actions of the members create the environment within which they continue to interact. Thus, for group members, their behavior is a function of their particular psychodynamics, their outside socializing experience, the resultant set of selective perception tendencies, plus the group culture of which they are a part. For the therapist, on the other hand, there is an extra factor explaining behavior. That factor is the theoretical model through which the therapist is selectively perceiving. Thus the therapist's behavior in a group is a function of the same factors that govern members' behavior *plus* his ability to cognitively structure the group phenomena through his theoretical discipline, training and experience. His particular psychodynamics are related to group appropriately through the analysis of the group's transference and his own counter-transferential response. His own outside socializing experiences are focused on group appropriately because of his training as a therapist, and the parameters of his selective perceptions are group appropriate to the extent that they permit group phenomena to be perceived, and not selected out.

Lewin's statement that an individual's behavior can be predicted from a map of the life space holds true for group behavior. The map of the group life space will predict how the group will behave next.

Group-as-a-whole perspective

The group can be thought of as having an environment, a goal, and driving and restraining forces relating to the goal. The concept of the group life space permits a therapist to think about group as separate from the individuals who make up the group membership. We had long known that this was possible because we had been able to predict that a needed behavior would occur in the group, but not predict from whom it would come. This fact has two implications. The first we have mentioned: working in the framework of group life space permits prediction of group behavior. The second is that knowledge of an individual life space in the group *does not* permit the therapist to predict that individual's behavior in the group with the same confidence that he would, for example, in individual psychotherapy. Thus we suggest that an essential adjunctive method for working in group is to use the group life space as the phenomenon to observe and to follow; to observe and diagnose; to observe and influence directionally by interventions related to group developmental goals.

Applications of this thinking lead to the therapist becoming more specific about developmental goals, and more familiar with the fixations in the phases of development through which the group must pass to reach those goals. It also leads the therapist to think about sub-goals; about goals that are set as a function of the level of group (chapter 6); about the developmental phase the group is in (chapter 5) and about the specific vicissitudes in the history of the particular group's development. It also underlies the therapist's decision as to whether and when to influence the individuals or the group-as-a-whole, or both. Focusing on an individual may be a necessary detour from group focus because the individual member is in need (which is not directly related to the group needs) and will get left behind by the group if not maintained at that time; or because the individual is on the threshold of insight and the therapist decides not to miss the opportunity. Focusing on the individual may also be in line with group focus, where the intervention made to the individual is powerful, both for the individual and for the group. In any case, influencing an individual also influences group process because of the interdependent nature of the individual and group life space.

A problem in interpreting individual or group behavior within the framework of the life space is the tendency to assume conscious goals (the goals that people in the group *say* they have). In contrast is the assumption that the behaviour we observe in groups can be better understood if we do *not* attempt to explain group behavior in terms of conscious goals but in terms of the construct of the implicit goal. Pragmatically, we induce our implicit goal from the way the group is behaving. Much as Freud interpreted parapraxes as 'slips of the unconscious' rather than slips of the tongue, so we interpret a group's 'as if' behavior as signs of an unconscious or unstated goal, rather than as coincidence. We infer the 'as if' goal by asking the following kinds of questions: 'What is the group behaving "as if" it is doing?' or 'What goal can I infer that explains more of the group's behavior than does the goal it says it has?'

In field theory, one begins by talking about the person (or group) in relationship to the goal. When we wish, instead, to talk about the goal in relation to the person or group, general systems theory solves some important conceptual problems for us by adding an additional dimension. When we apply general systems theory to the life space, we talk about the field of force in terms of system equilibrium. As we will explain more fully in the section following, systems analysis provides a method for describing how a level of equilibrium is maintained. One way of thinking about the 'as if' goal of a group is as a group level of equilibrium. Thus we use 'as if' goal and 'level of equilibrium' as synonymous terms, and the force field provides a model to define it (see appendix 2).

General systems theory

The simplest way of defining a system is to say that it systematizes something. For example, the 'system' of a thermostatically controlled room 'systematizes' the temperature by 'systematically' turning the heat off when it gets too hot, and 'systematically' turning the heat on when it gets too cold.

This system has a boundary (the walls of the room) which serves as a threshold between the inside of the system and the outside of the system. Transactions across the boundary have two directions. Transactions from within the system to the outside, called outputs, which in this case would be heat moving from inside the room to the outside, and transactions from outside the system to the inside, called inputs. The system boundary is characterized by permeability, and how permeable the system boundary is will affect the input and output transactions. In other words, if walls (boundaries) of the room are insulated (less permeable) heat and cold changes will be less than if the room is not insulated (more permeable).

How you define the system in relationship to its environment (of which it is a component sub-system) depends upon what you wish to understand. If you are talking about a group in relationship to the group's environment, for example a psychotherapy group in a clinic, then the group can be usefully talked about as a sub-system of its environment: transactions from the clinic affect the group, and transactions from the group affect the clinic. It is valuable, in this case, to think clearly about transactions across the boundary (the input and output relations between your group and the clinic) and also to pay close attention to the nature and character of the boundaries (in other words, permeability).

If, however, you are interested in exploring the relationship between the group and its members, then you will talk about the input and output relationships between the group as a system and the individual group members (or sub-groups of members) as sub-systems.

Why talk systems language? This is a fundamental question, particularly when there are almost as many interpretations of systems theory as there are people writing about it. Our answer is that when we conceptualize the dynamics of an individual and a group in systems terms we are able to provide a simplified way of describing complex phenomena.

Figure 2.7 is an example of general systems thinking applied to the complex 'event' of a group. It can be viewed the same way as a three-dimensional chess game. It is apparent that a move of a piece on the second board would significantly alter the whole game plan on that board. However, a move at any one level not only has meaning at that level, but it also has meaning in relationship to the other levels.

In our diagram we have called system 2 the 'system of group-role

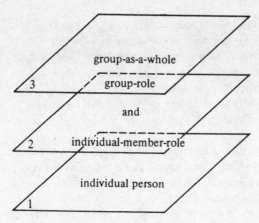

Figure 2.7 Three dynamic systems: 1, 2, 3, whose structure and function is isomorphically related and whose input and output relationships are such that a change in any one system changes any other

and individual-member-role'. It has been given this somewhat lengthy title deliberately, in order to make the relationship between it and systems 1 and 3 explicit. For example, when we talk about the relationship between system 2 and system 3, we talk about the 'group-role' relationship to the 'group-as-a-whole'; and when we talk about the relationship between system 2 and system 1 we talk about an 'individual-member-role' relationship to the 'individual person'. A move (or change) in system 2 has a special meaning in system 2 and that same move has one kind of meaning in relationship to system 3, a different meaning in relationship to system 1, and still another overall meaning in terms of systems 1 *and* 2 *and* 3. Just as in three-dimensional chess, a move on any one of the boards (for example, putting an opponent's king in check) will have a particular meaning for that particular board, a different meaning in relationship to each of the other two boards (check at one level must be resolved before any other play can take place), and yet another meaning to the overall game which is being played on all three boards. (The game-as-a-whole will be over if 'check' becomes 'mate'.) The rules of the game and the principle of movement is the same for each of the boards (the systems principle of isomorphy). What is more, just as scientists have discovered that whatever they learn from one system increases their understanding of systems in general, so, as many players of three-dimensional chess have discovered, three-dimensional chess has taught them some new and important ways of thinking about their unidimensional chess game.

The example above is intended to generalize in two ways. The most obvious generalization is the expectation that the group therapist who learns to 'play' group from the perspectives of group-as-a-whole and the group-role, as well as from the perspective of the individual-member-role and the individual person, will have significantly improved his ability to think about group psychotherapy.

The second intention is to introduce some important concepts of general systems theory. These are:

1   Each system (systems 1, 2 and 3) can be thought of dynamically in relationship to its own components, its environment (of which it is a component) and the other two systems (of which it is either a sub-system or supra-system).
2   Each system represents a focus for thinking within one level of abstraction.
3   The relationship between the systems can be conceptualized.
4   The crossing of system boundaries crosses levels of abstraction.
5   The input/output relationships between the systems can be stated.
6   The dynamic equilibrium (or 'goal') of each system can be distinguished from the goals of the other systems.
7   Each system is isomorphic with the others.

Helen Durkin (1978) noted that comparative study of systems in general yielded the revolutionary discovery that systems of all categories across the board share certain basic structural features called isomorphies, and also share their laws of operation (i.e., their function). This means that whatever one learns about one system will illuminate any other particular system one wishes to study.

Thus, the generality of systems theory is the major reason that we find systems concepts particularly useful to our theoretical argument: the way we think about a system at the general level remains the same, even when the particular system that we are thinking about changes.

At this point we pause to review the foundations that have been laid so far and to prepare for the concepts that we turn to next. We have discussed field theory and general systems theory. Field theory has been identified as a bridge between psychoanalysis and general systems theory. General systems theory has been related to two different levels of abstraction that we have called the individual and group perspectives.

We turn now to the relationship between systems. These we have labelled as input and output relations in the thermostat analogy. In the example of the three-dimensional chess game it is apparent that a move within any one system (on chessboard 2, for example) is equivalent to an input of information that results in a reorganization within that system, i.e., a move is in fact a communication that has meaning in relation to other moves on the board: the taking of a pawn is one kind of communication, putting the king in check is another. A move also potentially changes what moves can be made on other boards in the system as well as in the overall game in which each one of the boards is a system component. The move that is an input of information on chessboard 2 relates as an output of information from chessboard 2 to chessboards 1 and 3. When that output is received by one or both of the other boards as an input, it has meaning in terms of move potential there too. For example, in processing the information it may be that the move on chessboard 2 has put the king on chessboard 3 in check from chessboard 1, and therefore the move is invalid (in systems language, the original level of equilibrium or organization of information must be restored). Or the piece that is serving to check the king from chessboard 1 may be blocked by a move on chessboard 2. (Chessboard 2 reorganizes in relationship to the output from 1.) Thus, any reorganization of one system has a specific meaning within that system, and the output relationship from that system has specific input meaning to the system receiving it, as well as a different meaning to the system of which it is a component.

We now apply the principles explained in the analogy above to the systems that are the basic constructs of our theory. These systems are: the individual person system, the individual-member-role system, the group-role system and the group-as-a-whole system (labelled in figure 2.9 simply person, member, role and group). They are conceptualized at different levels of abstraction that are hierarchically related. The emergence of any one system is conceptually dependent upon the emergence of the system that precedes it. Each system is a complete system to the sub-system component that has developed at the stage before and is itself a sub-system component of the system that develops at the stage after.

The illustration in figure 2.9 represents the output relations between the four systems and will be used throughout the theory section to diagram different constructs in the theory of the invisible group. The form itself presents schematically the relationships that are described conceptually throughout this chapter and the next.

We would like to caution our readers at this point not to confuse the diagram in figure 2.9 with similar notions used in set theory, like Venn diagrams. A Venn diagram would define everything in subset C (see figure 2.8) by those elements which are in both A and B.

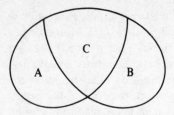

Figure 2.8 Venn diagram defining subset C by elements in both A and B

Should set theory logic be applied to figure 2.9, group would be interpreted as a subset, absolutely defined by the elements of person, member and role. This would be the equivalent of defining group as the sum of its parts and would make it impossible for us to develop the theory of the invisible group, which is based on the assumption that the group is different from, or other than, the sum of its parts. The reader should not, therefore, use set theory thinking or any approach based on Aristotelian logic in interpreting the diagram in figure 2.9. The diagram should be used only as a device to visualize different systems, related at different levels of abstraction through the principle of isomorphy.

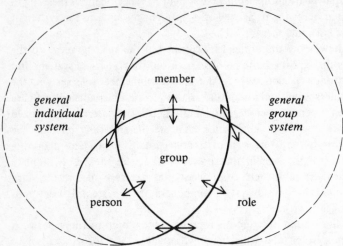

Figure 2.9 Input/output relationships between the systems of person, member, role and group

In figure 2.9 four systems are shown in relationship to each other. The arrows represent outputs from one system and inputs into the next. These input/output relationships exist between four co-existing systems in group psychotherapy. The input and output relationships and their effects on the levels of equilibrium within each system provide a way of talking about group dynamics.

We define each input and output relationship as a communication exchange. Each arrow can be thought of as a communication channel through which information can be transmitted. When the information transmitted through a channel is received by a system, it has an effect on the system. We describe this effect as a change in the level of equilibrium of the system, that is, a change in the balance of driving and restraining forces, just as in our earlier analogies, a heat exchange changed the level of the temperature in a room, or a move on one chessboard changed the game.

Talking this way permits us to analyze communication in a group in terms of input and output relationships between the systems that we define. It also permits us to talk about messages as changing the informational level of equilibrium within the system.

Systems in interaction and transaction

The model in figure 2.9 provides us with a method for analyzing communication among and within group in terms of input and output relationships between systems. The nature of the output messages from a system, and the nature of the input messages to a system, affect the level of equilibrium by differentiating and integrating information in terms of the system goal. Thus, certain input/output interactions can be described as directioned towards the therapeutic goals, and certain others can be described as directioned away from therapeutic goals.

George and Vasso Vassiliou of the Athenian Institute of Anthropes have pioneered much work applying these concepts to psychotherapy in Athens. They have also defined different types of interactions that occur between systems as dependent, independent and interdependent as follows.

Systems in interaction
Systems are defined as interacting when one system *acts upon* another, without either system's boundaries being permeable to the other system's output. System A and system B can react to each other's outputs, but neither will be any different afterwards in that they did not take any new information into their systems.

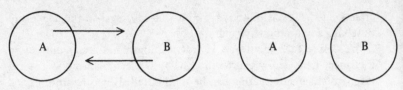

Figure 2.10 Two examples of systems A and B in interaction

Systems in transaction

Two kinds of transactions are defined: dependent and interdependent. In *dependent transaction*, one system's boundaries are permeable to the other's output, and one system's boundaries are impermeable. Thus the output of one system is received as an input into the other system and results in a change in the information store. Thus if system A has boundaries that are permeable to system B, system A will receive system B's outputs as an input, and will then have the potential for system change taking into account system A's information. System B, however, has boundaries that are not permeable to system A, and therefore may react to the act of output, but will not have the potential for change by taking in information.

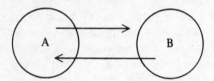

Figure 2.11 System A in dependent transaction with B; system B in independent interaction with A

In *interdependent transaction*, both system A and system B have boundaries that are permeable to each other and can therefore exchange information in their input/output relationships in a manner that carries the potential for change for both.

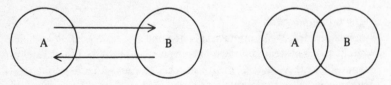

Figure 2.12 Two examples of systems A and B in interdependent transaction

In the visible group, interactions can be thought of as potential transactions (inputs and outputs) which are encoded in messages sent from one member to another or to the group, or even in messages sent internally to themselves. At the level of the invisible group, this process of communication is the interface of all systems: person, member, role and group-as-a-whole. Communication follows its own laws, and understanding these is crucial to both the inductive and deductive understanding of the behavior of people in groups and the development of the group itself. Information theory is the framework that we use to describe the process of information transfer that occurs in the communication channels (inputs and outputs) between systems in interaction and transaction.

Information theory

Information theory states that ambiguity, redundancy and contradiction produce noise (entropy) in the communication system. Without noise, a communication system is theoretically perfect. As all information contains ambiguities, redundancies and contradictions, and these factors produce noise in the communication channel (Shannon and Weaver, 1964), noise is therefore a problem inherent in the process of communication, between systems and within systems. Noise makes it more difficult to organize information and integrate it within a system. Noisy messages, therefore, increase disorganization in the communication process, within the systems that receive the noisy message and in the system environment. In information theory, this process is called entropic. Neg-entropic change entails organization and integration of information. The amount of 'noise' in the communications between systems will affect the potential for change within systems by affecting the level of equilibrium (or goal) of the system.

Those input/output communication transactions that are directioned towards therapeutic goals can be termed 'neg-entropic' in the sense that they transmit organized and organizing communication that contains the minimum of ambiguity, contradictions and redundancy. Those input/output communication transactions that are directioned away from therapeutic goals can be termed 'entropic' in the sense that they transmit disorganized and disorganizing communication that contains ambiguity, contradictions and redundancy.

Let us talk first of a conflict-free person in valid communication with himself. His sub-systems of psyche and soma are in harmony, his ego has no trouble mediating between his id desires and his superego rules for appropriateness in the outside world. His interaction with the environment is optimally responsive. A picture of his life space always portrays an accurate picture of his real environment and an ideal path to a personally and socially compatible goal.

So much for the ideal! The fact of life is that no one is in perfect harmony within himself, and a person's perceived environment is at best only a rough approximation of what is 'really' out there. Change is a basic law of nature. Therefore individuals are continually attempting to adjust to an environment that is changing even as it is perceived. A person's perceptions of the world are communications with himself. Ambiguities, redundancies and contradictions are characteristic of the perception process in the same way that they are characteristic of the communication process.

Howard and Scott (1965) in their theory of stress postulated that all human behavior could be described as problem-solving behavior, that either approaches or avoids a problem to be solved. Ambiguity, redundancy and contradictions are problems that are basic to all human experience, and, using Howard and Scott's framework, can thus be thought of as stimuli to problem-solving behavior.

For example: people tend to respond to *ambiguity* with attempts to organize it so that it has some kind of coherent meaning. Under stimulus deprivation, man makes coherent madness. People tend to respond to *redundancy* with attempts to change it. Faced with boredom, both individuals and groups generate problems for themselves to solve. People tend to respond to *contradictions* with attempts to explain away incompatibilities, as the double bind theory has illustrated (Bateson, 1956). (It is only in the laws of the unconscious that contradictions co-exist compatibly.) Thus the stimuli of ambiguity, contradiction and redundancy result in 'noise' within both the individual and the group-as-a-whole systems that serves both to create entropy within the system and to elicit a problem-solving response.

Festinger's theory of cognitive dissonance provides another framework compatible with information theory and stress theory, from which much work has been done on predicting the behavior of a person confronted with a perception of the world that does not fit his cognitive map of the world, and therefore confronts him with problems of violated expectations. Ambiguities, contradictions and redundancies are strong influences that contribute to the experience of this cognitive dissonance. The group environment is an environment that is differentially ambiguous, contradictory and redundant for its members. In the psychotherapy group, the therapist can significantly affect the ambiguity in the group by giving or withholding structure, can affect contradictions and redundancies by interpretation, intervention or silence. Thus, by intentionally influencing the level of ambiguity, contradiction and redundancy in the communication system, the therapist can reduce or increase the strength of the problem stimuli so that they can serve as driving forces to individual problem solving and to therapeutic goals.

For example, each member of the group will experience the group environment differently. Ambiguity for some members will be redundancy for others. Because of the interdependent nature of member interaction, the fact that some members will be responding to ambiguity while others are responding to redundancy will introduce contradictions at the group level. The therapist must decide whether or not the experienced ambiguity is too anxiety-provoking for an individual, and whether to reduce it by making a structuring or information-giving intervention. From the individual perspective, his decision may be based upon his perception of whether the conflict is contributing to membership work or not; from the group perspective, whether contradiction is serving as a driving or restraining force to group locomotion. Sometimes from both perspectives his choice will be the same. When, however, they are different, he will need to choose, based upon his overall perception of the group-as-a-whole as a developing therapeutic environment for the particular individuals in it.

In this chapter so far we have talked of the visible and invisible group and we have laid the foundations for the theory of the invisible group by describing the constructs that are basic to our thinking and relating them to the constructs that we have developed: person, member, role and group. One further aspect is important to the preparatory goals of this chapter, and that is an orientation to phases of group development.

Phases of group development

There appear to be certain aspects of group dynamics that are common to all groups, and certain manifestations in most groups that coincide with phases of group development.

Wilfred Bion is perhaps the most significant pioneer in viewing group as if it were a phenomenon separate from the individuals of which it was made. His original postulation, heavily influenced by his Kleinian orientation, was that group was in a part-object relationship to its members.

The aspect of Bion's work that is important to our argument is his theory that there are always two dimensions of group present: the work group and the basic assumption group.

The basic assumption group is an 'as if' term which explains group behaviour (much as the basic assumption that the world was flat explains why sailors sailed close to shore). Bion inferred three basic assumption groups from the way his groups behaved. There are dependency, flight-fight and pairing groups. He interpreted their function as a defense against the primitive anxieties that the groups aroused in their members. Bion described the work group as a property of the conscious level of group process, and the basic assumption groups as a property of unconscious group process.

The work group processes are those in which the purpose of the group is recognized, the task is defined, the structure facilitates task performance and leaders emerge when their resources are needed. The work group performance is consistent with survival of the group as well as the survival of the organization of which the group is a part.

The basic assumption groups manifest themselves with their goals unrecognized, and implied only by group behavior. The emergent leaders (or voices for the group) lead the group in the direction of one of the three basic assumptions, no one of which contributes to group work, and each one of which jeopardizes the organization of which the group is a part. The three implicit basic assumption goals are:

1   Dependency. The group behaves as if the members are helpless and know nothing, the leader is omnipotent, and the source of group survival.
2   Pairing. The group behaves as if the group will 'give birth' to a savior who will solve the group's problem. Two people in the group emerge to play reciprocal roles in this Messianic solution as the focus of the group's attention, support, affection, hope and fantasy.
3   Fight-Flight. The group behaves as if the group survival is dependent upon immediate action, either flight or fight. This pressure towards impulsive action results in the group behaving as if it were a mindless mass.

Bion's theory served as a springboard for many other theoreticians, among them Warren Bennis and Herbert Shepard, who built their theory of group development on Bion's constructs of the basic assumption and work groups. Bennis and Shepard observed dependency and fight-flight groups, predominantly in the early phases of group development, divided from the pairing and work group development by a 'barometric event' which changed the nature of the group's role with its leader.

Bennis and Shepard began by observing what happened in T-groups: training groups that were set up in a university setting, where students had come to learn about the dynamics of group. This provided a laboratory situation in which the task of each individual student was to observe the development of the group of which they were a part, and to identify the group level phenomena that emerged from this process.

This work is frequently disregarded in the literature of group psychotherapy, and understandably so, as it is not immediately apparent how theory derived from observations of large, fifteen-to-thirty-person T-groups comprised of 'normal' university students can be generalized to small, six-to-twelve-person patient groups. Several important differences have been identified.

1   The size of the groups are different. A T-group of fifteen to thirty is large enough to be talked about in terms of large group phenomenon: a psychotherapy group of six to twelve falls within small-group designation.
2   The population of the groups are different. The T-group population of students falls within the class of 'normal' psychology. Psychotherapy groups of patients fall within the class of 'abnormal' psychology.
3   The goals of the group are different. The goal of the T-group is to provide a laboratory situation within which the dynamics of groups can be studied. The goal of a psychotherapy group is to provide psychotherapy to its members.
4   Leadership of the group is different. The T-group leader serves as a consultant, and deliberately creates a power vacuum by abstaining from behaving in the ways that are expected of a classroom leader. The psychotherapy group leader serves as a therapist and behaves in ways that are usually expected of a therapist.
5   T-group leaders make mainly group-as-a-whole-level interventions. In the Tavistock method, the approach is similar to the T-group, but more exigent in that the Tavistock group leader makes *only* group-level interventions and never talks directly to an individual member. Group psychotherapists usually make interventions to the individuals in the group, and sometimes to the group-as-a-whole.

Parenthetically, in our experience, the Tavistock method is probably the single most effective method for training group psychotherapists in group process observation (as well as in boundary keeping which is frequently the therapist's weakest area), but it does not appear to be an effective style for group psychotherapy. The study by Malan (1976) has indicated that the deliberate avoidance of acknowledging the group member's identity as separate from the group is experienced by patients as sadistic and dehumanizing, and only a few are able to work therapeutically within the model. This, for us, is no criticism of the model *per se*, and it is a powerful illustration of one of our main contentions: that the group structure *must* be appropriate to the goals of the group and to the population of the group, otherwise, although the goals of the group *may* be reached, the goals of the individual members may *not* be reached (see chapter 5).

However, to return to our argument that generalizations *can* be made between the phases of development in T-group and the phases of development in a psychotherapy group: we wish to point out that the argument against generalization is based upon a confusion between *styles of leadership* and developmental dynamics. *Developmental dynamics* are independent of leadership style. Thus, whereas it is true that different styles of leadership are crucial to the achievement of different kinds of group goals (see chapter 5), it is also true that the phases of group development are predictable from knowledge of the dynamics of groups *in general.* Size of group, population, goals and leadership are variables that affect the dynamics of *how* the developmental phases of a group will manifest; they will not yield different developmental phases *per se.*

This is the rationale behind the fact that we have found Bennis and Shepard's description of group development generalizable to the beginning phases of *all* the groups that we have observed, and very specifically applicable to psychotherapy groups. In chapter 4 we discuss adaptation of Bennis and Shepard's phases of group development as they apply to the early phases of formation of the psychotherapy group into a therapeutic environment.

We are grateful to Dr Bennis and Dr Shepard for their generous support of our theoretical journey, and for their permission to reprint the summary tables of their theory in the same form that they originally appeared in their article introducing their theory of group development. These tables appear in appendix 1.

In the theory of group development as described by Bennis and Shepard there are two underlying assumptions. The first is that groups do follow a sequence of development from their inception to their maturity. This sequence can be divided into two parts, the first characterized by power relationships and the second by personal relationships.

The second assumption is that the catalytic forces in group development are provided by members of the group. Dependent, counterdependent and independent forces catalyze the initial power phase of dependence, flight and fight. Overpersonal and counterpersonal forces catalyze the personal relations phase of dependence and pairing.

From the individual perspective the labels dependent, counterdependent, overpersonal and counterpersonal are defined in terms of *people*. Thus, in observing a group, each individual member might be labelled as dependent or counterdependent, overpersonal or counterpersonal. This, in fact, it is quite possible to do. 'Dependents' would follow the leader. The 'passive' dependents would characteristically appear helpless unless told what to do, the 'aggressive' dependents would bully others into conforming. Counterdependents would appear nonconforming; in aggressively active or passively resistant ways they would show rebellion, by doing the opposite of whatever others tell them to do. 'Overpersonals' would form strong, affectionate attachments to members in the group, be sensitive to rejection, feel at peace and in harmony from belonging to the group, and claim that their identity was enhanced by merging. The 'counterpersonals', on the other hand, would fight to keep their psychological distance, finding the intimacy too close for comfort and fearing that the group will swallow them up.

The advantage of this way of labelling individuals in the group is that it provides a simple personality theory that can be helpful in the analysis from the individual perspective. The disadvantage is that it is simplistically limited and limiting. Real people do not fit neatly into two or three categories. What is more, a particular group member may behave like a dependent at one time and like a counterdependent (or independent) at another. We, therefore, confine the terms dependent, counterdependent, overpersonal or counterpersonal to behavioral components of people and sub-groups, and not as labels for individuals.

There are two advantages to our reserving these terms for the group-as-a-whole perspective. The first advantage is that we can use the much richer language of psychoanalysis when we talk about individual psychodynamics. The second advantage is that we reserve the terms personal, counterpersonal, overpersonal, etc., to refer to identifiable clusters of behavior that are independent of people, and thus independent of apparently bewildering individual role changes.

In this chapter we have differentiated between the visible and invisible group. There follows a summary of these two approaches, displaying the differences in the formulation of the dynamics of the visible group from the dynamics of the invisible group-as-a-whole which we see only through theoretical eyes. Before turning to the detailed exposition of our theory of the invisible group, which we do in the chapter following, we will first end this chapter by answering directly a question that we have not yet directly asked!

Why do we need a theory of group-as-a-whole that is different from individual personality theory? We need a theory of group-as-a-whole to differentiate group dynamics from individual dynamics; to permit group developmental dynamics to be described; and to permit groups to be classified. Classification of groups according to developmental level will then permit us to assess their relative maturity. For psychotherapists this means that we can assess our psychotherapy groups, as well as our patients, in terms of growth, in sickness and in health.

Comparison between the dynamics of the visible group and the invisible group

The visible group	*The invisible group*
A discrete collection of individuals	The group-as-a-whole system with sub-system components of person, member, role and group
Defined in time and space	Defined by theory
Group properties: demographic individual and group characteristics	Group properties: forces; vectors with direction, velocity and point of application
Group constructs: explicit norms, written rules, explicit or stated goals. Individual attraction to the group, individual member roles	Group constructs: implicit norms, implicit goals, group roles, role forces independent of individuals, that serve as vectors in relationship to (a) system equilibrium (system goals), (b) the direction of maturation, (c) vicissitudes of group development

Communication in terms of *why* people say *what, to whom,* interpreted on the basis of individual psychology, and/or interpersonal and/or social psychology	Communication in terms of patterns, like 'who-to-whom' which, when charted, provide operational definitions for constructs in group psychology
Individual communication styles provide operational definitions for psychologically or socially recognizable roles like martyr, bully, parent-adult-child, schizophrenic, etc.	Group communication patterns provide operational definitions for 'invisible' group constructs like voice of the group; 'as if' goals; driving and restraining flight-fight forces as roles in relationship to group goal
Cohesiveness as a function of individual member needs for satisfaction vs. cost of satisfaction	Cohesiveness as a function of energy organization and positive and negative bonding of system components
Individual behavior as a function of the person in interaction with the perceived environment (individual life space)	Group behavior as function of the group in interaction with the group's environment (group life space)

Chapter 3
The theory of the invisible group

This chapter is designed with two purposes in mind. First to provide
the novice group psychotherapist with a 'feel' for group dynamics, as a
step in bringing his expectations about groups into closer alignment
with the realities of therapy groups. Second, for all readers, whatever
their experience in group work, this chapter describes the framework
within which the authors think about group constructs. A conceptual
framework is rather like a map which serves as a guide to the real world
of group. When we have confidence in our map, we are less likely to
divert our groups back to territory that is familiar to us. We are more
willing to follow and less apt to lead. What a group psychotherapist
sees when he looks at a psychotherapy group will depend partly upon
his conceptual map, and partly on his experience. Whereas a map is
made from the ideas about what the group territory is like, experience
comes from having travelled it before.

The experienced group therapist has put together many new psychotherapy groups, seen the developmental phases of group life, worked
with co-therapists, modified his map in line with his observations, and
over the hours has seen old things in new ways, as well as new things in
old ways. As a result, most of the accommodating to the group that an
experienced therapist does is by an integrated, internalized, non-
conscious set of guiding responses. These responses develop rather like
driving intuition; as a function of the miles travelled, the kind of terrain
traversed, and the driving values that he holds. It is only when a situation
is puzzling, unexpected or unfamiliar that the therapist becomes
alerted; pays conscious attention to his responses and makes conscious
decisions about how to act, rather in the way that the analyst will
suddenly focus his free-floating attention. Even when alerted, however,
the experienced group therapist has past experiences against which to
relate the unexpected or puzzling situation; and a history which will

help him maintain a feeling of confidence while he analyzes the situation and prepares his response. Unlike driving, in group psychotherapy there are few emergencies demanding quick decisions or crisis interventions. Most often, time is on the therapists' side.

This flow and perspective is not available to guide the inexperienced psychotherapist. He is behind the wheel for the first time, with only his informal experience in groups to guide him. What is more, his intuitive expectations will most often lead him astray, since most social group experience is interpreted interpersonally and not in terms of group dynamics. The inexperienced therapist's expectations are destined largely to be violated. Even if told what to look for, he may not recognize it and has certainly not had the opportunity to internalize this understanding as part of his internal map of groups.

A vital part of the training of a group therapist is the acquisition of a cognitive framework that will permit him to 'see' both the visible and invisible group. This means literally being able to observe the *group-as-a-whole* as well as the individual people who are in the group. The emphasis in clinical psychology and group theory is still (and usefully so) heavily based on the interactions that go between individuals. The responses of individuals are interpreted in terms of their genetic, environmental, familial and social history as it has been modified through the particular personality structure that the clinician identifies. Thus, group is most often interpreted in terms of a 'collection-of-individuals' both in the literature and in training. This leads to an individual-oriented interpretation of what happens in a group expressed in the individualizing and sometimes cliché style of labels like some of the following:

- innate leadership
- one bad apple spoiling a barrel
- individual responses to power, influence and authority
- individual needs for inclusion, affiliation and control
- individual psychotic, neurotic or borderline responses
- transference manifestations
- individual 'games' played with a selected partner that ring the mutual changes along the dimensions of parent, adult and child
- individual acting out of member roles like pacifier, monopolizer, bully, martyr, Don Juan, seductress, little girl, mother, protector, big strong man, etc.

As we have emphasized in the preceding chapter, the labels we use to describe what we see, limit what we see. Interaction that is interpreted in terms of individual motivation gives a very different picture from interaction that is interpreted in terms of the group-as-a-whole. Thus, any and every one of the above labels can be very useful shorthand in our thinking, *provided* they don't confine us to the individual perspective at the expense of the group perspective that is needed if we are to be able to work with the group-as-a-whole as well as the individuals in it.

Broadly speaking, we encourage the group psychotherapist to use whatever psychological theory he holds that permits him to respond proactively, not reactively. To do this responsibly, however, he needs to understand the implications of his orientation. For example, if the group therapist uses Berne's orientation of 'parent-adult-child' it is important to understand that a 'transactional analysis' method of leading a group is likely to set up a pattern of predominantly therapist-patient interactions. This type of communication pattern inhibits other dynamics, like the development of group-level decision-making and independence. If, in another example, the group therapist uses the framework of the 'hot seat', then it is important for him to understand that change in the individual behavior will tend to persist only for as long as the group pressure persists. The recidivist rate will be high, because the group dynamics involved emphasize the pressure of external group norms upon the group members rather than the changes that occur as a result of emergent norms (norms that emerge as a function of changes within the group members). Therefore, the 'hot seat' techniques are useful provided the individual remains within the framework of therapeutic communities where the external norm pressure is maintained.

In addition to a framework for understanding and interpreting individual behavior, we argue that it is essential for a group therapist to have a coherent *group* theory from which to interpret what he sees in the group and from which he derives his attempts to influence the direction of the group-as-a-whole. Any intervention is an influence attempt and can be expected to modify the group in certain directions and away from other directions. The 'success' or 'failure' of an intervention can therefore be determined by what happens after the intervention is made. If the group moves in the direction of the group goal, then the intervention succeeded. If the group does not move, or moves in an opposite direction to the one intended, then the intervention did not succeed.

A conceptual group-as-a-whole framework will permit the therapist to formulate his group level interventions as a series of hypotheses that he is testing. Interpretations that are recognized by the therapist as hypotheses permit him to evaluate the face validity of his influence attempts and the construct validity of his theory.

In this chapter we present a theory of the group-as-a-whole which differentiates group dynamics from individual dynamics. We call this the theory of the invisible group. The invisible group can be conceptualized as four systems: individual person; individual member-role; group-role and group-as-a-whole.

Each one of these systems is capable of being modified by any one of the other three. In the sections that follow, these four systems will be described, defined and related in a hierarchical development that results in the emergence of the group-as-a-whole. Throughout this chapter we are using deductive reasoning, and are therefore describing the invisible group: the group that exists only in deductive theory. As with any theory, the test of its worth will be in its usefulness in application to the real world of group.

At this point we alert our reader to the realistic work of mastering a different theoretical approach to groups, with the necessary understanding of concepts that, though perhaps familiar in other frameworks, are used here in ways that are specific to this particular framework. We do not expect that the rest of this chapter will always be easy reading. This is our first presentation of our comprehensive group theory designed to explain the development of the group-as-a-whole and the relationship of the individual to it. Some difficulties may occur for our readers because this perspective is different from those that they are used to. Some difficulty may come from those areas in our argument which do not yet articulate as smoothly as we would wish. We hope, however, that our readers will accompany us on the journey, as we chart our conceptual map. Our intention is to define a group psychology that is different from individual psychology, which will thus permit group to be observed, described, classified, studied and researched as a phenomenon that is different from the individual phenomena who are its members.

Theory of the invisible group

Both Lewinians and psychoanalysts would agree that it is possible to understand and describe a person's intrapersonal dynamics by correctly understanding and interpreting the meanings of his communication behaviors. From the frame of reference of psychoanalysis, a person's free associations lead to interpretations of the person's life space. But whereas the psychoanalytic perspective focuses on the dynamics of the individual, a systems application of field theory applies to the dynamics of both the individual and the group.

In individual psychotherapy, when one requests a person to verbalize or to follow the laws of free association, his communications are a reflection of his internal individual dynamics and his transference relationship to the therapist. Some important, different things happen when we, as group psychotherapists, request people to verbalize and then listen with our third ear to individual associations and also to the group associative themes. Whereas initially people's communications in a group can be interpreted in the same way that we interpret their communications in individual therapy, very soon we come face to face with a 'foreign' feel to their associations. Initially, indeed, people's communications in a group reflect their intraperson dynamics. Very soon, however, their communications reflect also their interpersonal dynamics, and finally, the group dynamics. At this point the group themes may well be at least as, if not more, important for understanding individual dynamics than the individual themes.

Lewin, as we have mentioned, defined a person's life space in terms of the person in interaction with the environment as he perceives it. The life space, then, is a map of the world as the person himself sees it in relation to his goals: both the goal the person tells himself he has, and the inferred goal that a person behaves 'as if' he has. In analyzing the map or life space, it is possible to predict the most probable path (or alternative paths) that the person will take to the goal. Thus, to depict accurately the life space is to be able to predict the person's behavior. The paths available to a person are determined by the permeability of the boundaries between the regions in his life space: the permeable boundaries he can locomote through, the impermeable boundaries he must locomote around. To understand a person's behavior is to be able to draw a map of his life space. This leads to Lewin's (1951a) equation: behavior is a function of the life space; or $b = f(L. Sp.)$.

Lewin's life space provides a map of the person in relationship to his perceived environment. When a person first enters a group, he functions as an individual system. The person component of this system is a product of the specific intrapersonal dynamics that we understand from the psychoanalytic point of view. Instead of the psychoanalytic constructs of conscious, pre-conscious and unconscious, however, we are using Lewin's constructs of reality and irreality for the purpose of developing our schema.

The differentiation of the Life-Space also increases the dimension of reality-irreality . . . The different degrees of irreality correspond to different degrees of fantasy. They include both the positive wishes and the fears. The level of irreality in the psychological future corresponds to the wishes or fears for the future; the level of reality, to what is expected. (Lewin, 1951a, p. 245.)

Everyone's memory store contains information that has elements of both fantasy and reality that exist at the level of the unconscious, pre-conscious and conscious. In addition, everyone's perceptions of the world are selective; and the storage of information is related by some association to what is already stored. Simplistically, it is easier to file information when there is already a file ready to receive it. Thus there are two important aspects to each person's selectivity in perception. One is the compatibility of the new information with that already in the memory store, and the second is the style of reality testing that is idiosyncratic to the person. Perceptual style is an important reflection of a person's psychodynamics as the Rorschach test has shown.

Using general systems theory, group can be conceptualized from different perspectives, each one of which is a different level of abstraction, hierarchically related to the others. Lewin's construct of the life space can, through the principle of isomorphy, be applied to each one of the four systems. These four systems are: the individual-person system; the individual-member-role system; the group-role system; and the group-as-a-whole system. The first two systems are sub-system components of the individual system and the second two are sub-system components of the group system. The life space of each system is different. However, each system's life space is characterized by the same basic structural features and the same laws of operation as every other system's life space (see figure 3.1).

These four systems are in a hierarchical relationship to each other: the system *person* being in a sub-system or component relationship to the system *member*, which in turn is in a sub-system relationship to the system *role*, and so on. Each one permits us to delineate a system with boundaries and components that differentiate it from the other three systems. The boundaries between each of the four systems are potentially permeable to the outputs from each of the other three systems, and each one is therefore capable of being modified by any one of the other three systems.

In addition, each system is capable of being defined by an equation representing the life space. The life space equation for each system

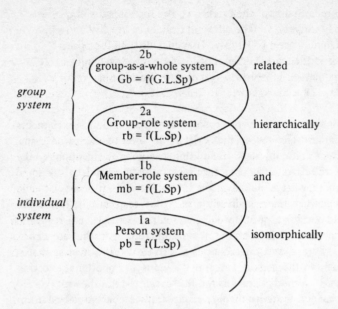

Figure 3.1 Group and individual perspectives, representing different
levels of conceptual abstraction defined via general systems theory as
(1) individual system with sub-systems (1a) person and (1b) member-
role; and (2) group system with sub-systems (2a) group-role and (2b)
group-as-a-whole; related hierarchically and isomorphically. Output
behavior of each system is defined in the life space equation

therefore defines the behavioral output of that system. Since we have
defined system outputs as communication behaviors, in these life space
equations 'communication behavior' and 'system output' are synonymous terms. All systems (and their particular life space equations) are
related hierarchically in terms of levels of abstraction. Finally, because
according to systems theory each system shares basic structural features
and the same laws of operation, increasing one's understanding of any
one of the systems will increase one's understanding of every other.

To illustrate, let us trace the journey of Ann, as she enters a group as
a new member. She enters having no direct experience of this group.
From her preparatory interview she knows that the group has been in
existence for three years; that there are seven other people in the group
and that she will be the eighth, that the group meets for an hour and a
half at the same time and on the same day each week; and that she has
been asked to agree to work with the group for a minimum of six
months; and if at any time after she should decide to leave, she should

be prepared to work through a six week separation period. That is the sum of her information.

Even before Ann joins the group, her 'member' self has begun to emerge from her 'person' self. In other words, a new focus of awareness has begun to exist for her: her expectation, her wishes and her fears of 'the group' have been mobilized. These expectations will be determined by her past psychological experience with significant people and with other groups, and by her present psychological state. For example, she might enter the group eagerly expecting it to be warm and cherishing, much as her father was to her when she was growing up. She might enter terrified, expecting the group to be cold, rejecting, and angry, much like her mother. She might arrive with a chip on her shoulder, expecting to have more in common with the therapist than the members, much as she felt at school when she was 'teacher's pet' and unpopular with her peers. She might feel 'nothing', expecting to be ignored, crowded out and overlooked, much as she was as the youngest member of her family.

Thus the content of her 'reality' and 'irreality' memories have already influenced her expectations, and she already has a (probably unconscious) fantasy in her mind of what to expect in group. We can expect her unconscious fantasy to generate a self-fulfilling prophecy.

When Ann does enter the group therapy room for the first time, her behavior will reflect both her person and her member systems. As a 'person' she will have available all those behaviors that she usually uses in new situations, that have worked for her in the past, and that are available to her under stress. As a 'member' she will select those behaviors which seem appropriate to the group situation *as she sees it.* As we have said, the situation as she sees it probably has more to do with the group that she has projected or displaced from her unconscious expectations than with the actual group that exists.

Ann-the-person will react (probably unconsciously) to several of the people in the group. Something about the way they look, sit, talk or speak will remind her of people that she knows. These reactions will be the basis of her transference responses. She will also tend to respond to these selected people more in terms of her expectations than in terms of the way they respond to her.

Behaving toward people 'as if' they are going to respond in a specific way is a powerful influence in eliciting the response that is expected. It is probable that at least some of the other people in the group will resonate with Ann's behavior. A nurturing man will experience the impulse to protect Ann. An aloof woman will experience an impulse to withdraw. In our group theory language, interactions have become complementary transactions at the psychic level, between person systems. The potential now exists for mutual acting out, each person being stimulated to repeat a mode of relating that belongs in their own past history. So far we are dealing with inputs and outputs between person systems, and the same phenomenon could occur if Ann was interacting with these people on a bus or at a party.

Ann-the-member will use these transference responses to 'typecast' these people so that they play out the roles in the group situation that she expects. In other words, Ann behaves in the group 'as if' her perceived group was the real group. The more the people in the group 'dance to Ann's tune', the more Ann's perceived group becomes acted out in the actual group. Those people whose member systems are compatible will sub-group with Ann in those role relationships: Pam, for example, whose perceived group is an environment where other siblings are continually tugging at her skirts, expecting her to put their needs before her own, and who is continually prepared to give them the cold shoulder in the hope that they will leave her alone; Bruce, whose basic stance is that of a protector of all mother-child and child-mother womankind and whose unconscious fantasy demands that he provide a strong supportive arm lest 'mother' collapse and let him fall into endless nothing. Ann and Pam, Ann and Bruce, and Bruce and Pam, can form a strong alliance in a triangular sub-group of member systems whose interaction is now predictable. Pam will reject Ann; Bruce will champion Ann; Ann will take Bruce for granted and solicit Pam's attention. Bruce will feel rejected and will chide Pam for rejecting Ann and Pam will become still colder. Each of these three people are now acting out their membership in their irreal groups, and the effect of their acting out on the real group is to create a repetition *in vivo* of their worst fears. Hence the repetition compulsion; the *folie-à-deux* (or *à-trois*, or *à-plusieurs*) and the self-fulfilling prophecy.

What happens next will depend upon the many factors of the group's dynamics. For some members, the sub-group of Ann, Pam and Bruce will serve a complementary function, and they will locate themselves in roles that are compatible both to their own person system dynamics and member projected groups. For other members, Ann, Pam and Bruce's sub-group will make no sense in terms of their projected groups, and they will question what is going on. Questions can serve to stimulate exploration and reality testing in the group, or they can go unheard or ignored.

Now to translate Ann's journey into theoretical terms. Ann-the-person is viewed against the matrix of her own past history and her transferences in the group are based upon the object relationships, developed with her original nuclear and extended family members as well as other significant relationships. In Ann's member-role, projections and displacements occur onto her psychotherapy group from her previous social experiences (her primary family group and her secondary groups such as church, school, social and work groups) which form her past group history, and act as a secondary source of transference. Her perceptions of the actual group environment is filtered through the wishes and fears that she has of 'groups' in general. This leads us to define the first of our two theoretical perspectives which we call the individual perspective.

From the individual perspective, 'group' is a collection-of-individuals, and its dynamics can be discussed in the language of individual and social psychology when group is defined in terms of 'the sum of' or 'greater than the sum of' its individual members. The individual systems perspective is shown in figure 3.2.

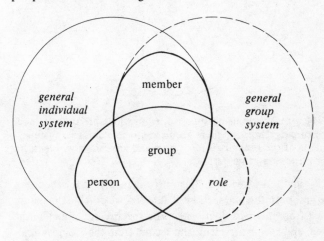

Figure 3.2 The individual systems perspective: from which group is defined in terms of individual and social psychology where person and member systems are components of the general individual system and group-of-individuals is equal to or greater than the sum of its parts

When we observe group from the individual perspective, as we do above, we are observing the stimulus of individual behavior upon group behavior, as we did in the case of Ann. When we view group from the second of our two theoretical perspectives, however, we observe the obverse of this. We call the second perspective the group perspective, where group is the stimulus to individual behavior. It is from this perspective that Foulkes writes: 'the individual patient and his disturbance is only a symptom of the conflicts and tensions within his group ...' (Foulkes, 1965, p. 291).

The group systems perspective is illustrated in figure 3.3 where, in contrast to the individual perspective, group is called the group-as-a-whole and its dynamics can be discussed in the language of group psychology when, and *only when*, group psychology defines group as *different from* or *other than* the sum of its parts.

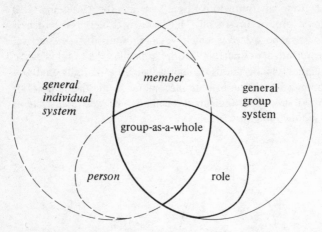

Figure 3.3 The group systems perspective: from which group is defined in terms of group psychology where group-as-a-whole and role systems are components of the general group system and group-as-a-whole is different from the sum of its parts

Figures 3.2 and 3.3 provide an illustrative summary of the theory of the invisible group. In the two sections that follow we develop the theory in detail: first from the individual systems perspective as defined by the person system and member system; and second from the group systems perspective as defined by the role system and the group-as-a-whole system.

Individual systems perspective

An individual in a group can be conceptualized as a system whose boundaries have thresholds of permeability and impermeability, and whose behavioral outputs will reflect the individual psychodynamics that have developed from his particular gene pool, and his sociopsychological history.

The boundaries of the individual system define the system. Dynamically, boundaries can be thought of as thresholds which either keep out, or let in, information from systems in the same field. Boundaries can be characterized as permeable, i.e. as relatively open or closed. A system whose boundary is permeable has a relatively low or open threshold; a system whose boundary is impermeable has a relatively high or closed threshold.

Person system

The person system is a component of the individual system. The *person* system is defined by the individual's life space. Lewin defined the life space as a person's *perception* of his environment. In systems language, the person and the perceived environment are sub-systems of the life space system.

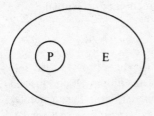

Figure 3.4 Person (P) and perceived environment (E) as components of the life space

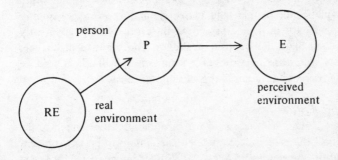

Figure 3.5 Perceived environment (E) as a perception of the person's (P) real environment (RE)

Perception is the process by which inputs from the real environment as well as resulting outputs from the person modify the total life space. Thus environment components of the life space represent the map that the person has made of the world, which is modified by the ongoing process of his perceptions (see figure 3.4).

There are two factors in the perceptual process that explain the particular life space that is mapped: (1) the person's discrimination style: how he discriminates similarities and differences; (2) the person's perceptual filter: the reality/irreality filter which determines his interpretation of environmental perceptions (see figure 3.6).

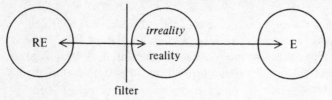

filter

Figure 3.6 Perceived environment (E) as a function of perceptual discrimination style and reality/irreality filter

1   Discrimination style
Discriminations between similarities and differences provide basic bits of information that can be integrated into perceptions. Discrimination involves two operations: perception of the similarities in the apparently different, and perception of differences in the apparently similar. Each person performs these operations at his own individual rate. Some people discriminate quickly and integrate quickly; others discriminate slowly and integrate slowly; still others discriminate quickly and integrate slowly or vice versa. Each person performs these operations in his own style. Some people tend to see similarities in the apparently different, and have difficulty perceiving differences in the apparently similar; others have the opposite tendency, and perceive differences immediately, whereas similarities take them longer. Still others perceive both similarities and differences almost simultaneously.

2   Perceptual filter
The person system has access to an information store which is the product of all the person's accumulated perceptions of his environment throughout his development. These perceptions are classified by Lewin (1951a, p. 245) in terms of past, present and future ideation; and in terms of reality and irreality (or goodness of fit between the ideas of the environment and the environment).

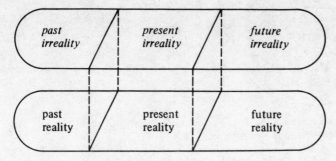

Figure 3.7 Past, present and future perceptions at the level of irreality and reality

The reality level stores those perceptions that have a greater goodness of fit with the real world. Outputs from the reality level have a greater potential for reflecting the actual probabilities and possibilities of the real world. The reality level also has a greater potential for its information store to be revised congruently with inputs from the real world. The process of information transfer between the reality level of the person and the real world has the characteristics of reality testing. In other words, the boundaries of the reality life space and the actual environment are permeable to inputs and outputs from each other. Thus there is a relationship between permeability of boundaries and the reality level of the life space.

The irreality level stores those perceptions that are characterized by information that does not have a good fit with the real world. Outputs from the irreality level have a greater potential for carrying information that reflects fantasies and distortions. The irreality level also has a greater potential for its information store to be revised congruently with internal wishes and fears which, projected onto the real world, distort perceptions, and are retrieved and stored 'as if' they were inputs from the real world. Ann, for example, perceived Pam's aloofness as a personal rejection. The process of information transfer between the irreality level and the real world has the characteristics of projection and other defense mechanisms, unmodified by reality testing. The boundaries of the irreality life space are relatively impermeable to environmental inputs. Figure 3.8 defines the person component of the life space in terms of reality and irreality.

The person will thus have (at any particular time) a tendency to process information (similarities and differences) in his own particular style, and a perceptual screen (organizing principle) which determines the reality/irreality nature of perceptual integration.

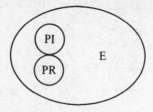

Figure 3.8 Life space showing person components of irreality and reality (PI) (PR) in the environment (E)

The organization of the stored information will define the person's characteristic manner of sending and receiving information. In other words, the organizing principle behind the manner in which present and future information relates to reality and irreality governs the outputs from the individual and also governs those inputs which the individual can receive. This organizing principle, in systems language, is a function of level of equilibrium, and changes in this level of equilibrium or organizing principle permit new organization to occur. A particular individual's style of selective perceptions defines both the way he perceives his environment and also the way he behaves in it. Changes in either permit change in both.

However, every individual has variable functioning. For example, when Ann is less vulnerable she may interpret Pam's aloofness as Pam's self-defensiveness rather than as a personal rejection. Therefore at any one time a person may be more reality oriented or more irreality oriented. Also, at any one time, a person's map of the world may fit to the reality actual world, or more closely fit to the irreality component. Thus, both person (P) and environment (E) of the life space have two components: a reality (R) component and an irreality (I) component. Thus a person's life space can be usefully defined as b = f(PR, PI; ER, EI). This is schematically expressed in figure 3.9.

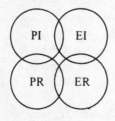

Figure 3.9 Life space components: person reality (PR) and irreality (PI) components in transaction with the person's reality (ER) and irreality (EI) perceived environment

The person's perceptions of his environment are influenced by the degree to which information about the environment is processed in the realms of irreality or in the realms of reality, which in turn is influenced by the permeability of the boundaries between the reality and irreality components of the person and the environment. When the irreality component has boundaries that are relatively impermeable to reality information, then there will be little modification of the perceptual distortions, and only inputs from the environment that are compatible with the irreality distortions will be received. The irreality component will be large, and the reality component small. In a group, the person's behavior will be little influenced by actual group behavior; and the influence exerted by his behavior on the group will be to elicit a complementary irreality, which then simulates the environment that the person is behaving 'as if' he is in. Hence the 'martyr' gets scapegoated, the paranoid finds himself talked about and isolated and Ann participates in a triangle of futility. If, however, the boundaries between the reality and irreality systems are permeable, then the person can modify his perceptions, and complementary reality transactions can take place, both within the person, and between the person and the group.

The more the irreality principle governs the processing of information, the more the person's environment will be mapped as a function of his irreality wishes and fears, and feedback from the environment will be distorted. In this case, permeability of the boundary will be selective, relatively permeable to inputs that synchronize with perceptions, relatively impermeable to inputs that do not. This results in the creation of a perceived group that is a function of the person's idiosyncratic ideational system.

The more reality in the processing, the more the person's perceived group will reflect the actual group (real environment). The more irreality in the processing, the less the perceived group will reflect the actual group and the more it will be a reflection of the person's irreality component. This constitutes our definition of the member system and its reality and irreality components.

Member system

The member system is defined by the person's perception of the *group* as the environment in his life space. The process by which this occurs is that the individual develops an ideational system *group* with which to interact. At this stage the *group* is almost entirely a perception from the person system, and how closely *group* approximates the actual group will depend upon whether the person's perceptions have been characteristic of the reality or the irreality level. Thus the more anxious Ann is about entering group the more likely she is to experience *group* in terms of her irreality wishes and fears and to interpret group events in terms of them.

As we have said, perception will be determined by the individual's psychodynamics, his social dynamics, his family memberships and his other overlapping membership experiences. Another influence on the closeness of fit between the perceived group and the actual group will be environmental factors, such as the ambiguity, redundancy and contradictions inherent in the environmental situation. For the member new to a psychotherapy group, the ambiguity of the situation will be high, and the wish to get something from the situation will also be high. Ambiguity, coupled with high expectations, is a factor that stimulates regressive distortion. Therefore, for the new psychotherapy group member, the probability is that the person's perceptions of group will be greatly determined by regressive wishes and fears of *group* based on expectations deriving from past irreality (as in our example of Ann) and relatively unmodified by the actual, present and as yet unknown group.

Whereas, in the person system, the person's life space represented his perceptions of his general environment, in the member system, the person's life space is represented by the person system in interaction with his perceived group environment.

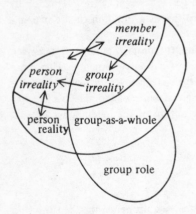

Figure 3.10 Dynamic systems in group illustrating the relationship between the person irreality system and the member system

In figure 3.10 the person system transacting with the irreality group system now represents sub-system components of the member system. The outputs from this new system are 'member' communications. The boundaries between the sub-system's member and group irreality are relatively permeable to each other.

Outputs from the member system are the source of the 'self-fulfilling prophecy'. By acting out the perceptions of the relationship to the irreality group, enough responses are stimulated from within the group to re-create in the actual group the social system which the member expects. Thus it is, for example, that scapegoating in the group can serve both individual dynamics as well as group-as-a-whole dynamics, as we shall see.

We have already talked about the dyads that can be formed when two people act out complementary transference interactions as occur, for example, in Berne's parent-adult-child combinations. In transactional analysis (TA) psychotherapy groups, sub-group relationships are encouraged to develop in this manner, and interpretations of parent-adult-child transactions are an example of an interpretation of an irreality group. Some TA and gestalt therapists externalize this irreality group through the multi-chair technique. A group of empty chairs set up for the critical and nurturing parents, the adult, the adapted, rebellious and free child and the little professor, etc., with an individual moving from one empty chair to another in response to his internal member-role is an excellent illustration, *in vivo*, of an irreal group.

The member system construct illustrates the transference relationship. The transference phenomenon can be described as the patient being in an independent transaction with the analyst. Transference resolution is the shift towards an interdependent transaction. In group psychotherapy, the members' irreality group component is modified toward reality in exactly the same way that transference is resolved. As the level of equilibrium is modified in the member system, so through the interdependent transaction between the member and person systems is the level of equilibrium modified in the person system towards reality. When this same dynamic is applied to member interaction with real and irreal group components, we have change in the person as a function of group membership which in psychoanalytic terminology we would talk about in terms of resonance and amplification.

For example, if in the process of the group in which Ann is engaged in acting out transferentially with Pam and Bruce, the sub-group gains insight into their co-operative triangle of rejection, Ann-the-member will gain insight into the irreality of her member role, and Ann-the-person will gain insight into her personal dynamics. This is shown in figure 3.11.

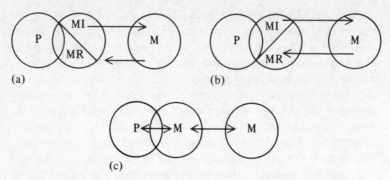

Figure 3.11 Dynamics of transference (independent member irreality interaction) (a); transference resolution (interdependent member transaction) (b); and transactions between member systems related to change in the person system (interdependent person/member transaction) (c)

From the individual perspective, there are the member systems and the person systems. These two systems have boundaries that are potentially permeable to each other, and can therefore relate in transactional dependence and/or interdependence as well as in interaction.

When the boundaries of the member system are permeable to the person system, but the person system is impermeable to the member system, then no feedback loop has been developed (as with the analyst, who has counter-transference information through the projective identification of the patient, but is not yet able to communicate it to the patient).

A similar dynamic operates when the member system continues to receive inputs from the person system, and to interact on the basis of projections with other member systems in the group. The characteristics of these interactions is a closed feedback loop (positive feedback in systems terms) governed by repetition-compulsion, and/or delusion, relatively isolated from the dynamics of feedback from the actual environment. For example, if Ann enters group feeling terrified, unconsciously expecting it to be cold and rejecting like her mother, and in spite of a warm and accepting group response does not modify her expectations, or her behavior, or her terror, the system dynamics would approximate the diagram in figure 3.12.

As we have said, person system output is a function of the person's individual psychodynamics in interaction with the person's perceptions of the environment. Present (here and now) output can be understood in terms of a person's experience of (a) the particular past associations that are available at the particular present moment; (b) his perceptions of the present; and (c) his expectations of the future. Present perceptions are strongly influenced by the quality of both past memories and future expectations. The degree to which a person's output is reality oriented depends upon how related to the irreality level past memories are. The more past memories are activated in ways that are relevant to the present reality, the less distorted the person's perceptions of the present environment will be and the more accurately will he be able to map the path to his goal in the future (based on probability, rather than on wishes or fears). This process determines the goodness of fit between the person's map (or life space) and the real world.

Figure 3.12 Dynamic systems in group illustrating positive feedback between member and irreal group system

Dependent transactions between member and person systems

Dependent transactions occur when only one of the system's boundaries is permeable to the other. When member systems are largely a function of inputs from person systems, and when the person system is characterized more by irreality function than reality function, then the member boundaries will be relatively impermeable to any communications from any systems that are characterized by reality. On the other hand, it is probable that these same member boundaries will be relatively permeable to outputs from other member systems that are characterized by the same compatible irreality communications, thus the *folie-à-deux*. In the case of Ann, for example, the triad of rejection between Ann, Pam and Bruce would be diagrammed as in figure 3.13. Thus transactions between member systems are likely to be selective, one set based on communication outputs that are characterized by reality communications, and the other sets based on compatible irreality outputs. This explains the mutual acting out and the development of a *folie-à-deux* (or *à-trois*) at the member level, and the formation of sub-groups based on shared transference.

Figure 3.13 Dynamics of *folie-à-trois* described by interdependent transactions between compatible irreality member systems and independent interactions between incompatible reality systems

To summarize, systems whose dynamics are more characterized by reality will have boundaries that are relatively permeable to both reality and to irreality based systems. Thus irreality systems will not interact with reality systems; but reality systems can enter into dependent transactional relationships with irreality systems, and can enter into interdependent transactional relationships with other reality systems. Irreality systems will transact across boundaries with other, compatible irreality systems.

This is a systems method for describing the transference neurosis within group psychotherapy. For example, during the phase of the authority issue, the group-as-a-whole manifests a paranoid episode in relationship to the therapist. When this episode is acted out it results in the 'death' of the leader. This can occur either symbolically, or in reality if the group splits off this scapegoated component of itself and forms again.

How does successful psychotherapy take place? Successful group psychotherapy modifies the reality/irreality system interactions from dependent to interdependent. This can happen in several ways. For example, let us say that Ann comes to understand that she is experiencing Pam as her mother, and this leads to insight into her own dynamics. Insight changes the reality/irreality level in the person component of her life space, which changes her perception of her environment from past irreality towards present irreality. This in turn leads to an increase in the permeability of the boundary between her person system and her member system, and her member system becomes more permeable to inputs from the real group (see figure 3.14a). Ann-the-member's behavior changes towards Pam. This behavioral change is received in the triad member systems as reality inputs which modify the member systems' transactions (figure 3.14b).

However, as the irreal 'triad' group was a function of the member system transactions, so the irreal group also becomes modified towards reality (figure 3.14c). The result is to change the feedback system from positive (maintaining) to negative (changing). Thus the total system is 'unfrozen' and the potential for insight and change increases for the person, member and group systems previously involved in a positive (fixating) feedback loop (figure 3.14d).

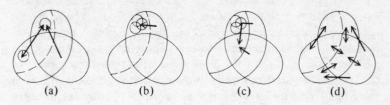

(a)   (b)   (c)   (d)

Figure 3.14 (a) Ann's person and member system modified towards reality. (b) Triad member system modified as a function of (a). (c) Transactions between member and irreality group systems change. (d) 'Unfrozen' group

For Ann specifically there is increased permeability for reality information in both her member and person systems. Her initial insight, through her interaction with Pam and Bruce, and her understanding of the group system that they had set up together, may lead to still further insight. For example she may understand that she tends to set herself up in triangular relationships where she turns away from the accepting person in her pursuit of the rejecting one.

Up to this point, Ann's insight has been explained as a function of transference resonance and amplification in a group that is formed by its individual members in transaction. This sequence has a different set of implications from the group-as-a-whole perspective as we shall see in the next section. For example, the shift in the reality/irreality dimension of the group-as-a-whole reflects upon the potential for group role development. Different potential in the group role system influences *all* person and member systems at the level of reality and irreality as well as influencing the potential for the development of the group-as-a-whole. As we will explain fully in the next section, the development of the group-as-a-whole maturity depends upon increased differentiation of the group life space. Changes in the group role potential in range and flexibility of locus permits increased discriminations and integrations of group relevant communications. As the group-as-a-whole communication potential increases, so does the maturation potential for both the individual and the group-as-a-whole.

Group systems perspective

From the individual systems perspective we differentiated between the person and member constructs and traced the development of the 'irreal' and the 'real' group as it emerged from transactions between member systems. For example, Ann's self-fulfilling prophecy was acted out in a triad with Bruce and Pam. From the individual perspective this triad can be seen as an example of an 'irreal' group that emerges as a function of the transactions between the 'irreal' components of the member systems. 'Group-of-individuals' does not need the concept of the 'group-as-a-whole' to explain its dynamics. It is sufficient to explain the group dynamics in terms of the resonance of individual member transferences, amplified in the interactive process between the members.

The question then arises why there is a need to define the group as something other than a transference resonance and amplification phenomenon. What is the need for a group systems perspective? The first major reason is that unless group dynamics are differentiated from individual dynamics there can be no true psychology of group as different from the psychology of individuals.

There are many obvious comparisons that can be made between individual and group systems, and rightly so: as we emphasized in the beginning of our theoretical exposition, the systems of group and individual are isomorphically related and share similar structure and function manifested in different orders of abstraction. It is no accident, therefore, that when we discuss the individual system many of the things that we say lead to insight into the group system. The reverse, however, is not true. Group and individual systems are not yet sufficiently differentiated for group to be discussed clearly enough as a separate phenomenon for insights into the group system to be transferred to the individual system. This is the first major reason that we stress the importance of being able to differentiate the individual perspective from the group perspective.

A second major reason is that of classification. Classification is an important operation in understanding human systems. For example, through the process of classifying people, the similarities and differences between types of people are formalized in ways that permit us to observe and study the implications of those similarities and differences. This leads us to being able to compare and contrast human behavior in ways that we could not, if we were not able to type and classify. We are then able to learn, not only about different types of people and their behavior *per se*, but also to connect the influence of environmental factors upon the ways that their behavior manifests. Anthropologists, through classification, compare the differences between the human product of different cultures. They also compare similarities between simple and complex cultural systems that are independent of geography. The importance of being able to make similar kinds of comparisons and contrasts in terms of individual patients and group psychotherapy cultures is obvious from this argument. It is also relatively unexplored.

At the end of this chapter we will take up the classification aspects of this argument and relate it to different types of groups along the dimensions of development and sophistication. First, however, we shall deal with the practical application of the classification of group from the group systems perspective. Having argued that being able to discriminate group-as-a-whole from a group-of-individuals is an important thing to do, the first question is: how does one observe it and describe it?

As we have said, when one requests a person to free-associate, his uncensored associations are responsive to his internal, individual dynamics. Something very different happens when one asks a group of people to free-associate. Whereas people in a group may start to associate in tune with their individual dynamics, over time a different phenomenon takes place, in which group dynamics serve as the major catalyst for these free associations.

Thus the potential for interpreting the individual's communications in a psychotherapy group changes over time from being obviously related to individual dynamics to being obviously related to the group dynamics. This change parallels the development of the group, from a group whose dynamics represent a collection of individuals in interaction; to the dynamics of a group-as-a-whole whose members are in inter-dependent transaction. Recognizing this phenomenon makes it important to understand the group-as-a-whole as a catalyst to individual associations that cannot otherwise be explained.

In order to 'see' the invisible group-as-a-whole, one observes the complementary relationship between group dynamics and the group role. We ask ourselves different kinds of questions, make different kinds of connections, view things from a different perspective, and the result is a different understanding of group, and the definition of a different system: the group system. In the sections following we apply the group systems perspective first to the group-role system and second to the group-as-a-whole system.

Group-role system

The group-role system is hierarchically related to the individual member system but is a property of the group-as-a-whole. While its influence upon the individual system can be explained, its derivation as a product of the individual system cannot. In the group-role system aspects of group function continue to be predictable, even when significant changes, such as the absence of members or the addition of members, occur in the group.

For example, however much Ann's perception of the group was a function of her own distortions, an actual group environment did exist. This actual group will manifest stages in development that are independent of Ann's membership. In the group's developmental phases, certain sets of behavior function as forces that drive the group forward toward the next phase and certain others function as forces that restrain or fixate the group in its developmental movement.

When we left Ann in our original example, in the triadic group, the issue that remained unanswered was what would determine whether the group-as-a-whole would pause and explore this sub-group phenomenon or ignore any invitation to do so. Let us postulate that the group ignored repeated questions, including the therapsits'. It is not enough to say that members want to act out the behavior more than they want to understand it. It frequently occurs in even quite skilled and sophisticated groups that all members claim that they do not want an event to continue, yet continue it does. Therefore this phenomenon cannot be explained as a 'sum of member behavior' or even as 'more than the sum of the member behavior'; rather it must be explained as a dynamic that springs from a different source.

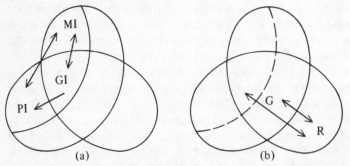

Figure 3.15 (a) Triad, illustrated from the individual systems perspective as a *folie-à-trois* (see figure 3.13). (b) Triad, illustrated from the group systems perspective as a role in transaction with the group-as-a-whole

The difference in the dynamic reflects the difference in definition between the individual systems perspective and the group systems perspective. This is illustrated in figure 3.15, using Ann's triad as the example. It will be noted that from the individual systems perspective, the irreal group is a function of the member system transactions at the irreal level; and from the group systems perspective, the irreal group serves as a role in transaction with the group-as-a-whole.

The fate of Ann's triad will depend upon the role it is playing for the group-as-a-whole. For example, in the flight phase of group, dependent behavior is likely to be supported by the group, either overtly or covertly, as a driving force towards the dependency goal of flight, and Ann's dependent behaviors together with other members' dependent behaviors will form the dependent role. In the fight phase, if the group expresses fight by scapegoating dependence, Ann alone might represent the group role whose function would be to 'contain' the group dependence while the group disowned its own dependency by attacking Ann's. In the pairing phase of intimacy, Bruce's nurturing response might well be joined by the entire group. In this case, Ann or any other member or sub-group might become the nurtured object of group. In the phase of alienation, Pam's withdrawal might well express the underlying feeling of the whole group, and Pam's role would thus be a voice for the group-as-a-whole.

From the group-role perspective, therefore, both the fate of Ann's sub-group and the group's response to Ann's behavior has more to do with the behavioral clusters that define a role in the group process than it does with the individuals who are contributing to the role.

In an earlier illustration (figure 3.13) Ann, the potential victim, was described as a person-member system whose transactions in the group resulted in complementary scapegoating at the level of an irreal group formed by complementary member systems. We reproduce this in figure 3.16a to illustrate the same phenomenon from the perspective of the group-as-a-whole. To do this we use different language and different systems definitions. Forces that maintain the group level of equilibrium (in this case, scapegoating as a driving force toward the goal of fight) are represented by complementary transactions between role systems. Ann may or may not participate in the scapegoated role. From the individual perspective, it was sufficient to explain her as a scapegoated member through knowledge of her person-member dynamics. Her person-member system dynamics have not changed. But they are no longer sufficient to predict how her behavior will manifest in a group-role system. The system role is a function of the system group, not a function of the system member or system person.

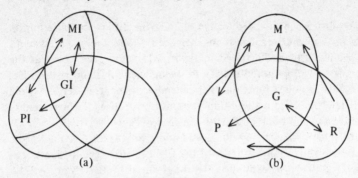

Figure 3.16 (a) Transactional interdependent relationships between person-member systems and the irreality group. (b) Transactional interdependence relationships between the group-role systems, and dependent transactional relationships between the person and member systems and the group and role systems

In figure 3.16 transactions between the person-member systems and the irreal group, which describes scapegoating as a function of self-fulfilling prophecy, are contrasted with transactions between group and role systems. It will be seen that person and member systems are in dependent transactional relationships with the group-as-a-whole and group-role systems, which are themselves in interdependent transactional relationships. 'Insight' for the person can come as a function of insight into the function of group-role relationships; as a function of insight into the incompatibility between member expectations of the group and the actual group; or insight as a function of an effective response to group process that changes the transactional relationship between the reality and irreality of the person.

In the case of Ann, figure 3.16a serves as a diagram of the triangle of rejection between her and Bruce and Pam. Figure 3.16b is viewed from the group role and group-as-a-whole systems. If the group-as-a-whole is engaged in an unconscious simulation exercise of 'no exit' futility, demonstrating to the therapist that a group hell has been created, the arrows from the group-as-a-whole region to the person, member and role systems would illustrate the forces that maintain this direction. The group role that is played by the triad towards this goal might be interpreted as an expression of the 'play-within-a-play'. As the group passively watches the triangular expression of futility, it reinforces its continuation by its silent attention and disowns the responsibility through refraining from intervening. The triangle is thus the voice of the group; demonstrating to the therapist futility in action, word and feeling. An interpretation at either the group-as-a-whole or group-role level could yield insight at any one, or all four, of the systems for Ann or any of the group members.

Outputs from the group-role system have a potential influence on the person and member systems, both at the level of reality and irreality. The *reality* component of the role system is related to the *work* group. The irreality component of the role system is related to the basic assumption group. It is possible for person and member systems to be influenced by inputs from the reality and irreality components of the group-role system at the same time. An example would be if our member Ann got insight into the meaning of her behavior through input into her person system from the group-as-a-whole which modified the reality component of her member system and communicated her insight from the perspective of her part in a group-role system function in the group. In this sense, she would be a 'voice of the group'. Her input at the level of group role would be a reality work communication, as well as reality work at the person and member system levels, in that in the process of integrating the insight she would be changing the irreality-reality equilibrium in each of the three systems.

Should Ann recognize the same type of phenomenon a second time and 'teach' the group what she was observing, at the level of group role, her communication would still be a reality work input and voice of the group. At the level of individual member, her communication would also be a reality input in that it would modify her perceived group in line with the actual group. At the level of her person system, however, her communication is redundant. She 'knows it already' and to repeat it is therefore an avoidance of further insights. Thus what is 'work' at the group level can be 'flight' at the individual level, as it would be in this case.

The reverse can also be true. Groups frequently pause in their developmental tasks in order to regress and thus help an individual member gain mastery over an aspect of group behavior that the group has already mastered. Going over old ground is redundant for the group. It avoids new insights, and in this sense the group role serves a flight function from the developmental task. At the member level, however, group developmental work is being done. Thus it is that what may be described as regression or fixation from the group-role level, may be in the service of work at the member or person levels.

The group-as-a-whole

The voice of the group is expressed through the group role. The group therapist gains insight into the group-as-a-whole by listening to the 'group' that is behind the group voice, much as the individual therapist gains insight into the individual by listening to the 'person' that is behind the person's voice. Just as different types of people will talk with different 'voices', so will different types of groups.

In the previous section we illustrated group-role dynamics by describing different aspects of the group's response to the voice of the 'triad'. In this section we will view the group response to the triad from a different perspective to illustrate group-as-a-whole dynamics. The most obvious example of different group-as-a-whole responses were (1) when the triad was serving as a voice for flight, contrasted to (2) the responses when the triad was serving as a voice for fight. In the first case, the group-as-a-whole would be classified as a flight group and the triad would be serving the group-as-a-whole as a force in the group goal of flight; in the second case the group-as-a-whole would be classified as a fight group and the triad would be serving the group-as-a-whole as a force in the group goal of fight. Both flight and fight groups are 'basic assumption' dependency groups, or, in our language, 'irreal' groups-as-a-whole.

From the group perspective, the group role is the communication behavioral output of the group system. Within the group-as-a-whole life space, the group roles serve as driving forces in relation to the group-as-a-whole goal. Thus the group role serves as negative or positive feedback function within or between the irreal and real group components of the group-as-a-whole. Thus, when the group role is a single voice for the group-as-a-whole it serves as positive feedback to the *status quo* (or level of equilibrium) of the group, and therefore as a driving force in relationship to the irreal group goal. When, however, there are conflicting group roles, then the group-role voices reflect discord, and serve as disequilibrating negative feedback to the group-as-a-whole. This can be represented as a field of force in relationship to the group-as-a-whole goal. For example, if there are two group-role voices, the voice of flight and the voice of fight, then there is negative feedback and the irreal dependency group is in disequilibrium, and thus there is a potential for change; like a shift in development. If the group, on the other hand, is in equilibrium in either flight or fight, then there is a potential for fixation.

Take, for example, the triad as a group role, or voice for the group. The therapist is observing the 'play-within-a-play' against the matrix of the group. If the 'play' occurs in a group whose history has been to passively watch sub-group interactions, and the sub-group interactions typically portray futility, to a passive, apathetic, uninvolved and helpless audience, then the therapist could develop a good working hypothesis that this is a dependent group, fixated in dependency in that the solutions to the group frustrations are repetitive and predictable. The sub-groups change, the role does not.

Where there is a diagnosis of fixation in dependency, further hypotheses arise. The dependency group could be occurring within a specific maturational phase which the group-as-a-whole is experiencing significant trouble in mastering. In this case there is a question as to whether the group will be permanently fixated at this stage, or whether it has the resources to work through the dependency fixation as a developmental vicissitude. Alternatively, the dependency group might be expressing an initial group fixation to which it regresses under stress. In this case, the kinds of goals that the group can achieve will be limited to those that are attainable for dependent groups. As a psychotherapy group, this is a sick group.

Which hypothesis fits for a particular group will depend upon the group history. Let us refer again to the triad, and place it against the matrix of a different group history. If the play-within-a-play manifests in the context of a group whose characteristic behavior in the past is to spontaneously produce 'plays' that contain the symbolic elements of whatever problem the group is working on, and if the therapist has observed before that the group tends to first watch, then analyze, and then use their insight to work through issues in the group, the therapist is certainly observing a mature group which has developed a method for using the group role as the vehicle for making the unconscious elements of the irreal group conscious. 'Mature' groups will develop different methods for transforming the unconscious content of the irreal group into the work goal of the real group. Criteria for differentiating between the manifestation of irreal group problems in the service of work, and manifestation of irreal group problems as signs of fixation or developmental vicissitude reside in the group history.

At this point a theoretical discrimination can be made, using the triad in its role of group voice for the irreal group as an example. If the symbolic content of the triad was 'oedipal', and if it is the voice for the group-as-a-whole, conveying the latent content of the group as a work goal, should the group-as-a-whole then be labelled an oedipal group? Our answer is no. We do not use psychoanalytic labels for group-as-a-whole phenomena for two reasons. The first reason is in the service of differentiation. We reserve psychoanalytic terminology for phenomena that we interpret from the individual systems perspective. To do this is particularly appropriate in the light of our interpretation of group-of-individuals system in terms of transference resonance. Our first reason is thus a matter of differentiation, clarity and convenience. Our second reason is in the service of theory. Psychoanalytically labelled groups, like 'oral' groups, 'anal' groups, 'oedipal' groups, manifest against different group-as-a-whole contexts. Thus a sub-group play-within-a-play may well give voice to an oral, anal or oedipal group issue. The context in which it is raised, however, can be in any one of the different classifications of group-as-a-whole. From the perspective of the relationship between group role and group-as-a-whole, an oedipal group role serves as a driving force in relationship to the goal. But, as always, a role is only one force in a field of force that represents the group-as-a-whole life space. Thus, where an oedipal group can play a role in the group-as-a-whole, the reverse is not true. Basic assumption and work groups (and other classification labels for group-as-a-whole systems) are a higher order of abstraction than psychoanalytically classified groups, by the definitions and assumptions of our theory.

Classification of groups-as-a-whole

In the introduction to this section, we argued for a group perspective that would permit the classification of groups-as-a-whole as different from groups-of-individuals. Group-as-a-whole is a classificatory label that defines group phenomena that cannot be adequately described in terms of individual dynamics and can be defined independent of individuals. Transactions between role systems yield group-as-a-whole phenomena just as transactions between member systems yield group-of-individuals phenomena. There are thus two major classificatory dimensions, individual and group, each one of which can be defined in terms of its systems components. The individual dimension is already rich in classification. Within the developmental hierarchy, for example, there is a psychology of infants, children, adolescents, young and mature adults, etc. In the psychology of group, however, there is not even a general acceptance of the phenomenon of group development, let alone a generally accepted sequence of phases of development from the infant to the mature group which could be classified.

Thus a group perspective which permits the classification of a group-as-a-whole as different from the group-of-individuals is important, not only to permit group psychology to be clearly differentiated from individual psychology, but also so that group developmental dynamics can be defined and observed, the vicissitudes of development understood, fixations diagnosed, and the healthy and mature group differentiated from immature or sick groups.

We offer our first pass at a classification system in the pages that follow. To do this, we have applied our theory of the invisible group as a tool to define group as a separate phenomenon from individual, and therefore classifiable in its own right. We hope that we are not alone in this task, as to do it successfully would make it possible to assess the goodness of fit between a specific type of person and a specific type of group for a specific type of goal. This, of course, is particularly important in group psychotherapy. Independent criteria for assigning certain types of people (patients) to certain types of group (psychotherapy) to obtain certain results (therapeutic change) is a prerequisite for a therapeutic prescription that can be evaluated by criteria other than patiently waiting to see the results.

In the pages that follow we define three classificatory areas:

1   *types of group culture,* which parallel the anthropological classifi-
    cations of simple and complex cultures;
2   group *maturation,* within which there can be fixations and vicissi-
    tudes along a developmental sequence which can be defined
    discretely in the ways that individual developmental phases can be
    defined and classified; and
3   classes of *real and irreal groups,* which parallel the classifications of
    individual behavior in terms of (a) the real or conscious, secondary
    process perspective and (b) the irreal or unconscious primary
    process perspective. This third section is the least well formulated
    in that its development clarity depends upon continued theoretical
    clarity. However, our work here marches in step with psychoanalytic
    thinking, and yields two different manifestations of group-as-a-
    whole: the reality problem-solving group-as-a-whole, and the irreality
    problem-solving group-as-a-whole.

1   Types of group-as-a-whole

We classify types of group in a manner that parallels the anthropological classifications of simple and complex cultures in man. The character-istics of the simpler group cultures are greater role rigidity, more predictability of function, narrower behavioral range; less sophisticated manifestation of cognitive development; and a greater pre-disposition to magical thinking and animistic interpretations of forces that the group experiences itself as helpless against. In contrast, a complex group culture has greater flexibility of role, wider behavioral range, creativity of function, sophisticated manifestations of cognitive development and a potential for regression in the service of the group consensually validating (or ego) functions. When we apply this kind of classificatory thinking to the three classes of group that we define in chapter 6 as Level One, Level Two, Level Three, we define three group-as-a-whole systems, each one of which can be mapped against the matrix of its life space.

Each of these three group life spaces will have characteristically different regions through which to locomote to reach the goal. Looking at these three groups from the group-as-a-whole perspective, it becomes apparent that the goal of a Level One group is a sub-goal of a Level Two group which is in turn a sub-goal of a Level Three group. Thus the concept of three levels of group belongs to the levels of maturation from the group system perspective. Operationalizing the three levels of group requires an understanding of the role system and its relationship to the group-as-a-whole. With this understanding, specific types of group can be prescribed for specific types of people and for specific purposes.

The person and member input relationship to the group system will depend upon the social potential of each individual and vice versa. The individual with less or more sophistication in social dynamic potential will have an effect upon the potential sophistication of the group system of member-roles that can develop in the group. The less social potential the individual enters the group with, the less complex and flexible can the group's member-role clustering be; the more socially sophisticated the individual's potential, the more potentially complex and flexible the group role potential. Because the group role potential is fundamental to the speed, style and probability of therapeutic goal achievement, the selection of an individual for a group becomes crucial, both for the potential therapy that the individual can obtain, and for the nature of the therapeutic environment that the group can become.

2   Group-as-a-whole maturation

Maturation in the group system can be described, theoretically, in the same manner that maturation of the individual system can be described, i.e. by increased differentiation of the life space. Increased differentiation permits increased complexity of function which in turn leads to an increase in the potential for maturity.

There are parallels between the developing cognitive ability of the individual and of the group. The individual matures in relationship to the rate that he can discriminate and integrate information. This same principle can be applied to the maturing group. Thus, maturation of the group-as-a-whole can be expressed as a function of the rate of discrimination between similarities and differences and the integration of those discriminations. It is hoped, at this point, that the reader is experiencing *déjà vu.* For everything that we have said about perception and discrimination at the levels of reality and irreality when we described the person system applies to the group-as-a-whole system.

Thus a mature group has increased complexity and flexibility of function; diversification of roles; permeability of boundaries between systems, inputs and outputs that convey information through a communication system that has a high potential for organizing it. Negative and positive feedback, in the mature group, serves to keep the group in balance between over-organization and under-organization, and thus in a state of free energy to work through developmental tasks (which in a group are never-ending) and to solve problems (which in living systems are ever present).

There are two aspects of maturation at the group level and also at the individual level. One is maturity of socialization in relationship to cultural norms and the other is maturity in interpersonal relationships. Developmental phases occur in group in both these aspects, but with an important difference in sequence from that in individual psychology. Whereas the maturational phases of the individual start with symbiotic infancy and progress through stages of separation and individuation to socialized maturity, the developmental phases in group occur differently at both the real and the irreal group-as-a-whole manifestations.

The first stage of development of a group has the superficial characteristics of 'mature' social functioning with dependency at the irreal level. Defenses against symbiotic dependency manifest as an overemphasis upon social structure which superficially 'looks like' socialization. Thus, within the first stage of group development, there is a regression from social maturity to social immaturity, culminating in a simple group culture where good and evil are animistically split. The phases in this process we have labelled as (1) dependent flight; (2) counterdependent fight; and (3) power-authority classes of groups-as-a-whole.

The second stage of development of group has superficial characteristics of mature interpersonal functioning. These manifest first in interpersonally harmonious and non-aggressive interactions and second as reactive individuation. Both these modes of interpersonal relating perform the defensive function against the irreal group manifestation of primitive wish/fear of incorporative aggression and fusion. These we have labelled as overpersonal enchantment, for the first, and counter-personal disenchantment for the second. The third is the interdependent work stage where the group-as-a-whole reaches a level of maturity which permits the working through of both individual and group problems that are inherent in the existence of all living structures.

Chapter 5 details these six phases of group development. Each phase represents a group-as-a-whole system, and each phase is resolved through the transactional relationships between role systems, thus making it possible for change at the individual systems level to occur as a function of this process. Maturation of the group-as-a-whole system is a function of the potential for maturation of the individual systems which become actualized through the interdependence transactions of group-role systems.

3   Reality and irreality groups-as-a-whole

There are two discrete yet interdependent sub-systems of the group-as-a-whole, the reality system and the irreality system. We have used Bion's basic assumption and work groups as examples of these. Let us emphasize, however, that the work group and the basic assumption group are examples only, and not definitions of the reality group system and the irreality group system.

The reality and irreality systems are two discrete classes of group-as-a-whole. Outputs from the reality group-as-a-whole reflect the laws of primary process in that paradox is inherent in the communication. Communication from the irreality group is connected with inner world problems. Communication from the reality group solves outer world problems.

The therapist who is able to discriminate between the individual perspective and the group perspective can apply the knowledge of both individual psychology and group psychology to his work. The therapist who can classify the group process in terms of the reality group-as-a-whole and the irreality group-as-a-whole is then able to make the *group* unconscious conscious. Thus group psychotherapy parallels at a different level of abstraction the process of individual psychotherapy, where change is a function of making the unconscious conscious and thus subject to the laws of secondary process.

Conclusion

It was the need that we felt to be able to distinguish clearly between the phenomenon that we now call the reality and irreality groups-as-a-whole that led us to develop the theory of the invisible group. In the process of developing the theory, we found that when we had defined reality and irreality for the individual systems perspective, we had also defined reality and irreality for the group systems perspective.

The components of reality and irreality are common to all the four systems defined by our theory. The reality and irreality groups-as-a-whole, to the extent that they do exist in the actual world, derive their existence as a function of the developmental nature of living structures.

The principle of development from simple to complex which is inherent in the nature of living structures must be reflected in any general systems theory. This principle is reflected in the hierarchical development of the four systems which are the constructs of our invisible group theory. The assumption is made in field theory that greater differentiation occurs within the life space as the system which it represents matures. By defining each system in terms of its life space, an illustration of the complexity of the life space also becomes the operational definition of the level of maturation of the system.

The reader will note that the group-role system stands in relationship to the group-as-a-whole system as the person system stands in relationship to the member system. The member system is a product of the person system. However, the person system serves as only one source of input to the member system once the member system has become differentiated. Initially, the discrimination style and perceptual filter of the person system determines the reality/irreality components and nature of the boundary permeability of the member system. Once differentiated from the person system, the member system functions with the potential for input/output relationships with all systems in the system hierarchy. Thus the discriminatory style, perceptual filter and boundary characteristics are capable of being modified in the member system – as they are in all systems as soon as they are differentiated.

From the perspective of the individual system, the sum of member-system transactions between the real and irreal components yield group systems that can be defined and classified from the perspective of individual psychology. From the perspective of the group system, individual perspective groups can be redefined as roles (sub-group phenomena) or as group-as-a-whole (role transaction phenomena). The role system is a product of the group-as-a-whole, which, through transactions at the level of reality and irreality with other systems in the hierarchy, is capable of modifying and being modified.

When the transactions *between* the reality and irreality group-role systems (as well as between the reality and irreality components of a specific group-role system) are outlined, it can be seen theoretically that there is the potential for the group-as-a-whole to change from a simple to an increasingly complex system; given that the group-as-a-whole system is a function of the interdependence of group roles. This developmental complexity exists both at the levels of group-as-a-whole reality and group-as-a-whole irreality.

Table 3.1 Theory of the invisible group
a The individual system: group is equal to, or greater than, the sum of its parts

	Person system Group = f(sum of parts)	Member system Group = f(more than or greater than sum of parts)
Theory Hierarchy of isomorphic systems	*Definition* Type of person is a function of intraperson dynamics deriving from: a projection from psychosexual development b ego-development c object-relations development d idiosyncratic (wish/fear) screen	*Definition* Manifestations in group of member as a function of interpersonal dynamics deriving from: a projection of socio-psychological history and expectations of particular groups b response to experience in particular group c responses to cognitive dissonance arising from group environment
Communication behavior Inputs/outputs Intra and inter systems	*Person communication behavior is a function of the person in interaction with his perceived environment defined by his reality and irreality information store:* pcb = f(L. Sp.) or pcb = f(P, E)	*Member role communication behavior is a function of the person's irreality and reality perceptions of the group environment modified by irreality and reality inputs from the group environment* mcb = f(M, G)
Types of theory and Constructs	Field theory where pcb = f(L. Sp.) Psychoanalytic or any valid personality theory Howard and Scott theory of stress Constructs: personality tests	Field theory where mcb = f(M, G) Bennis and Shepard theory of group development Howard and Scott theory of stress Psychoanalytic transference concepts; resonance and amplification; object relations theory Constructs: projective tests; FIRO B & F (Schutz, 1978)

Table 3.1 (cont.)

b The group system: group is different from, or other than, the sum of its parts

	Group-role system Group = f(interdependence of parts)	*Group-as-a-whole system* Group = f(different from sum of parts)
Theory Hierarchy of isomorphic systems	*Definition* Manifestations in group of group-roles is reflection of inter-role dynamics deriving from: a Interdependent communication between reality and irreality components of role systems b Dynamics of group development	*Definition* Type of group is a function of intra- and inter-group dynamics deriving from: a Group system component input/output relations b Group input/output relations with environment
Communication behavior Inputs/outputs Intra and inter systems	*Group role communication behavior is a function of the group-role in interaction with the group-as-a-whole environment:* $rcb = f(R, GW)$	*Group communication behavior is a function of the group life space: input/output relationships in relationship to a) group goal; b) environment* $gcb = f(G. L. Sp.)$ or $gcb = f(GW, E)$
Types of theory and Constructs	Field theory where $rcb = f(R, G)$: group development roles Bion's basic assumption role behaviors Foulkes's group-as-a-whole theory Constructs: Force field; Gaussian curve	Field theory where $gcb = f(G, E)$ Information theory General systems theory Bion's basic assumption groups Constructs: SAVI patterns of communication (Simon and Agazarian, 1967)

Chapter 4
The constructs of group dynamics as they apply to the visible and invisible group

In chapter 2 we introduced the visible and invisible group. When we stop talking about individual people and start talking about the group-as-a-whole, we are talking about the invisible group; a group that can only be seen if we *don't* see it in terms of people. When we stop talking about group and start talking about individual people in a group setting, then we are talking about the visible group, a group that can be seen if we *do* talk about people. We understand the visible group through understanding the dynamics of individuals. From this individual perspective we understand that the group is equal to the sum of its individual members' behaviors. We understand the invisible group through understanding group dynamics. From this group perspective we understand that the invisible group is dynamically different from its individual members.

In this chapter we talk about norms, goals, roles, cohesiveness, and structure. We discuss each of these constructs generally in relation to group dynamics and specifically in terms of the visible group and the invisible group.

Every construct in group dynamics is interdependent with every other construct. Let us use the construct of norms as an example. Group norms are the explicit and implicit rules that govern behavior in a group. A comprehensive understanding of the group norms provides an understanding of the particular pattern of acceptable behavior and unacceptable behavior in a particular group. That particular pattern defines the kinds of behavior that people will use in the group, which in turn determines which kinds of task can be done successfully by that particular group. Thus, norms are related to the construct of goals, and when talking about goals, norms can be defined as 'behavioral pathways' by which goals can be reached. When people do not conform to the norms of the group, when they break the rules, they are behaving as deviants. When people deviate from group norms, the group attempts to reimpose conformity. If the group succeeds, the deviants again become 'members in good standing'. From this point of view, norms can be described as behavioral modifiers. Every group member, whether new or old, gains and maintains his membership by 'modifying' his behavior according to the norms. If the group does not succeed in modifying a deviant's behavior, he is either excluded, or the group norms adapt to include the deviant's behavior. In this second case, the deviant has become a 'leader' who has 'led' the group to change.

In the sections that follow, we have chosen five constructs from group dynamics to define at both the conceptual and operational levels. Four of these five constructs are the same as those that have been defined by Lewin and his students. These are cohesiveness, structure, norms, and goals. Our fifth construct is roles, and under role we have discussed leadership, as a special facet of role behavior.

Structure is most often talked about in terms of communication structures. We certainly agree that it is easier to talk about communication structures, and ways of demonstrating them, than it is other types of group structures, and for this reason we do devote a large part of our structural section to models that structure communication. But we do want to emphasize here, as well as in our structural section, that structure is a construct in its own right, separate from communication, and can be discussed as such. Communication also has existence as a construct separate from structure.

Changes in communication affect the dynamics of group. It is equally correct to observe that changes in group dynamics affect communication. However, the purpose of our theoretical explanation is to provide a framework for operationalizing, at the behavioral level, the constructs that can guide the therapist's action; in other words, what he sees and what he does following his interpretation of what he sees. We are paying attention in this book mainly to how changes in communication affect changes in group process. Treating communications as the independent variable permits the therapist to manipulate his own communications in order to influence the process of group development and to influence the development of cohesiveness, structure, norms, and goals.

Norms

Social norms are the 'rules' that govern behavior within each society.

Social norms differ, not only between societies, but between different groups within the same society. Infants grow into members of their society by learning the social norms. Each individual learns to co-operate with his society's particular boundaries of time and space, as they apply to eating, eliminating, sleeping, and relating to family, community and strangers. The function of social norms is that of a lubricant, which permits the smooth running of social occasions, and which programs the expected series of responses into a pattern of communication that is as predictable and familiar as a folk dance. These acquired social skills manage most occasions, and define the boundaries of what is proper and improper social behavior. Without such skills, individuals are deviants in any group, They will then cause the group's members to experience dissonance, and the group itself will manifest disequilibrium: the deviant member will either be pressured to conform or be ostracized.

In the process of learning the rules, and learning where and how to bend or break the rules, the individual learns to belong to more than one of the small groups that make up his particular society. The norms that govern acceptance in the nuclear family need to be adapted in the extended family. Norms that govern acceptance in the extended family may or may not be compatible with the norms that are adaptive at school, a fact that is particularly well known to children of immigrant families.

Overlapping membership behaviors are those behaviors that people bring from one group to another. Sometimes the overlapping membership behaviors help the person fit into the new group, sometimes they hinder. People from the dominant American middle-class background, for example, will fit more easily into Harvard or Yale than will people from an immigrant background.

It is important for the group therapist to identify those behaviors which group members manifest that are appropriate to their outside social norms, and to distinguish them from those behaviors that emerge in conformity to group norms. The purpose of group therapy is to change those aspects of the individual that result in either over-socialized or under-socialized behavior in outside social settings. Change is accomplished by the individual member's experience of developing and conforming to the social norms of the group *in vivo*. Thus, any stereotypic behavior is antithetical to the individual's therapy in that it is automatic, stimulates little anxiety within the person, and prevents change or growth. The outside social norm behaviors that the member brings to the group with him, that are appropriate to other social groups at other times, will *always* perform a defensive function within the group.

Although the 'good' group member who uses familiar 'helpful' behaviors from everyday life may be very useful to the group therapist and to the group, he himself will gain little therapy. It is thus that the 'work' leader of a group can function as a 'flight from work' leader for himself.

From the perspective of the visible group what makes a therapy group work is confrontation with the unexpected and the unpredictable. A new member expects the behavior that has been successful in achieving his goals to work again; in a therapy group, this does not happen. This failure stimulates several individual dynamics. Repeated failures lead to clearer and clearer manifestations of maladaptive life strategies, which can be interpeted in terms of self-fulfilling prophecy. Individual needs for inclusion, affiliation, and control are stimulated, and frustrated. Frustration stimulates anger and fear, which in turn provoke a wider range of adaptive and maladaptive behavior in the group, The anxiety that is brought on by the experience of frustration in understanding and mastering the membership role in the group leads to regression, and thus makes new experiences and material available to the individual for work. Therapy occurs as the individual gains insight into the dynamics that underlie these experiences, undergoes a corrective emotional experience, and gains mastery of the group environment.

From the more abstract perspective of the invisible group, norms can be described as those portions of group energy which are devoted to the control of all other group energy expenditures. Conceptualizing group as a system, norms perform the regulating function of determining when and how dynamics occur. For example, norms determine the *mode* of group work; when a group will scapegoat, when it will pair, when it will flight.

Norms function as implicit modifiers or prescriptions for group behavior. An analysis of their relative flexibility and their appropriateness to the group goal is an index of group maturity and effectiveness.

Norms are so powerful that identifying them permits the group therapist to predict behaviors that will and will not occur in a group, and to decide which specific norms to influence when he wishes to modify the group behavior.

Group norms are developed by the *group*. This apparently obvious statement is made to emphasize the fact that the rule that is *stated* by the therapist for the group is very different from a rule that is enforced by the group. This is such a trenchant fact in group life that our experience has taught us to start a new group with only those rules that *we* can enforce. Thus we can and do start and stop the group on the scheduled time on the scheduled day. But, much as we would prefer the group to begin its life with certain norms, such as no social-izing outside group, we are aware of our inability to enforce them. We therefore rely on the group to build the norms that make therapeutic sense, and they usually do.

'Obedience' to the group norm develops from the responses that people in the group make to the behaviors of others. Those behaviors which fall within the group norms are reinforced by the group in recognizable ways. There is a neutral or positive response from members to other members as long as the members' behaviors fall within the norms. When a member's behavior breaks a norm, the group will respond in verbal and non-verbal ways that inhibit or punish the new behavior. The simplest non-verbal cues are changes in attention, eye contact, and body availability, all of which add up to a subtle with-drawal of the group from the offending member. Verbal responses are more explicit. The group member may be interrupted; the group may suddenly stop talking to the offender and start talking to someone else. The most explicit sanctions involve direct confrontation of the member in ways that express the group negative reaction. Such confrontations range from sophisticated to primitive, supportive to antagonistic, strong to mild.

Goals

Goal is a concept which provides a framework for talking about behavior in terms of direction and velocity. The concept goal implies a location, or a preferred state, and this location provides an impetus to movement toward such a state or location. All behavior can be described as moving in relation to a goal, either away from it, or toward it.

When the behavior of the group is observed and interpreted in terms of group dynamics then we are talking about group goals in the group-as-a-whole, i.e., the invisible group. When individual behaviors are being observed in the context of the group and interpreted in terms of individual dynamics, then we are talking about behavior in terms of the individuals' goals in the visible group.

The major contentions in group psychology about how to concep-tualize group goals lie in the 'sum', 'greater than', 'different from', argument, of which there are three postulates: a group goal is a composite or sum of the individual goals of the members in the group; a group goal is greater than the sum of the individual goals in the group;

a group goal is different from the sum of the individual goals in the group.

Which of these three perspectives the group therapist adopts is important because each leads to a different kind of thinking about group goals. Thinking about group goals as the 'sum' of, or greater than, individual goals binds thought within quantitative parameters. The therapist who sees the goal of his therapy group as dependent upon summing up group members' goals is going to tend to overreact to any member's goal which is antithetical to his therapy goals. At best he will work at understanding the psychodynamic implications for the individual member: at worst he will discriminate against the member in his concern for the survival of the group.

On the other hand, the therapist who understands group goals as dynamically 'different from' individual goals has, as the raw material for his understanding, the different individual goals which he also sees as manifestations of group dynamics. He will understand the individual's implied goal behavior in terms of both individual psychodynamics and group dynamics.

The dynamics of a group and its goals are different from the dynamics of an individual and his goals. The attainment of a group goal, for example, may or may not provide explicit satisfaction for every member, but will manifest itself in 'satiation' behavior, where the group behaves as if it is no longer energized to pursue what was, a few minutes previously, a clear goal. For example, a group may reach a decision that does not please every member, but, once the decision is made, all the members of the group will show relief. They will lose the tension they manifested during the decision-making process; this is demonstrated by relaxing, changing the subject, stretching and yawning, chatting to their neighbor, etc.

At both the group and individual level, goals can be defined as explicit and implicit. At the group level, the explicit goal of a therapy group is to be therapeutic: to develop and maintain itself as a functioning change agent to individual maturation. However, when a psychotherapy group is observed, it frequently behaves 'as if' it is in pursuit of a quite different goal. This 'as if' behavior leads us to infer an implicit goal, the goal the group acts 'as if' it had. We have talked at some length about inferred constructs in chapter 2; suffice it to say here that being able to talk about implicit goals (like the goals of flight, fight, pairing, etc.) provides the group therapist with a framework for thinking which permits interpretation at both the group and the individual level.

Both explicit and implicit group goals can serve simultaneously as motivators for behavior. The relationship between the explicit and the implicit group goals can be congruent or incongruent. These same attributes apply to individual goals. Individual goals can also be explicit or implicit. Individual implicit goals are often referred to as hidden agendas in group dynamic literature. Individual implicit goals can also be referred to as unconscious goals or unconscious motivators, and as such are a parallel to constructs in psychoanalytic theory. Individual explicit (conscious) and implicit (unconscious) goals can be congruent or incongruent with each other and, in addition, they can be congruent or incongruent with the group's explicit and implicit goals.

These aspects of group and individual goals are contrasted in figure 4.1 below. This figure represents the four regions created by explicitly stated and publicly acknowledged goals of the individual (region A) and the group (region B), and by implicit goals that are inferred from the behavior of individuals (region C) and the behavior of the group (region D). In the case of both explicit and implicit individual goals, there can be as many different goals stated and/or implied as there are individuals, or there may be relative agreement in the goal statements of the individuals – and/or their behavior.

	individual goal	group goal
explicit goal	A	B
implicit goal	C	D

Figure 4.1 Implicit, explicit, individual and group goal regions

For example, the therapy group has the explicit goal of providing therapeutic experience for its members (region B). Let us say the group is behaving as if it wants a magical cure instead of a therapeutic experience, and is in flight from the therapeutic task (region D). In this case, the explicit group goal, to do therapy, is incongruent with the implicit group goal, to have magic done.

Let us say that most of the individuals in the group share an explicit individual goal of 'getting cured by getting therapy' (region A). There may be one or two exceptions. For example, one member says she is in the group 'only' because her husband will leave her if she doesn't attend, and another member is in the group because he is 'only' fulfilling a training requirement and wants to learn group process.

For neither of these two members is the group goal of flight incongruent with their announced, explicit individual goals.

Now let us return to the individual goals of the members whose explicit purpose is to get better by getting therapy. There may be as many unconscious meanings of 'getting cured' as there are individuals in the group. For one member it may mean entering a state in which he is never taken by surprise, and never confronted with anything that he feels is out of his *control*. For another member it may be the experience of 'oneness' with the group, which will fill up the emptiness inside with a *loved* feeling. For another member, it might be the experience of being part of a therapy group for the *secure* feeling that nothing in the world can really hurt or threaten when there is a group to return to. For yet another, group is a place to *belong*. Each of these implicit individual goals is in region C, and is incongruent with both individual and group goals in regions A and B.

If we take these individual goals - being in control, feeling loved, feeling secure, belonging - it is clear that the explicit group goal of therapy is in fact *not* the sum of the individual goals, but is an 'ideal' goal that has been postulated, and that as yet has little reality.

If we ask these members how what is happening in the group is helping them to reach their goal of 'getting cured' they will probably say that they are trying to get help from the therapist. This stated goal, common to all group members, might be more convincing as an explicit goal if the members were behaving as if they really wanted such help.

Let us consider again the six members we are describing and look at their behavior. The 'keeping a husband' member has spent many sessions attacking the men in the group for being passive and weak, and is now turning her attention to the male co-therapist complaining that he is ineffectual, 'flabby', and that his interpretations 'do not turn her on'.

The goal implied by her behavior appears to have more to do with rendering men impotent (and herself less frightened) than it does with keeping her husband. The 'student', who says little and keeps his eye on the therapists most of the time, is admonishing other members to listen and do what the therapist says if they want to get the help they say they want. His behavior appears to have more to do with being a good second lieutenant than it does with learning group process. The member whose concern is control is insisting to the group, as he does session after session, that the therapists' suggestions work like a magic charm, and, if the group would just do as the therapists say, they would get the benefit too. His behavior implies insistent belief in the therapists' magical control rather than concern in gaining his own. And so on . . . the member who wants 'love' consistently does the opposite of whatever anyone suggests, which results in group rejection; and the member who wants to 'belong' maintains a distant, cool stance, making comments like 'you all seem frightened of committing yourselves to trying to change'.

It appears that identifying the goals that the individuals say they have, and comparing them to the group's explicit goal, does not always make sense of the way the individual is behaving. What such analysis does yield, however, is insight into the individual's dynamics, and some delineation of the therapy work that each person faces.

Let us look now at the same example from the view of group dynamics. The explicit group goal is 'to provide therapy' and the group is behaving as if that means that the therapist will magically make the therapy work without their having to do very much except be there.

We infer an implicit group goal of flight from work into magical thinking. Dependency is the dominant mode, expressed either aggressively or passively. When we look at the group, we find that it has divided into two sub-groups. The sub-group following the student admonishes other members for interrupting, and not listening to the therapist. The sub-group following the member concerned with control asks him to explain what is going on, to interpret for them, to suggest what they should do. The dissatisfied woman and the rebel do not seem to make any impression on the group: what they say seems to disappear into the group without leaving a ripple.

Later, in fact, the dissatisfied woman will pair with the rebel, and the group will voice dissatisfactions through supporting the pair (we will infer a goal of fight). Still later, the cool commentator will find, with bewilderment, that the group is taking her observations as the wisdom that they had previously assigned to the therapist (we will infer a goal of 'replace the leader'). But that is in the future. At this time the goal is flight, the group behavioral mode is dependence, the theme is magical solutions, and all member behavior that does not fit is ignored.

To summarize: group goals are a group level construct. There are two kinds of group goal, the explicit goal and the implicit goal, which may be congruent or incongruent. Implicit group goals are inferred from group behavior, as Bion did when he formulated his basic assumptions. The implicit group goal is inferred by observing the dominant in the group. The theme is 'what' the group is talking about, which, when listened to with the third ear, parallels the major issues in the group. The dominant mode is 'how' the group is behaving, and how the group behavior clusters into roles. In the case we have presented here, both the theme (magic) and the mode (dependent role behavior) support a flight goal picture.

Explicit goals at the visible group level are the goals that people in the group say they have, for themselves and for the group. The implicit goals, goals that people behave 'as if' they have, can be interpreted in two ways. One way to interpret implicit goals is in terms of psychodynamics of the individual. This level of interpretation leads to better understanding of the individual but does not contribute anything to the understanding of the group. The second way to interpret implicit goals is as a function of the dynamics of the group. From this perspective group dynamics are sufficient to explain the behavior of individuals in the group without referring to individual dynamics.

Roles

From the perspective of the invisible group, a role is a set of interrelated functions that contribute to group movement. These functions can be located at the individual level, the sub-group level or group level. A role has flexibility of locus, that is, different members or combinations of members can perform it. It is this quality that makes it easy to understand a role as a function of the group rather than as idiosyncratic to an individual. For example, a group may have been working for weeks with the predictable factor that when a group summary is needed, Sam will summarize. From the visible group perspective we can observe Sam's summarizing role and can talk about Sam's dynamics that result in summarizing. From the perspective of the invisible group, however, if Sam is absent, we can predict that the summarizing function will be taken over by another member, by several members working co-operatively, or even by the whole group. It is as if the functional hole that Sam's absence has left in the group is automatically filled in some other way by the group.

Two other regular group occurrences elaborate on this point. Suppose, for instance, the group member, Sam, who typically plays the summarizing role, is engaged in work and, as he and the group work, there is a need for summarizing. If Sam is busy doing something else important, the group therapist can expect that some other member or sub-group of members will perform the summarizing role. The therapist may not be able to predict who will perform the role, or how it will be performed, but will be able to predict that it will be performed. Again, suppose the group is in a period of passive resistance, where on the surface the group appears to be working very hard indeed, but nothing comes of it. The group is badly in need of some summarizing. The group's implicit goal, however, is to 'look as if it is working while in fact it refuses to work'. Our summarizing member, Sam, will probably not only fail to summarize but, should any other member do any work which looks like summarizing, will join the anti-work sub-group in making the work futile. Should he, however, play his usual role and start to summarize, he will be treated like a deviant, and silenced, whereas previously he was supported in this task. Group members come and go; group roles remain and get performed.

A role cannot exist in the group as a function of the individual alone. Every role in a group is not just a reciprocal relationship between two or more people, but is also a manifestation of the group dynamics. It is for this reason that we interpret 'roles' in terms of the 'voice' of the group when we are deliberately influencing *group* dynamics, and we interpret them in terms of 'self-fulfilling prophecies', 'individual repetitive role relationships', or 'personality styles' when we are deliberately influencing individual dynamics.

The concept that each member is a voice both for himself and for the group is fundamental to understanding roles. When the therapist is dealing with the visible group, he hears individual voices. When he is listening to the invisible group, he hears the voice of the group. For example, the most dependent member will often give voice to the dependence in the group, just as the most aggressive member will most often voice the anger and the most solicitous will voice the concern. When the therapist is working with the visible group, he will be aware of the individual member's dependency or aggression. When the therapist is listening to the invisible group, he hears only the voice of the group. It will be as if the group has allocated to members in the group 'parts' in a play by type-casting. These role dynamics, however, by no means always manifest so simply. An example of the complexity and subtlety with which they can manifest is the case of Vanessa. Vanessa is the member who wanted to belong but whose cool and critically objective stance isolated her from the group, and was surprised to experience that the group was suddenly hanging on her every word. The group had assigned her the role of leading them away from the feelings that the therapist was interpreting. In this case, no great harm would have been done had the therapists not been aware of the 'role' that the group had assigned Vanessa. Another facet of group role phenomena, however, if overlooked, does have serious consequences for the group. One solution that groups frequently use to a group problem is to assign one member to voice it, and then to silence that voice. For example, all groups have a tendency to avoid working directly with the projective and suspicious aspects of paranoid members, tacitly assigning them the role of 'group paranoid' and then silencing the 'voice' for the group paranoia by refusing to listen. If the whole group is successful, the *status quo* is maintained. If, however, the member, or the therapist, continues to surface the issue and the group is not ready to deal with it, then the group is likely to solve the problem by extruding the member. It is only when the therapist is able to help the group deal with the paranoid layer in the group that the paranoid member can join in the group work rather than be the 'silenced' group voice.

Roles contribute to structure, and structure contributes to the security that members experience in a group. Whether they like or dislike the structure they have, structure yields predictability, and predictability makes for a feeling of safety and security. Thus, groups tend to be very tenacious of their roles. One of the most seriously fixating tendencies in some groups' dynamics is the tendency of the group to develop roles and to maintain them at all costs.

Think a moment, for example, of a member who has been encouraged by the group to change his behavior. Let us say that, habitually, this member is silent, and tends to speak only in the last few minutes of group when there is no longer time to deal with what he wants to say. The silent member yields to the group pressure, and speaks up earlier in group. The group not only refrains from acknowledging or rewarding the change, but behaves in such a way as to re-elicit silence on the part of the member, perhaps by interrupting him, talking over him, or generally behaving as if he were still silent and hadn't talked at all. This happens most consistently in groups who resist change, and whose security rests in functioning in a predictable pattern.

A group's resistance to change is a very different phenomenon from the group need to have a role taken as part of a reciprocal role pattern. We have described one aspect of the reciprocal pattern when we talked about the voice of the group. A further important aspect is the group duet, in which the group sets up a reciprocal role relationship which acts out a particular group dynamic. Take, for example, the role of 'bully' as a manifestation of the group's sado-masochistic dynamics: the reciprocal role is 'bullied'. Or take the active and passive aspects of group performance, which is often manifested by the group passively encouraging a member to monopolize. From the point of the invisible group, it doesn't matter *who* plays the reciprocal roles as long as the roles are played. For example, the same person can play the role of monopolizer (and sometimes the therapist does!), group after group after group. Or first one person, then another will monopolize in a sequence of long monologues. Or half the group will monopolize and the other half of the group will watch. Or the whole group will 'monopolize' a single member.

The particular manifestations of reciprocal roles in a group reflect the dynamics that are governing the group at that time, and also reflect the specific developmental task that is present in the group at the time. As members take their roles in the group developmental dynamics, aspects of their own individual dynamics will be aroused.

For example, the roles of 'monopolizer-monopolized' may be a group-level manifestation of the individual early symbiotic refusal to discriminate differences, and may be in the service of the implicit individual goal of fusion. This relates to the level of development where there is a poor toleration of differences, and this in turn will carry a high potential for arousing separation-individuation issues in the membership. Each member will respond differently to the group dynamics, and how they respond will be a function of their individual readiness for change together with the intensity of involvement in the group role reciprocity. Thus, some members will resist, some will deny, some will rationalize, some will gain insight, and some will be swept along with the group development, ready or not! Thus participation in the role dynamics of the group is participation in the behavioral forces reflecting group developmental dynamics, which are experienced at the individual level as potent stimuli to associations and insight. The above explains why some members will experience the apparently innocuous experience of monopolizer-monopolized as deep separation-individuation issues, apparently much more regressive than the manifest content of group would appear to warrant. Others will associate to adolescent separation-individuation issues, or to issues in genital, phallic, oral or anal developmental phases. It is as if the group dynamic stimulus amplifies the underlying group dynamic, and reverberates at a level appropriate to the individual dynamics.

Understanding groups from both the individual and the group perspective provides the therapist with two complex and distinct, but not discrete, phenomena. Thus in the example above, group dynamics of homogeneity, as a phase of group development along the fusion/defusion dimension, emerges in the form of the problem of group monopoly. From the individual perspective, it is important for the therapist to understand these dynamics at the conscious, pre-conscious and unconscious levels, because at each of these levels the individual will be responding to the dynamics of the group and of the other individual members.

The therapist having both individual and group dynamics in mind can choose how to influence the processes that result in individual insight. He may choose to influence the group's reciprocal role relation-ships and thus influence the group environment that is serving to stimulate the group members' dynamics. He would do this in the case of monopolizer-monopolized if he wanted to encourage further group development before individuals analyzed their separation-individuation issues. Or he may interpret the underlying theme of fusion in order to make explicit the goal which the roles were serving, and thus encourage work on the underlying issues. Or he may interpret directly to an individual about the reciprocal relationship between that individual's dynamics and society (every monopolizer requires a monopolizee and vice versa), thus encouraging both individual and group develop-ment at the same time.

Leader: role or label?

So far we have discussed roles without discussing the role of 'leader'. We have done this deliberately. Our definition of role is dependent upon behavior and not upon people. However, the title 'leader' is a significant one in our culture, and is important to group therapists who are typically referred to as the leaders of the psychotherapy groups. In the pages that follow therefore, we relate our thinking about leadership to the title of leader on the one hand, and to leadership roles in the group on the other.

Leader: the label

The word 'leader' is a title publicly designated within a system such as a group, carrying with it the *potential* for power, authority, responsi-bility, and accountability. In any system, the person who fills the formally designated role called 'leader' can be observed in terms of the degree to which he actualizes power, influence, authority, responsibility and accountability. Actualization of these attributes is only potential in the title 'leader', and may not in fact manifest itself.

For example, an individual may have the title of leader but be without followers over whom to have authority; have no duties for which a system requires accountability; have no specified goal against which his behavior can be judged responsible; have no power to give or withhold rewards from any other person; and be someone with whom no one identifies and therefore have no one to influence.

Every group therapist is the designated 'leader' of a group. Whether or not the group therapist actualizes his title in the *role* of leader depends on whether in fact he has any power over, authority in, responsibility to, or accountability for, the group. The title 'leader' is filled by an actual leader only when someone 'follows'. It is not the *title* but the *role* that has impact upon a group, and *role* is not an individual attribute, but a group function.

Leader: the role

The therapist's 'role' as leader is influenced by: (1) the meaning that the title 'leader' has in the culture in which the psychotherapy group exists, (2) the meaning that the title 'leader' has in the psychotherapy group, (3) the particular meaning of 'leader' that emerges as a function of (a) different phases in group development and (b) different individual and group transference manifestations. How effectively the therapist actually *leads* the group will depend, at any one time, on how effectively the group *follows*. In other words, whether or not the therapist's behavior functions as a driving force toward the therapist's explict goals – both his individual goals and the group goals – depends upon whether the group moves towards these goals or away from them.

There is a difference between 'effective' and 'successful' leadership. If, for example, the effect of leadership behavior is to move the group away from the explicit goal, the leader is still leading. His behavior is an effective act of leadership in the group, even if it is unsuccessful in terms of the direction that it led.

Leader behavior is defined in terms of movement in a direction toward or away from a goal, irrespective of the conscious intention of the leadership. The effect of the leadership behavior on the group provides data for inferring the implicit goal, which in turn explains role behaviors.

Everything that we have said about leadership of the therapist, except for the designated title of 'leader', applies to every member in a group. In fact, one of the goals for every member in a therapy group is to enable him to develop skills of self-leadership. Self-leadership enables a member to use his own resources to lead himself and the group of which he is a part in a direction which is constructive.

This point is particularly relevant to our culture, as the Vassilious pointed out when they contrasted leadership in simple and complex cultures (Vassiliou, G., and Vassiliou, V., AGPA presentation, 1979). In relatively simple sociocultural groups, where the goals are collective survival through interdependence (like the Greek village), leadership is initiated by a request for help or teaching. The led take it for granted that both nurturance and exploitation are built into leader potential, and therefore that the responsibility for choosing, maintaining or *cancelling* the leader rests with the led. The group is the basic cultural unit and defines the roles. Those in the designated roles are treated as the experts in the group. Thus, to ask a Greek village mother about mothering practices would get the reply, 'ask the teacher', whom the group has assigned the role of child rearing.

In more psychosocially differentiated cultures, like ours, the *individual* becomes responsible for processing information, setting goals, etc. Every member of society is thus an expert in everything. The individual, not the group, is the responsible unit and so takes on what in a simpler culture would be the group system responsibility. Thus the individual needs to contribute to both his own individuation and to the structure for his individuation, otherwise he is oppressed by the group. Individuation is defined in terms of setting goals, priorities, and values for oneself, as well as choosing the types of group member-ship for actualization of those individual goals.

It is in the above context that dependent or conforming group members are very bad group members. Therapy groups are made up largely of people who are conforming to authority, either by over-compliance or rebellion. (The person who *must* do what he is told is no more conforming than the person who *must* do the opposite of what he is told.) Thus therapy group members join a therapy group with some of the characteristics of members of a group whose norms are collective survival under adversity. They therefore take the nurturance function of leadership for granted. However, they deny the fact that there is also exploitation potential in nurturant leadership; therefore they deny their own responsibility to be non-exploitable. This denial leaves both the choice of leader and the cancelling of leadership in the hands of the leader and increases the member potential for exploitation. It is therefore the group therapist's task to reactivate self-leadership in the members. This is the first function that is restored by the group developmental process. As the group develops through phases of flight and fight, manifesting first compulsive compliance and then compulsive rebellion, it gradually develops sufficient cohesiveness to confront the exploitive potential of the leadership position. This is step one in recognizing that the responsibility for exploitation rests, not with the leader, but with the individual. The second step is taken when the group develops through the positive and negative pairing phases, manifesting symbiosis, followed by premature and precocious separation-individuation. Final phases of mature group development become possible when the group develops sufficient reality testing to work towards developing a group environment which will facilitate their task of defining their own goals, setting priorities, etc.

If the therapist in the psychotherapy group is both an effective and a successful leader, then every member in the group eventually emerges as a self-leader. Only thus can the individual in this sophisticated culture take up the responsibility of his social role, which is to maintain himself as a viable system and to choose viable systems to relate to, and finally to create new systems for his own and for cultural survival.

The goal of the psychotherapy group and the goal of the leader is to reactivate the self-leadership properties within each individual so that they can enter into reciprocal role relationships that contribute to the task.

Cohesiveness

Of all the group constructs, cohesiveness is the one that is most clearly a group property, and is also the one that, once it has been observed, is most unmistakable. For example, a group has finished work, time is up, but the members remain as if 'glued' to their seats, leaning forward, interacting non-verbally. They shift about, each one in his or her own struggle to pull away; first one and then another collects things, straightens clothes, pushes a chair back, stretches. Then the group breaks up, some people sub-group, others stand around, and still others start to leave. Once seen, this phenomenon is never forgotten. It looks 'as if' the group is held together by an invisible magnet, from which the members can only detach themselves with a struggle. That is in fact how we define cohesiveness. Cohesiveness is the magnetism that a group has, the force that it exerts upon its members. Cohesion keeps the group together. A measure of group cohesion is the amount of energy it takes to move group members away from the group, the amount of energy it would take to pull the group apart.

From the group perspective, cohesion is the internal force that maintains the group as a system. It maintains the group system through phases of group development and defines the connectedness between the components of the group system and sub-system in terms of negative and positive bonding. Cohesiveness affects the available energy for bonding in reciprocal role relationships; the energy available for the enforcement of group norms, the energy available for group movement in relationship to goals, and the energy available for the maintenance and modification of group structure. The relative strength of the driving and restraining forces is effected by cohesiveness. Of all the constructs in the invisible group, cohesiveness is the least invisible! Its manifestations can be observed, its effects can be experienced, but it is best defined by analogy; for example, to a magnetic field.

From the individual perspective, cohesiveness in the group appears to be related to members' expectations that the group will provide need satisfaction or fulfillment of individual goals. Every member of a group gets something from a group and gives something in return. A measure of individual cohesiveness can thus be defined in terms of a satisfaction/cost ratio, i.e., the ratio between the satisfaction that a member expects from membership in the group and the cost of belonging to the group.

In his early days as a psychoanalytically oriented group researcher, William Schutz defined three primary needs in membership: inclusion, affection and control (1958). Postulating these needs as factors in the satisfaction/cost ratio provides a basis for interpreting individual behavior in a group as it contributes to cohesiveness.

Individual satisfactions that contribute to cohesiveness can 'sound' the same from one person to another, but can mean very different things in terms of individual dynamics. For example, a group may be working with the issue that one of the co-therapists is going away on vacation. Different members may say 'I will miss you'. When analyzed in the group, however, one member is expressing his wish for affection, and is wondering if the therapist cares about him and will think of him during vacation. Another member may be expressing control, concerned about where and with whom the therapist is going, and resentful that the therapist is leaving 'without permission'. A third member while talking about missing the therapist may actually be concerned with inclusion, wondering whether his own vacation will in any way alter the status of his own membership.

From the group perspective, 'we will miss you' expresses the rift in the group's cohesive 'skin' that will have to be repaired during the therapist's absence. The more cohesive the group, the more all the properties of group are energized. Thus, in a cohesive group, there is more potential kinesthetic energy to channel into movement toward group goals; more energy available to build, maintain and enforce strong norms; more energy available to follow or resist leadership; to resolve or refuse to resolve group issues; to 'work' harder, to 'fight' harder, to 'flight' harder.

To say that a cohesive group is one that functions with more energy is to say that it carries a higher potential for activity within the group. This is not to say that this potential is necessarily actualized. A cohesive group is a group that has a lot of energy. That energy may be 'free' or 'bound'. For example, a group may be highly cohesive and highly inert, almost like a mass which is too heavy to move. Cohesive groups with energy that is bound are groups that are fixated, or resistant to change. We have often experienced the inertia of a group, and been awed by the strength and heaviness of the group resistance to intervention and interpretation. In such cases there can be no doubt that the group is strongly cohesive; no doubt that members of the group are strongly bonded to the group; no doubt that the group does not want to leave, either during the session, or afterwards.

A cohesive group tends to continue to be cohesive over time, through membership changes and through the vicissitudes of development, as well as through the vicissitudes that individual members experience with their own cohesiveness. This can be observed by noting that even though the entire membership of the group is claiming to feel disenchanted, disinterested and apathetic, the group continues to manifest itself as magnetizing; and although individuals may experience their own energy as blocked, they behave 'as if' magnetized.

The climate of a group is often talked about as if it is synonymous with cohesiveness. We have found it useful to differentiate between climate and cohesiveness, reserving cohesiveness to describe the magnetism the group has for its members and the strength of that magentism as it affects other group variables. We see climate as an affective variable. A climate can be warm or cold, friendly, loving, angry, fearful, defensive, hostile, anxious, or apathetic. Climate emerges as a sum of how the group members 'feel' about the group, and is a key construct when group morale is discussed. When group morale is high, members experience greater satisfaction and may feel more cohesive, and vice versa. However, this phenomenon should not be confused with the group cohesive magentism and energy.

Structure

The word 'structure' is frequently used in the literature of group dynamics. By and large, the phenomena to which the word structure is applied appear to fall into three classes. The first class covers the broad usage, as when writers are referring to the 'structure' of norms, roles or other group dynamic terms. For our purposes, we will not use structure in this general sense.

The second common usage for 'structure' refers to the large class of analytical models which provide methods for collecting data and presenting them in a consistent and analyzable form. We will use structure in this sense to refer specifically to communication structures like interaction patterns, who-to-whom matrices, sociometric choices, etc. We will discuss this interpretation of structure under 'communication structure' below.

The third usage of the word 'structure' concerns the more literal sense of how the group is made up in time and space as well as in its member composition. We will discuss these demographic and temporal aspects of structure first, and then continue with structural models and communication.

The physical characteristics of group define the way the group exists in space. They may include, for example, the place where a group meets, the number of its members, their seating arrangements, etc. The way a group exists in time is defined by its temporal variables: when the group meets, for what length of time, how often, how regularly. The nature of the group is further defined by its type, for instance whether it is open-ended or closed, is a short-term or long-term group; whether it is a Level One, Level Two, or Level Three group; or whether its population is homogeneous or heterogeneous in terms of age, sex, race, culture, occupation, socioeconomic position, diagnosis, etc. A group's location in space and time, and the nature of its make-up, will tend to be reflected in the kinds of communication structure that can emerge in the group. In turn, the kinds of communication structure will influence the norms and goals and roles that emerge.

Another important aspect of the group as it exists in time and space is the group's environment. This important aspect of group process (which involves the boundary of the group, and the nature of the group's relationship with its environment) we think about in terms of systems analysis. The group is a system which is a component of other systems, with inputs from and outputs to the other systems which affect the group. It is important for the therapist to be aware of the need to manage the relationship between the group and the larger system of which it is a part.

For example, the need for management of the group as a sub-system is particularly important for the therapist who is working within a specific environment such as a given mental health system. If the group is part of an outpatient department, the therapist must be aware of the structure of the particular group, which is a component in a system of groups, which in turn are a component of the outpatient department, which in turn is a component of a community health service. By managing the input/output relationships between the group and the system of which the group is a part, the therapist can perform work which preserves the integrity of the group's boundaries and thus protects the structure of the group within those boundaries. It might be important, for example, to negotiate with the system to permit a former outpatient who is undergoing hospitalization to continue to attend the group, or to negotiate the continuing use of a particular therapy room at a particular time. If the group is a self-determining group, it might be important for the therapist to alert the in-patient staff to the need for special handling of acting-out behavior when such behavior is a function of the dynamics of the group and not just a function of individual psychodynamics. This approach is particularly applicable when an individual member, in reaction to group process, may appear to be either 'more sick' or 'more well' than he or she would be independent of the group. It might be crucial to have created a relationship that allows the therapist to explain to the unit staff that it would not be appropriate to modify a treatment plan at this time.

It is very important for the group therapist to understand the function of group boundaries. Group boundaries mark the transition between life inside the group and life in the outside world. Group is an environment where therapeutic risks are taken, however painful: these risks, even when they turn out badly, do not have real consequences in the outside world. Group boundaries are the border between the group norms that have been developed to facilitate experiential learning and psychodynamic insight, and the outside social norms which have been developed to reinforce socially acceptable behavior. Goup boundaries are defined by such things as time, location, money, and role; each of which has both dynamic and reality meanings within the group, and has many reality meanings outside the group.

If the therapist is ambivalent about maintaining boundaries, he is likely to condone the group's ever-present efforts to blur them. He may permit the group to run overtime, to come late. He may avoid confronting the group with the cost to group work of socializing outside the group. He may make significant changes in group time or location to suit his own needs without involving the group. He may change fees without involving the group, he may confuse the role of therapist with that of savior, friend, or teacher. All these are common ways in which a therapist joins the group wish to deny boundaries. Time, location, money, and role are realities both in the group and in the outside world. They provide stimuli for analysis of, and insight into, developmental issues that may well be missed if the meaning of real boundaries is not explored. These realities also provide material for real decision-making, which we have found to be the single group activity that yields the most therapeutic results for the individuals involved in it. Most important of all, group boundaries define the possibilities of group process and contribute to the controlled conditions within which member regression can be therapeutic and group work can be done. In summary, structural elements provide the means to open and resolve boundary issues.

Communication structure

A group's function is defined by its structure. Sometimes the structure modifies the function, and sometimes the function modifies the structure. For example, if concrete pathways are laid out to connect a cluster of buildings, a map of those pathways will define the formal communication structure between those buildings. This map will depict the way the communication structure was designed to function.

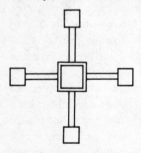

Figure 4.2

If we take an aerial snapshot some time after the cluster of buildings has been occupied, we will almost certainly find that trodden pathways have emerged in addition to the formal ones, as people have taken shortcuts.

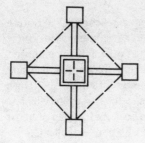

Figure 4.3

If we now amend the map to include both the original concrete path-ways and the new trodden ones, we have a map of the formal and informal communication network between the buildings.

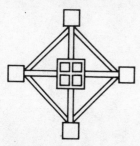

Figure 4.4

A different process would be observed if the builder had arranged for the people in the buildings to communicate freely across a grassy lawn, and then returned in six months and laid concrete pathways where the trodden ones had appeared. The builder would then have been formalizing the informal structure that had arisen functionally.

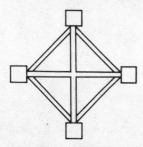

Figure 4.5

A different kind of analysis would arise from a helicopter observation of the way the pathways between the buildings were used. Some would be used more often, some less often than others. If the pathways to one building in the cluster were used more frequently than any other, that building could be described as 'most often chosen'. Once that inference was made, it would make sense to investigate why the building was so chosen. This is exactly how a sociometric map of 'most chosen group members' is made; the information is collected by observing 'who' chooses 'whom'. The results of the helicopter survey are displayed in figure 4.6 with the number of choices represented by units and figures.

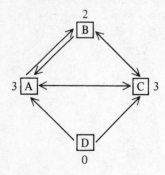

Figure 4.6

As a result, the same information can be displayed in a who-to-whom chart, as in figure 4.7.

	A	B	C	D
A		1	1	
B	1		1	
C	1	1		
D	1		1	
Total	3	2	3	0

Figure 4.7

Which group members talk to which others builds communication pathways between members through which group energy can flow. A member to whom no one communicates may have an energy relationship with the group in terms of cohesiveness, but does not yet have an energy relationship with individual members that can be described structurally. 'Member' D in figure 4.6 is an example, if we now use the lettered units in the figure to represent members instead of buildings. In other words, the communication network does not include a pathway for the isolated member.

It is important to distinguish between communication at the dynamic level and communication dynamics as they are manifested in communication networks. It is the manifestation of the dynamics of communication that can be charted in terms of a network. The network, however, is always only a map. It is not the thing in itself.

For this reason, when we talk about communication as a structural variable, we always mean the communication network that has resulted from the way that people have been communicating. We continue to define communication itself as an independent variable which manifests itself in different ways in structure, norms, goals, and roles. Changes in communication can effect changes in structure, norms, goals and roles. In other words, the nature of the communication can change the structural map of who speaks to whom; can change the nature of the sanctions and thus change the norms; can change the potential for information transfer and thus change the potential group goals; can change the nature of the behavior and thus affect roles.

The communication pattern to a deviant group member, for example, may be described in a structural map, which may then be interpreted in terms of norms, goals, roles, etc.: norms, when the group is applying conformity pressure; goals, when the group has a goal of consolidating membership; roles, when the group is using the deviant as a scapegoat and projecting onto him the aspects of group function that the group wishes to deny.

For our purpose, at the operational level, we have confined our use of structure to the models that we are able to derive by collecting information about the group in some consistent way, and mapping that information. Thus a sociometric diagram is a map of the sociometric structure of the group which emerged through the way in which people chose to speak to other people, and how their choices differed, when the topic was work, from their choices when it was interpersonal support.

Each therapist will feel differently about structural models. Some will feel that they are inhibiting the free-floating associative process of following the group without preconceived or predictive ideas to influence their intuitive understanding. Others will feel that using models to analyze the data from their group will permit them to organize their thinking about what is occurring in such a way that new kinds of understanding are possible that were not possible before. Still others will use a combination of the two kinds of experience. This combined approach is certainly true for us, where various models – like a force field, or a communication pattern, or a who-to-whom – will occur together with their diagnostic or predictive implications, as part of the associations that accompany free-floating attention.

For those who find structural maps useful, much work has already been done in the field of group dynamics, and considerable research has applied such models in descriptive, diagnostic and predictive studies.

Summary

In this chapter we have presented five group constructs that define different aspects of the group system. Norms perform a regulating function that determines the form that the group energy takes. Norms are modifiers of the behavior in the group that determine the range and type of behavior that the group is 'permitted' to use. Goals are a vector construct that describes the direction of group locomotion. A force field showing the vectors of group locomotion provides an operational definition of the system goal, or of the level of equilibrium of the system at any one moment in time. Roles are the parts or components of the group that are defined by clusters of behavior. These behaviors serve to operationalize the driving and restraining forces in the force field. Cohesiveness is an energy construct, like a magnetic field, that accounts for the relative strength of the bonding of components within the group system. Structure is the map of the pathways through which group energy flows.

In the summary table that follows, these constructs are defined from the perspectives of the individual system and the group-as-a-whole system. From these two perspectives, different aspects of each of the five constructs are explained.

Table 4.1 Summary: group dynamic constructs of (1) norms, (2) goals, (3) roles, (4) cohesiveness, (5) structure, (6) communication, defined from the perspectives of (1) the individual (a) person, (b) member; and (2) the group-as-a-whole (a) role, (b) group

	Individual perspective		Group-as-a-whole perspective	
	Person	Member	Role	Group
Norms	Individual standards and rules; values that person brings into group situation: the dos and don'ts that govern individual behavior independent of group norms may or may not be compatible with group norms	Individual overlapping membership norms as defined in groupdynamic theory, modified by person's member role in group	Explicit and implicit group norms that emerge as a function of group development and that influence both group and individual behavior Norms function as behavioral prescriptions that modify role performances	Modifiers of energy expenditure in the group system Boundaries or thresholds of behavior, relatively impermeable, that function to determine role emergence, patterns of communication, patterns of locomotion, etc. (norms of behavior define type of group: psychoanalytic, gestalt, Tavistock, etc.)
Goals	Explicit and implicit goals that are the property of the individual and may be congruent or incongruent with each other, i.e., explicit goal, to get better; implicit goal inferred from individual behavior; to be got better	Implicit and explicit goals developed as a function of 'member systems' imagined group	Explicit and implicit goals independent of individuals implied by, or stated by, group behavior that are the property of the group, which may be congruent or incongruent: explicit, add a new member; implicit, rebel by keeping out a new member	Directional construct: group locomotion in relationship to group goal region in life space; congruent goals have goal-directed pathways, incongruent goals have conflicting pathways

Table 4.1 (cont.)

	Individual perspective		Group-as-a-whole perspective	
	Person	*Member*	*Role*	*Group*
Roles	Individual can be talked about independent of group in terms of any valid personality theory (like psychoanalysis) which yields definable personality styles (like hysteric, obsessive-compulsive, etc.)	Individual can be talked about independent of group in terms of: (a) individual socio-psychological dynamics and overlapping membership roles; (b) roles developed as a function of transfer-ence in group; (c) membership responses to specific phases and group dynamic events	Role is a function of the specific dynamics of the specific group. Roles are clusters of definable behavior, independent of people, that serve as driving or restraining forces in relationship to group goals; may be located in member, sub-group or group-as-a-whole	Role dynamics can only be talked about in relationship to the interdependence of member roles specific to this particular group system and generalizable to group roles in general. Role behaviors serve as outputs of sub-systems and inputs to the group system. Group-as-a-whole in turn functions with a role in the system of which it is a component
Cohesiveness	Individual's perceived satisfaction and need fulfillment through membership in the group. Individual measure of cohesion equal to *satisfaction perceived* cost of membership	Positive and negative bonding as a function of salience for other members and the imagined group, and as a function of permeability of irreality and reality boundaries between components of 'member-persons'	Positive and negative bonding between sub-system role components of group	Group systems as a magnetic field of force Tension systems within group and valency for level of equilibrium related to strength of input/output relationships within group and between group and group environment

Structure	Location of people in time and space: who sits next to or opposite whom; number of people in group; demographic characteristics of people; homogeneity, heterogeneity characteristics, etc.	What can be known about group by summing information about individual members' behavior over time: rules, norms, goals, interactive roles, etc.	The role structure: what an observer can infer from observing group's sub-system boundaries defined and redefined in group process, independent of individuals	What an observer can infer from the overall function of a group. System boundaries between the group and the environment, as they relate to the input/output relationships and the effect on levels of equilibrium of systems
Communication	Patterns of communication that describe why an individual says what and to whom. Interpretation of the patterns is based on individual psychodynamics, transference, resistance and acting out	Patterns of communication that describe pairing and sub-group as a function of projections, transference and interdependent affective responses to particular shared conflicts resulting in resonance between individuals, sub-groups or total group and resulting in *folie-à-deux*, reciprocal role relationships, etc.	Patterns of communication, independent of individuals, that describe roles in the functional patterns of flight, fight, and pairing, etc. Communication patterns to deviant, development phases, etc.	Patterns of communication that can be mapped in terms of input/output relationships between systems, sub-systems and components, and qualified on the basis of reality and irreality content. Patterns characteristic of groups in general like flight groups, dependent groups, hot-seat groups, etc.
Communication behavior	Person communication behavior is a function of the person in interaction with their perceived environment, or: $pcb = f(P,E)$	Member communication behavior is a function of the member in interaction with the imagined group environment, or: $mcb = f(M,Gi)$	Role communication behavior is a function of the role in interaction with the group environment, or: $rcb = f(R,G)$	Group communication behavior is a function of the group in interaction with the environment, or: $gcb = f(G,E)$

Chapter 5
The phases of group development

There is no commonly accepted theory of group development in the field of group dynamics. This problem parallels the one we dealt with in chapter 2, when we delved into the implications of the lack of a commonly accepted definition for group. Just as the lack of definition for group brought the very existence of group as a discrete phenomenon into question, so the lack of a commonly held group development theory brings the very phenomenon of group development as a discrete process into question. Although most people who observe groups agree that groups *change*, not all people who observe groups interpret group change in terms of development. In other words, they deny that change in groups yield aspects of function that could not exist unless the change was in fact part of a developmental process. We, of course, disagree, and in this chapter we intend to demonstrate that groups change developmentally. By that we mean that groups organize themselves in ways that change from simple to complex, in a predictable and recognizable series of phases which meet the criteria for developmental stages in all groups.

There is a corollary problem to the lack of any unified understanding of group developmental phases in today's literature, and that is that group function is viewed from many different perspectives and described in many different languages. While specific observations about group events can and are organized into developmental sequences, there is no commonly accepted general frame of reference which is validated through this process. Finally there is the gulf between the literature of group dynamics and the literature of group psychotherapy. Research and writing on group dynamics has largely been published in the field of social sciences, and made available to students in organizational development, management consulting, business administration and educational psychology. Research and writing on group psychotherapy

124

has largely been published in the field of Mental Health Sciences, and even within the mental health field there is not always a correspondence between the discipline of psychiatry, social psychology, psychology and social work. By and large, with some welcome exceptions like Whitely and Gordon's test on *Group Approaches in Psychiatry* (1979), group psychotherapy is poor rather than rich in its range of resources.

Our choice of Bennis and Shepard's theory as the springboard from which we have formulated our own understanding of group development is subjective in the personal sense as well as objective. Both of us, separately and at different times, entered the doctoral program of the Group Dynamics Department at Temple University to study groups. Both of us, coincidentally, were already in training as psychoanalysts at the time, both of us were already practicing as psychoanalytically oriented psychotherapists. Both of us studied there with David Jenkins, one of Kurt Lewin's students, one of us intensively. What is more, when each of us began to work with psychotherapy groups, it was the Bennis and Shepard model, not the psychoanalytic model, that provided the basic framework for our observation and understanding of group dynamics. For over ten years, therefore, we have watched the development of psychotherapy groups through this perspective.

As we mentioned in chapter 2, Bennis and Shepard's theory of group development is extraordinarily compatible with psychoanalytic theory, influenced as it is by both Freud and Bion. Bennis and Shepard subsumed Bion's dependency and flight-fight modalities under their first phase of dependency-power orientation, and his pairing under their second phase of interdependent personal orientation. They related their understanding of these two orientations to Freud, quoting from Freud's *Group Psychology and the Analysis of the Ego*, 'each member is bound by libidinal ties on the one hand to the leader . . . and on the other hand to the other members of the group' (Freud, 1957, p. 52).

Both Freud's observation and their revision of Bion's basic assumption groups into developmental phases supports our own observations that the primary concern in groups in the initial phases is the response to authority, whether that authority be the person leading the group, or the rules that represent the 'authority' of socialization, and the second concern that surfaces only when some compromise is reached with the authority is concern with peer relationships.

There is one other element in Bennis and Shepard's theory that made it an ideal sequence in which to frame our own understanding of group. This is the phenomenon they call the barometric event. This is the symbolic removal of the leader. Bennis and Shepard are well aware of the psychodynamic implications of this phase, likening it to Freud's discussion of the myth of the primal horde and their totem feast (Freud, 1957, p. 112). Bennis and Shepard's barometric event thus serves us in our knowledge of the needs and potential of the psychotherapy group as the process of confronting the negative and positive transference. This psychodynamically applies to all levels of development: from early pathogenic introjection; the mechanisms of splitting; oedipal dynamics; to adolescent and adult resolution.

In the therapeutic task today these three aspects of psychodynamics are particularly relevant, perhaps because of our present cultural vicissitudes. Using this schema as an outline, we developed from it a description of group development (presented in the summary table at the end of the chapter). This also yields a diagnosis of fixation for groups who remain in the phase of dependency-power-authority without working through the barometric event. As we continued to observe our own psychotherapy groups from this perspective, working through the authority issues with us both at the level of individual transference, and at the level of the group, and as we experienced the exigency of our own counter-transference response, we began to formulate some notion as to why so many other group psychotherapists were not familiar with our understandings of the authority phase. First, had we not had the Bennis and Shepard schema to guide us, we are each separately convinced that we would have been unlikely to have believed that the process of the barometric event was therapeutic. Had we not 'believed' that following the barometric event, the group would have the opportunity to do work that it would not otherwise do, we doubt that we would have felt that the anxiety and rage that the barometric event generates could be justified.

Second, we became aware that it took experience, knowledge and skill to facilitate the group's movement through the barometric event. We learnt, through trial and error, that judicious applications of both interpretation and silence were necessary if the group was to proceed through the sequences entailed in their confrontation with authority.

It cannot be over-emphasized how applicable to group psychotherapy is a group development theory that parallels, not only the developmental vicissitudes of each individual, but that permits intense working through of precisely those aspects of development that are most problematic in our present culture.

The parallel between group development and the resolution of adolescent issues and the resistance to adult life is extraordinarily clear in the Bennis and Shepard schema. So is the work entailed in maintaining consensual validation parallel to issues in adult life, and the decisions that contribute to the ability to work and to love.

Having been fortunate in having Bennis and Shepard's theory as a developmental guide (see appendix 1), we in turn came to understand that in their final phase called consensual validation, there were probably a separate and different set of developmental dynamics that defined phases of work. Whereas their theory had been developed from observations of short-term groups, ours has been drawn from long-term groups whose norms and structure persist, with changing membership but constant norms, over years.

In this chapter we have outlined our adaptation and Bennis and Shepard's phases of group development. These should enable the group therapist to recognize the phases that a group must enter and master if they are to reach the maturity of the consensual validation phase. Observing and formulating developmental issues in the work of the consensual validation phase is an ongoing task for us.

Group development

The dynamics of group growth can be outlined with the same requirements for descriptive rigor and psychodynamic and empirical explanation with which the dynamics of an individual's growth can be described. Just as the anamnesis of an individual carries the data base for explaining the vicissitudes in the development of the ego, so the anamnesis of a group provides the data base for explaining the mode of functioning of a group.

There is, however, an important difference between group and individual development. For every individual, the passage of time serves to provide stimulation for attempts on the part of the ego to master the relationship between the self and the outside world. Thus, the defenses that are in the service of both ego growth and psychic mastery are elaborated within the psychic economy of the person. However serious the vicissitudes of development for an individual, however much an individual's energy remains bound in fixations of stages of development along the way, all but the sickest individual will proceed, at least in part, from one phase to another until a functioning maturity is reached. This is *not* true of group development. Group growth offers a different kind of economy. Unless there is specific input stimulus to group growth, the passage of time does not necessarily serve a group as a stimulant for new solutions to old problems, but rather serves as a cement that consolidates fixations in the development and precludes further growth. Unless the group therapist is sufficiently knowledgeable about group dynamics to facilitate the emergence of each subsequent phase, group 'maturity' will be confined to the parameters of a specific phase. This, in our understanding, means 'fixated' prematurely.

One explanation for the difference between groups and individuals is that, whereas an individual is a self-contained system only in the sphere of fantasy, and by virtue of being a social being must continally process a series of input and output stimuli and responses between himself and others and the changing environment in which he and others live, the group can provide an unchanging environment for its members. This unchanging environment encourages repetitive and predictable responses to input and output stimuli and thus serves as a regressive force toward the mean of normative behavior, which is both a self-fulfilling prophecy and an actuality.

This is why there is a significant difference between the therapy group whose therapist does individual therapy within the setting of a 'group' of people, without the understanding of group development theory, and the therapy group whose therapist understands group process and employs group developmental theory. The group process therapist is able to influence deliberately the process of group development therapeutically at the same time that he deliberately chooses to influence individual development therapeutically; thus contributing both to the interdependence between the individual therapeutic potential and the potential for the group environment. The individually oriented therapist is not able to influence group development deliberately and will not have that choice until he has become familiar with group process as distinct from individual interests.

As we have said before, Kurt Lewin emphasized that the behavior of an individual is a function of the person's interaction with his perceived environment. By this he means that the person, with his individual psychodynamics, behaves as a resultant of this psychodynamic potential as it is influenced by the environment that he perceives. In other words, what he responds to and how he experiences it will be influenced by his particular matrix of selective perceptions, together with the impact of incoming stimuli from the environment on those selective perceptions.

In a group, an individual's psychological perception of the group is heavily influenced by the group culture of which he is a part. A good example of this phenomenon is the Asch (1951) experiment, where it was demonstrated that an individual's perception of the length of a line could be influenced by the way his group stated their perceptions. In this experiment, two lines of unequal length were displayed to a group of people. All of the group members were 'in the know' except for the last person in line, who was 'the subject'. One by one people reported the shorter line as the longer. The 'subject' was faced with the dissonance between his perceptions of length and the increasing pressure that built up as person by person stated reality differently.

Only a few individuals were in fact able to maintain the correct perception, and then many of those that did maintain their own perceptions 'excused' themselves by attributing their difference to some other cause, like their vision, their state of mind, the light, or their ability to discriminate spatial relationships. The majority of the individuals misreported their perceptions, and reported the length of the line in the same way that the group reported it. Of these, only a relatively few knew that they were misreporting; most solved the dilemma by misperceiving. Thus, although it is certainly true that a person's perception of his environment is heavily influenced by his own psychodynamics, it is equally true that both his ability to perceive, as well as the ability to 'own' his perceptions, are heavily influenced by group dynamics.

This fact, that in the group the individual's psychological perceptions of his environment are heavily influenced by the group culture, is particularly important because, in a psychotherapy group, the therapist can prevent the group culture from becoming too predictable. When the therapist does this, the individual has to interact with a continually changing culture which is continually surprising and disconfirming. Group psychotherapy offers the patient a unique experience in that it does not permit the patient to re-create the world in the way he does in everyday life. It is thus true for the patient that he enters group expecting to make of it the self-fulfilling prophecy that he does in the rest of his life, expecting his experience in the group to be yet another series of repetitions of his interactions outside, with the same disappointments and satisfactions, and it is not. Although the therapy group is a microcosm of society, it it not a microcosm of the real world, and therapy begins when the self-fulfilling prophecies fail.

For group psychotherapy to take place, the therapist needs two sets of skills: the skills of intervening at the individual level in such a way that individual group members gain insight into themselves as they relate to the events in the group life, and the skills of intervening at the group level which permits the group to develop as a therapeutic milieu with norms of behavior that are conducive to individual insight and growth.

The group process therapist deliberately introduces interventions that are designed to change group function. This is accomplished by the therapist selecting different aspects of group activity to encourage or discourage. The kinds of things that a therapist will encourage or discourage at any one time will depend upon the group's phase of development and the specific individual and group issues that are relevant to the moment.

We emphasize the importance of the group therapist being primarily concerned with guiding *group* development because each particular phase of group development provides specific and discrete opportunities for the insight and growth of each individual member. As a group moves from one phase of development to another, the individual members are involved in a process that stimulates certain psychodynamic responses in themselves. Thus, the working-through and mastering of group development phases induces the working-through and mastering of individual developmental phases. Among the many other things that a psychotherapy group offers, it provides a corrective emotional experience.

The process by which the group grows is predictable and recognizable. Its particular course can be described, and although there will be idiosyncratic deviations from the norm of development for each group, each and every group will follow, in general outline, the same course. But whereas the group developmental course can be charted with some confidence, the same cannot be said for the individual's inner experience while the individual is contributing to the general group development. Although the specific phase of group development is characterized by certain identifiable behaviors that are common to most, if not all, of the members who are participating, the particular psychic significance for each member is different. The development of a group can be characterized spirally, with phases of development recurring throughout the group life at ever more sophisticated levels. The experience for an individual member therefore has the potential of carrying a different meaning, and a different therapeutic potential, at each recurrence.

Phases of group development

All groups develop in a predictable sequence. Only those groups that are structured so that phases in the predictable sequence can be resolved and succeeded by the next phase are able to complete the sequence that we present here.

The reason for this is that fixation at one phase precludes the kinds of learning that are necessary conditions for the manifestations of the next phase. This is not to say that fragments of all phases are not identifiable in even the most immature of groups, but it is to say that sustained work that is typical of a later phase of development is impossible without some mastery of early phases, just as the skills of walking are impossible until the child has learnt the co-ordination of standing upright.

The phases in a psychotherapy group are precipitated by the individual members' reactions to the ambiguity of the situation. Every person enters a group with expectations that are based on past experience, and with some personal predictions about the kinds of things that he will do and see in the group. Every group therapy member enters a therapy group with heightened anxiety. Every patient has unconscious, pre-conscious, or even conscious expectations that the therapist will cure him. However sophisticated, every patient will respond to the ambiguities of the therapist and the group situation with projection and displacement. It is the projections, and the struggle to validate these projections, that precipitate the group into the phases of development.

Problem-solving responses are stimulated by the internal dissonance aroused by the ambiguities, contradictions and redundancies existing in the verbal and non-verbal communications between members. Problem-solving responses also occur from the need to tolerate and make tolerable the internal dissonance that each member experiences aroused by discrepancies between his expectations of what will happen in the group, and what he perceives to be happening.

Predictably, therefore, initial member behavior will probably be 'safe', adaptive and socialized. Equally predictably, these stereotypic social behaviors will not solve the problems that the new member is faced with in a group any better than they solved his problems outside the group. The next set of behaviors that can be predicted will be the first reserve style – a regression from casual social coping to second line of defense. As line after line of defenses do not resolve the problem, members run regressively through their repertoire of coping behaviors and ultimately are compelled to develop new ones. This, in a nutshell, is what group psychotherapy is all about: individual group members develop more socially and psychologically adaptive responses within this microcosmic society (the group) which they can then generalize to their everyday life outside.

When people go into a new group experience, they face an ambiguous situation. To the extent that what they expect to happen does happen, then to that extent the ambiguity becomes 'structured' in terms that are familiar to them, and they are able to use effectively the kinds of behaviors that have worked for them in similar situations.

To the extent that people's expectations are not met, however, as in the psychotherapy group - to the extent that their stereotypic ideas are violated - then to that extent the ambiguity of the situation increases for them. People will then tend to use the kinds of defensive behaviors that they fall back on when they are confronted with the unknown or unexpected. Stereotypic ideas and defensive behaviors have one thing in common. They both have more to do with a person's reaction to his inner experience (fears or wishes) than they have to do with the situation itself. Therefore, they tend to be less adaptive than exploring, problem-solving kinds of reactions.

Defensive behaviors are characterized by the kinds of interactions that avoid confronting the problem situation. Sometimes they successfully reduce stress; sometimes they help increase it. These kinds of interactions characteristically avoid confronting the problem situation that is generating the stress. There are three kinds of defensive behavior - flight, fight and pairing - that can be described as different kinds of evasive actions in response to stress. These three modes of behavior operationally define the 'basic assumption' cultures that Bion describes as alternatives to 'work'.

In the pages that follow, six phases of group development will be discussed. These are (1) dependence: flight; (2) counterdependence: fight; (3) power: authority issue; (4) overpersonal enchantment; (5) counterpersonal disenchantment; (6) interdependence: work.

First phase in group development - dependence: flight

Flight behaviors lead a retreat to some place else in time and space into the past or the future and far away from 'here' and 'now'. A leap into abstractions, generalizations, or 'oughtitudes', that define the way things 'ought' to be, keep the group safe from defining specifically what *is*. Other kinds of flight help a group detour into narratives about things that are relevant only to things that are irrelevant to group issues. 'Solving' a problem immediately can be an effective method of avoiding the task of defining it. Changing the subject into one that turns everybody on and the issue off is another effective flight tactic.

The first phase in any group exhibits the kinds of behavior that we have called flight. The more sophisticated the group, the more sophisticated the flight pattern – and the less sophisticated the group, the more regressive and primitive and autistic the flight pattern.

The theme of the flight phase is that all will be well if only no one rocks the boat, and the basic assumption of the flight phase is that the benevolent leader will somehow rescue the group and each and every one of its members. The dynamic force is that of dependence and the wish is for conformity.

Typical of this phase is the emphasis on rules and regulations and proper behavior. The new member who is greeted by a listing of the 'rules' of the group is entering a group that is manifesting itself in the dependent phase. Rules are a flight maneuver away from the interpersonal restructuring that must take place if the new member is to be incorporated. An outside authority, personified by 'the rules', is relied upon to maintain the *status quo*.

The phenomenon of flight appears in relation to several individual psychological dimensions: flight from involvement with others (object relations); flight from the here and now (external reality); flight from feeling (internal reality); flight from controversy (autonomy); flight from change (fixation). Which function the flight performs can usually be interpreted from the content of the flight talk, which parallels at a symbolic level the issues that the group has taken flight from. Listening to the themes in parallel talk provides material which can be interpreted at the group level by the therapist, much as the analyst listens with his third ear and interprets the pre-conscious or unconscious determinations in the associations of his analysand.

In every new group, the beginning phase is characterized by flight behavior. However, the beginning phase of group development is not the only time that flight occurs. Flight occurs as a defensive maneuver when the work in hand gets too difficult, or as a group goal whenever the dependency issues in the group remain at the unconscious level. Flight is also predictable at the start of each group session; when it is not uncommon to see the group recapitulate all its developmental phases before beginning to work. The same recapitulation is characteristic of the period after any task completion, whether that task be to finalize a decision, surface an unconscious goal, resolve a fixation, or work through a phase.

Some major work gets done in the flight phase of the beginning group. Members become familiar with the sight and sound of each other, develop expectations of different kinds of responses from different other members, and start to pair in alliance. These alliances are based partly on the similarities and support that members see in other members, and partly on transference manifestations.

The word pairing in this sense is used differently from Bion's definition, in which he uses pairing as the label for the basic assumption group, where an interactive role relationship arises between two people representing a solution (through the birth of a Messiah) to the unconscious group problem. We have never yet observed pairing with a messianic goal. We have observed interactive role relationships, equally powerfully induced by the group process, that represent other kinds of solutions to unconscious group problems. Thus, we see pairing as a system phenomenon, independent of the purpose of pairing. For this reason we do not reserve the term pairing as a label for Bion's basic assumption group, and use it instead to describe a phenomenon that occurs in all groups for many purposes, sometimes as an individual or group solution to unconscious problems, and sometimes not.

For example, a member may pair with another because both intellectualize away from the threats of disagreement (pairing on similarity of defense mechanism); because both are Catholics (pairing on overlapping memberships); because both are young and of the same sex (homogeneous pairing); or of the opposite sex (heterogeneous, sexual pairing); or because both are supportive of each other (pairing by identification); or because one perceived the other as nurturing and protective, and the nurturer needs someone to protect (transference pairing).

Pairing behaviors manifest in all phases of development. They are the behaviors that reflect the interpersonal collusion that attempts to avoid the stress in the group. 'Teaming up with the strongest', 'making nice', 'pouring oil on troubled water', 'doing it for your sake', 'not wanting to hurt anybody's feelings', or 'flying to the rescue of poor troubled you' are all effective evasions that require the co-operation of other group members and that help to avoid the tension inherent in the task of building working relationships.

Second phase in group development – counterdependence: fight

The fight phase in group develops when the mechanisms of avoidance that characterize the flight phase fail to create a safe *status quo*. The alliances formed through pairing also form the basis of support for opposition. Whereas it is relatively difficult to stand alone and take on a group in disagreement, it is relatively easy to challenge another group member, secure in the support of at least one other member.

Fight behaviors avoid confronting controversial situations by stirring up controversy between people. Shouting the person down avoids hearing the problem. Blaming oneself, someone else or the system, scapegoating the bad apple in the barrel, or the bad barrel, are all good battle maneuvers. 'You always' and 'why don't you' and 'if only you would' and 'you ought' are all fighting words that avoid confrontation with what *is* that needs to be dealt with.

Where phobic and pervasive anxiety is more characteristic of the underlying dependency issues of the flight phase, stubborn or angry passive-aggression is more characteristic of the counterdependent and aggressive dependent issues of the fight phase. Just as the manifest content of the flight could be read as parallel talk symbolizing the basic issues relevant to the here and now issues in the group, so the manifest fight content also parallels the pressing group issues. The basic group forces at work in these two early phases in group development are the forces of dependence in the first phase and counterdependence in the second.

Dependence behavior results in compliant followership of the leader's wishes (real or imagined). Aggressive dependence is the behavior that induces the conformity of other members to the leader's imagined or real leadership, and counterdependence is the behavior of non-conformity or rebellion against the leader's real or imagined rules. The common theme in dependence and counterdependence is that the inferred wish of the leader is the reference point around which group process revolves.

These three sets of behaviors, dependence, aggressive dependence and counterdependence, can be seen in a group as different roles, carried for the group by a single individual or a sub-group.

Third phase in group development – power: authority issue

In the first two phases of group development the group has responded to its problems predominantly through flight and fight. Although from one aspect these phases are characterized by a mindless scramble into activity, from another aspect the foundations of group work and group development are being laid.

Members are becoming familiar with each other and developing expectations of the kinds of responses that they can expect. They have had the experience of working together to resolve group issues. They have learnt to look to certain members for support and alliance, to others for contention and disagreement.

In the flight phase the 'good' leader is seen as some sort of beneficent savior, whose power will protect the group from anything bad happening to them. In the fight phase, the projections on the leader turn 'bad', and the leader is seen either as the malevolent cause (scientifically manipulating the group and watching it squirm like a butterfly on a pin, or like an amoeboid colony on a slide under a microscope), or else as an incompetent who is irresponsibly fiddling while the group, like Rome, burns.

Scapegoating is the overt manifestation of the fight phase, with competitive sub-groups scapegoating each other, an issue or a particular member. Moreover, scapegoating performs a group function. It becomes a unifying group force that unites the members against the leader.

The behaviors of the group as it approaches and enters the phase of the authority issue are so distinctive that, once they have been experienced and identified, they are recognizable and unmistakable even in their most subtle forms. Just preceding the authority phase the group builds its solidarity. This is the time when membership work is done, unfinished business is taken care of, and strong support bonds develop between members. The uninitiated therapist may mistake this sudden group unity for group work, and congratulate himself and the group for having resolved the dependency that they had been manifesting such a short time before in flight and fight. But the group is not working, in the sense of doing the work that they are in group to do. What the group is doing is consolidating, gathering its forces so that it can turn once again to the authority and resume the power struggle, but this time from a position of unified strength rather than fragmented helplessness and turmoil.

The first clear signs that the group is about to enter the authority issue phase is at the content level. Oblique references are made, first about authority figures in general, and then about the therapist in particular. The group may argue, one faction criticizing the therapist and the other faction defending him.

At the level of parallel talk, the content of the talk will be 'leaders': well-meaning, bumbling politicians, brutal policemen, esoteric and obscure professors, cold and distant fathers and mothers, warm and soothing grandparents, etc. This level of parallel talk can be inter-preted directly by the therapists as oblique references to the group conflict about the therapists' leadership. When this intervention is successful, the group will make indirect references to the therapists by a series of condemnatory 'they/them' statements. '*They*' won't answer questions, '*they*' won't help; '*they*' know it all and enjoy watching the group squirm; *'they'* don't really know how to help, and won't own up to it, etc. At this stage there is little that a single group therapist can do to facilitate the process. Anything he says will be taken as evidence to support whatever 'they' hypothesis the group is generating at the moment. (In the co-therapy situation, however, one therapist can often 'mid-wife' the group's accusations of the other, supporting the group in its anxiety and guilt.) This pattern has its prototype in both the flight and fight phases, but with a difference. In the flight phase the attack is intellectualized and aloof, and in the fight phase the therapist is more a bone of contention in the fight than the object of rage. However, in the early stage of the authority issue, the therapist is clearly the target. Sometimes the references to the therapist are amused, affectionate and teasing. Sometimes they are sarcastic and sneering, sometimes they are dazzlingly intelligent and witty. However the group expresses the issue, the effect is to continue to build a strong family feeling among the members. The particular style the group uses reflects the particular issues with authority in the particular group. The content, however, is the same in nearly every group. The group leader is being tried and found wanting.

The precipitating event between the initial oblique attack on the therapist and the final direct attack is nearly always heralded by a confrontation question. Either a member of the group asks a question spontaneously or the whole group encourages one or other of their members to question the therapist. What the actual question is, is usually irrelevant, for what may sound like a question is in fact an act of power. An answer will not and cannot satisfy the group. It is at this point that nothing the therapist can say will make any difference. If the therapist answers the question, the group will find that the information is somehow deficient and will ask more questions, demonstrating each time they get an answer that the therapist has not in fact given them what they wanted. This of course is true, because what the group wants is control over the therapist, not information. If the therapist refrains from answering the question, the group will voice its outrage at the inappropriate treatment, the unthinking or deliberate cruelty in the necessary deprivation, or the weakness in the therapist in being unable to meet the group's needs. Whether the therapist responds or does not respond is immaterial. In either case the group is now riding the wave of the authority issue, and unless there is some serious diversion, they will continue on its crest. As the authority issue breaks around the therapist's head, the group is carried out of its depth.

Bennis and Shepard point out that, even in a T-group, the deep level of the authority issue experience is on the level of that of the primal horde who consume the leader in order to incorporate his power. For the psychotherapy group, where the goals are not primarily insight into group process but rather insight into self, the basic issues are focused around the primary pathogenic introject. Oral sadistic and cannibalistic fantasies are aroused; annihilation and pre-oedipal castration anxiety is experienced. It is precisely the strength of the authority issue stimulus to deep underlying conflictual dynamics that makes the procedure of facilitating the group's entrance into, and resolution of, this phase such a potent therapeutic process. The group as a whole provides surrogate ego support for all members, which is particularly necessary for patients whose egos are weak or brittle, or who have serious developmental deficits.

Just as the authority issue arouses primitive transference issues in the members, so it does for the therapist. The counter-transference issues that are inherent in the positive or negative transference neurosis are always difficult for the therapist, however experienced, in individual therapy. In group psychotherapy, transferential feelings resonating between group members are amplified through the group and become focused upon the group therapist as a function of group dynamics as well as individual dynamics. Thus the intensity of the counter-transference response is increased multidimensionally. One of our students in group psychotherapy, after his first experience of the full force of the authority issue, returned and said that to his surprise he had experienced the kind of terror that would have been appropriate had he really been about to be killed and eaten – quite so! Even though each therapist will experience his own psychodynamic response to the authority issue, annihilation anxiety is not, by any means, an uncommon counter-transferential response.

For the therapist, working through the counter-transference will provide potent material, not only for understanding his role in group process, but also for his own self-analysis. We have found that each authority issue results for each of us in more knowledge about group psychotherapy, *and* about ourselves. Each authority issue gives us the opportunity to use the skills that have resulted from our previous experiences in working through the authority issue as well as clues to the need for new skill development for the next.

The therapist needs to be able to gauge the readiness of the group for working through the authority issue, both on content and in depth. It is important to remind therapists that from the aspect of their own group membership it is particularly important for them to gauge their own readiness. The group therapist who, for whatever reason, attempts to facilitate the group through the authority issue before he is ready to take his own role in it, will not only be unlikely to facilitate the group work, but will run the danger of jeopardizing group development.

The therapist who has no experience of the authority issue, either at the practical or at the theoretical level, will almost certainly prevent it, by sending a clear, non-ambivalent message to the group that he will not tolerate the power struggle. One of our students, for example, before understanding the implications of confrontation with authority, reported that on entering the group one day he found one of the male members sitting in his chair and the group in a state of tense exhilaration. He touched the member on the shoulder, and said 'your chair is over there'. The member moved, and the group subsided. After having been in supervision for some time, he recognized how clearly he had aborted the group authority issue. He also gained insight into his own need to control the group by coercing their dependency through benevolent paternalism.

A less clear and more ambivalent response was implied in a discussion that we had with a group therapist at a conference who talked of the 'ingratitude' of a group who, after all he had done for them, turned on him and rebelled. He put the rebellion down, firmly pointing out that they were behaving like adolescents, and after that he had no more trouble with them. Almost certainly his group continued to work within the therapeutic conditions that existed within the prescribed limits (which we would label fixation), and equally certainly the group did not work, as a group, on separation-individuation issues.

Although the authority issue most frequently takes the form of the group attempting to control the therapist and incorporate his power through aggression, groups are by no means limited to one strategy. One group, having attacked savagely but incompletely, and backed away from the issue in guilt and confusion, returned to the issue again in a different guise. This was a time-limited group of ministers before their ordination. Their next strategy was seduction. Not sexual seduction with which group therapists have plenty of counter-transferential experience, but religious. The group passed a peppermint patty around from member to member, each one breaking off a piece and eating it in the spirit of group communion. When the therapist's turn came, she experienced an almost uncontrollable desire to join the group in mystical unity, and merge her identity with the group's. It was only by remembering her role, her function and the group goal that she was able to abstain and stay constant to the group development issues through the loving reproaches of the group.

Even the well-trained *and* experienced group psychotherapist is challenged through the group's entrance into, and resolution of, the authority issue. The major task for the well-trained but less experienced group therapist is to gain experience of the authority issue process by experiencing it, and by learning to tolerate the counter-transferential turmoil that will be set off. Just as the authority issue is an experiential crisis for the group, so it is for the therapist. The entire group must be ready to work through the relevant dynamics. Sometimes the therapist is ready and the group is not. Sometimes the group is ready and the therapist is not.

As we have said, for both of us, experienced as we are with the vicissitudes of individual transference resolutions, it is clear that the power of evoking violent counter-transferential responses that can be found in the group transference is a quantum jump in intensity from that of individual therapy. We are also aware that the ability to tolerate and work through, within ourselves, the counter- transference reactions to the authority issue are significantly different when we are working with a group alone as contrasted to when we are working as co-therapists. As co-therapists we can support each other silently during the attack and facilitate our partner's individual working through and resolution of narcissistic hurts (in the case of the negative transference) and omnipotent fantasies (in the case of the positive).

As co-therapists we also have immeasurably greater tools in helping group resolution, as at any one time one of us can facilitate the individual and group expression and exploration of frustration, hatred, disappointment, pain, confusion, hurt, sense of abandonment, and helpless love and rage, guilt and despair, using the other as the object. When only one therapist is working with a group, he is in the anomalous position of both facilitating and enduring the group attack. This has consequences on the potential of the guilt reaction experienced by the group that is so often a consequence of group confrontation, and which, in and of itself, can abort a working through if it is mishandled.

Resolution of any instance of the power struggle that exists in the authority issue must, by its very nature, be a major victory for the group in an ongoing process which, in and of itself, never comes to an end. It is impossible for us to imagine a group of a level of sophistication and maturity that would preclude the need to continually and cyclically work through issues of power and authority; not because it is impossible to conceptualize the ideal, nor because that ideal may not in fact have a potential for actualization, but because as a matter of practical fact we are children of the culture as we know it, and in this culture issues of power and authority are woven into the everyday fabric of living.

The authority issue centers around the issue of power and influence, of outer-directedness versus inner-directedness, of separation and individuation at the level of adolescence, of separation from fusion at the level of infancy. Each time a group works through a crisis in the authority issue, the potential for work on separation and individuation is increased. This work is usually done in two distinct and successive sub-phases, enchantment and disenchantment.

Fourth phase of group development – overpersonal enchantment

The phase of enchantment is organized around a sense of mastery and independence. The group in general, and individual members in particular, feel potent, resourceful, accomplished, and triumphant. It is during this period that new kinds of alliances are made between members and individual members receive positive, affirmative feedback from the group of the ways in which they are particularly resourceful to group growth and function. It is a time of cohesive good fellowship in psychotherapy group development. Characteristically, the group will work independent of the therapists – and whereas the therapists were under severe attack for withholding help and resources during the authority conflicts, the therapist's help is not only not sought, but apparently not needed during its aftermath. For those individuals whose formation of object relations was a delayed experience, the phase of enchantment provides a repetition of early symbiotic gratification. Their striving to become fused with the group, and to merge their identity into the group identity, intensifies the forces of group cohesion. For those individuals whose early object relations were formed in disappointment and deprivation, or for those for whom too early splitting of the object precipitated pre-conscious independence, the intense group cohesiveness arouses fear of fusion in the form of fear of merging with the group at the cost of identity.

Cohesive euphoria shortens the distance between members. If this (overpersonal) force is strong enough to overcome (counterpersonal) resistances to bonding the group enters into a strong phase of enchantment where the bonding is very strong. To maintain this equilibrium consumes tremendous amounts of group energy and maintaining the level of cohesiveness becomes the task. Should the group reach a level of equilibrium in this state, there is group fixation. The amount of energy required to maintain the group structure in this state is so great, however, that for most groups in a relatively short time the homogeneity of the structure cannot be maintained (personal communication with Michael Fryd, Rutgers University, New Jersey).

Whether the group has a short or long, mild or intense phase of enchantment will depend upon many factors: the composition of the group; the strength of the membership work during the flight and fight phases, the underlying trust in the therapist, the amount of guilt generated, the intensity and effectiveness of the phase of authority, the nature of the individual transference and psychodynamic issues that are stimulated by confrontation of the authority, and intimacy with peers.

The euphoria of the phase of enchantment is based upon denial: denial of guilt, denial of anxiety, denial of mistrust. Omnipotence, grandiosity, overestimation and blissful symbiosis defends against fear of fusion, loss of identity, homosexuality, sibling rivalry and suspiciousness.

As the work of the group centers more closely around maintaining the euphoria rather than expressing it, 'closeness' becomes 'too close'. The counterpersonal roles become activated and dominant. Conflict returns to the group. Group cohesion is disrupted and the group is precipitated into the phase of disenchantment.

Fifth phase of group development – counterpersonal disenchantment

The sub-phase of disenchantment is organized around a sense of disappointment and failure. The group in general and individuals in particular feel let down, anxious, distrustful, isolated. For the optimists the disappointment is acute, and is expressed in depression or rage against the group and against its members. For the pessimists, there is almost a relief that their predictions have been confirmed, and that the world is as untrustworthy and disappointing as they had always believed.

The phase of enchantment looked like a group flight into health. The phase of disenchantment arouses fears in the therapist of group suicide. Patients come late, miss sessions, report depression and disillusionment and loneliness, alienation, futility, hopelessness and depression. Whereas the phase of enchantment was marked by great cohesiveness, the phase of disenchantment is discohesive.

A group that is basically cohesive can survive a phase which is characterized by non-cohesiveness. It is important for the therapist to use his understanding of cohesion to manage his own and the group response to the phase of disenchantment, when attendance may very well be sporadic and apathetic. A group with a background of strong cohesion will be unlikely to lose members at this period. A group with a non-cohesive background may not only lose members, but may disintegrate under the stress.

The behavior in the phase of disenchantment 'looks' the same for both cohesive and non-cohesive groups, but the prediction and prognosis is different. Unless the group psychotherapist knows the difference, the loss of his own internal cohesiveness (which he *will* experience as his own needs for control, affection and inclusion are threatened) may motivate him to act out his own disenchantment in the group. Acting out his own disenchantment would most likely manifest itself in running after absenting members with phone calls or letters. More extreme manifestations would be the punishing of late or absent members when they come back to group, or joining the underlying pessimism of the group members' prognosis for the survival of the group.

If the therapist is not able to discriminate between the phase of disenchantment and a disintegrating group, it will be impossible for him to respond appropriately. It is important for a group therapist to be able to build different intervention strategies aimed at individual members based upon whether the member behavior is a function, predominantly, of the dynamics of the group phase, or whether it is a function of the member's individual dynamics. For example, pursuing members during the phase of disenchantment, when lateness and absences are predictable, will only increase the individual fears of fusion and loss of identity and lack of trust. But, for example, for an individual member whose attachment and commitment is tenuous at best, and whose grandiosity or narcissism, when injured, arouses such pain or shame or rage that he is unable to face the group, a letter or phone call might be a very appropriate and even necessary intervention if the individual is to become able to return to group.

The phases of enchantment and disenchantment have the character of cyclothymic swings. Much depression and elation are experienced by group members. Individual members are stimulated to confront issues in their early development as well as needs for inclusion and affiliation and control, which apply not only to their own membership but also to the need for group work.

The outcome of the resolution of these phases is the 'mature group' that can work on a reality-testing level with a language that has been consensually validated and a communication medium through which information can be exchanged and distortions can be processed.

Sixth phase of group development – interdependence: work

This final phase of group development ushers in the therapeutic environment. The mature work group has a history upon which it can draw. It can recognize characteristics of earlier phases when they recur. It has a memory of successful methods that have been used in working through phases and the experience of previous mastery of vicissitudes in development. It has the ability to support and facilitate the work of an individual member when the member has to do personal work so that he or she can again function at the group level.

This mode of working has significant implications for the group energy that is available for group work. The mature group expends less energy in maintaining the therapeutic environment and in working through temporary regressions or mastering new aspects of old problems. The mature group can, therefore, direct more energy to exploring and resolving issues that are relevant to individual insight, or to understanding the depth and relevance of group experience.

A mature therapy group has a high synergistic potential which provides a unique therapeutic environment for the therapy of the individual. Some of the therapeutic gains that the individual achieves come almost as a 'side-effect' of good group work.

The creation of the particular kind of therapeutic environment that exists in a mature group creates a high potential for individual therapy to take place within the group. This does not imply, however, that the individuals who helped to build the group to its maturity have necessarily reached maturity themselves, nor does it say anything about the members' individual therapy goals other than that their therapy is progressing well, and the prognosis is good.

In fact, for some group members, the level of functioning that they experience in the therapy group exceeds the level that they can individually achieve in everyday life. This delay of generalization can be very frustrating for members, and it is important that group therapists be aware of this particular source for a reactive depression. For other members, the level of maturity of function that they achieved in the process of building a mature group is not only generalizable, but is in effect a quantum leap in overall function. For them, termination of therapy, or transferring to a different group which offers different challenges more appropriate to their next therapeutic steps, may be necessary to maintain for them an environment that continues to be therapeutic, rather than becoming redundant. Group function becomes redundant for an individual when it ceases to provide the necessary stimulation for the deeper levels of psychodynamic working through that are the ongoing task of every individual member in a 'mature work group'.

Discriminating between the dynamic potential of a 'mature' work group and the dynamic potential of a developing group was a relatively new insight for us in our work together. We had some five years of co-therapy experience before we began to recognize that the *themes* that were familiar to us in the phases of development of a new group were now recurring themes in the mature group, and no longer constituted developmental phases *per se*. As we continued to observe and discuss this phenomenon, we came to the conclusion that the main function of the recurring themes in a mature group had more to do with the needs for development of individual members, and the general deepening of group experience than they did with the phases of development as we had originally understood them.

It is now clear to us that this is often a subtle difference, but one that is important for the group therapist to recognize. It is almost as if the group, like a body, pays attention to the regeneration or generation of new parts of itself to replace those that are weak or malfunctioning. This analogue is a useful one in that it makes clear some of the similarity of group dynamics to individual dynamics, and also emphasizes the dissimilarity between group and individual dynamics. An individual can 'heal' certain kinds of wounds, both in the soma and the psyche, when the individual is in a state of overall psychic and somatic health. However, unlike a lizard, a human being cannot grow a new limb when the limb is either lost in trauma, or when, through epigenetic malfunction, the limb never grew in the first place.

A group, however, seems to function more like the lizard than like the human being. It is almost as if, in the dynamics of group, there is some unconscious recognition of an aspect of the process that is malfunctioning, and consequently is in need of regeneration or of generation. Those individuals in the group whose personal developmental deficits have come to play the role of group deficit or to represent a group trauma, become amenable, in the group, to a regenerative role. It is perhaps in this way that some of the group 'cures' that we would not have predicted can be explained. The effect of the maturely functioning group is to 'heal' its members.

For example, a group may function at a paranoid level for several sessions while, at a different level, individual members will work at resolving issues in basic trust, issues of homosexuality, or other issues that are integral to the working through of paranoia. Sometimes it will be one member who will manifest paranoia within a group environment of basic trust; at other times the whole group will experience a manifest ambivalence between trust and suspiciousness, using both individual egos and group reality testing and consensually validating mechanisms to analyse both sides of the ambivalence and to create a climate in which some individuals will get insight into personal issues of basic trust, others into personal issues of suspiciousness and still others into both kinds of issues.

This working through is very different from the developmental phase preceding the authority issue, where group suspiciousness is relatively non-ambivalent, in that the membership work has induced high pairing trust between the members while the therapists have been the recipients of projected or displaced distrust.

Appropriate therapist interventions which facilitate therapy for individuals in the two kinds of group 'paranoia' are very different. Interventions that are appropriate when the group is moving through the pre-authority issue phase are largely the skills of providing a neutral screen on which to project the transference. In paranoid 'theme' development, however, the therapist must be prepared to respond with a range of appropriate interventions: as a neutral screen for one member or sub-group at one time, as an interpreter, supporter, confronter or group-level interpreter at another.

Discrimination between the dynamics which can be recognized as developmental phase work, and the dynamics which can be recognized as theme work, is an ongoing task for us. However, we offer an example of the difference between the developmental phase and the recurrent theme in the dynamics of the authority issue.

Developmental phase

As we have described earlier in this chapter, the developmental phase of the authority issue is preceded by strong group membership work, with members pairing and sub-grouping until they are secure enough to experience their paranoid projections at the group level; first at the level of parallel talk, later in direct paranoid attack.

In the final group confrontation of the authority issue, the group will demand a response from the therapists. This demand will not be for the purpose of getting information, but for the purpose of gaining power. Should the therapist be unwise enough to attempt to give the group the information that it so emphatically insists that it needs, the group will deal with it as if it is irrelevant (which it is to the group process) or as if it has not been given, or even as if the therapist has not spoken at all. The authority issue is an issue of who has the authority and power, the therapist or the group. We have dealt earlier in this chapter with both the difficulty and the importance of facilitating the group's mastery of this phase. What is relevant to the discriminations between developmental phase of power-authority and the theme of power that we are drawing here is the different therapist responses to the different symptoms that emerge from group paranoia as part of a developmental phase, as contrasted to group paranoia as a theme.

Recurrent theme

The sequence that occurs when paranoia is part of a recurrent theme is frequently preceded by the acting out of individual members. Individual members will attend group and report problems in their lives during the week, the themes of which reflect the dynamic conflicts that exist at an unconscious level in the group. In the meantime, the group itself will apparently be working well - but strangely without results or insight. As the members introduce material, a common theme becomes apparent. They have been ill-used and discriminated against by bosses, husbands, wives, parents, relatives, perhaps a neighbor - or even another group member. When the group discovers the common plight, either through their own work or by therapist intervention, they recognize the strange similarity between issues of suspiciousness inside and outside the group. The group's ability to work with the material is significantly different from the group response in the authority-issue phase where the group uses *all* material as ammunition in an acting out attack. Insight into the recurrent theme provides opportunity for one or more members to achieve deep and significant insight. When insight is shared with the group, the group is ready to resume productivity and effective work.

Summary

The phases of group development occur reliably and sequentially. The group therapist who understands the vicissitudes of group development can facilitate the group movement in the direction of its goal. The skills that the therapist needs to accomplish this leadership task are the theory and practice that permit him to facilitate the resolution of fixations within any one phase. He must know how to differentiate between regression in the service of group development from regression as a symptom of fixation; how to interpret resistance to the transitions from one phase to another; and how to discriminate between the occasions when interpretations should be at the individual level so that the individual insight will serve as a driving force for the group, and occasions when the appropriate intervention is at a group level.

We have used the Bennis and Shepard theory as the basis of our presentation of group development as a map, being aware that the map is not the territory, but an overview which permits us to organize our observations of group events into an understanding that guides our behavior and permits us to generate hypotheses, make predictions and test them. Any other good *group* developmental theory that explains group developmental dynamics will permit the same therapeutic moderation. The phenomena of group development exist, and a mature group is apparent and recognizable, whatever developmental explanation is used to describe its growth. We do not have a vested interest in all group therapists using the same theory; in fact, it is probably true that a growing understanding of group phenomena is dependent upon work with many different approaches.

In groups that have reached maturity, we now recognize a different aspect of group dynamics; our ongoing task is to understand this more comprehensively. For many group therapists, the group that is fixated before the resolution of the authority issue *is* what a psychotherapy group 'is'. For these therapists the goal of a group is its development to a dynamic equilibrium between fight and flight modes, within which equilibrium other group work can be done. Further signs of development will inevitably be understood as regression to fight behavior. Preliminary membership work will be interpreted as defensive pairing behavior. The election of the 'sickest' member will predictably be interpreted as a symptom of the sickness of the group, rather than as a reflection of a particular phase and a step in the rebellion that results in the confrontation of the therapist and the initiation into the exploration of power, authority, responsibility, and accountability. For us, some years ago, a 'mature' group that had reached the working mode of 'consensual validation' was a group that had reached its goal. However, our continuing experience confronted us with the teleological nature of our thinking. We consistently made the attempt to interpret what we saw, not only within the framework that had become familiar to us, but also outside the framework in terms of what it 'could be' that we did not yet understand. We became eager to see what kind of therapy is available to people in a therapy group that has reached and continues in the consensual validation mode – à mode that many groups never reach and a mode that few groups have the opportunity to function in.

Some ten years later we are continuing to explore what a psychotherapy group can become when what it is is a group that functions in consensually validating maturity. We are aware that in mature groups we observe phenomena that we have not observed as a consistent underlying dynamic in groups functioning at the level of pre-maturity. For example, a group in its maturity works to activate the leadership potential *both* in the members of the group and in the group-as-a-whole.

It is into this arena of exploration that we hope other group psychotherapists will enter in future, and that researchers will describe, explore, develop hypotheses and predictions about. This kind of effort will contribute to the next steps in understanding and in creating new possibilities in the field of group dynamics. We owe a debt to Lewin, Freud and Bion, for their pioneering quality, and we use their theoretical formulations in our foundations not as the boundaries of exploration but as the first charting of unfamiliar territory which guides other explorers to new discoveries.

We owe a debt to Bennis and Shepard for their theory of group development – the summary table of which they have graciously permitted us to reprint in appendix 1. In the summary chart that follows we present our version of the phases of group development. We have retained Bennis and Shepard's six phases, and their labels for each. We have, however, substituted our own variables for theirs. Thus, each of the six phases: (1) flight, (2) fight, (3) power-authority, (4) enchantment, (5) disenchantment, and (6) interdependent work are described in terms of (1) the implicit group goal, (2) the group organization, (3) the group role, (4) the voice of the group, (5) the group theme, (6) the group focus, (7) content themes, (8) the group activity, (9) individual member defenses and (10) major membership concerns.

Table 5.1 Phases of group development
Stage one: dependence, power, control, pseudo-socialization

	Phase one: dependence: flight	*Phase two: counterdependence: fight*	*Phase three: power: authority*
Implicit group goal	Flight	Fight	Incorporate power by rebellion or seduction
Group organization	Group organizes around homogeneous pairing	Group organizes into warring sub-groups around negative and positive transference	Individuals, sub-groups and/or group organizes around scapegoating therapist and seizing power
Group role	Dependent, conforming compliant roles	Counterdependent, aggressive-dependent roles	Controlling, contending manipulative roles
Voice of group	The most conforming and/or controlling member or sub-group	Scapegoats and warriors. 'Tug-of-war'	'David' against 'Goliath'
Group theme	Therapist as benevolent, all powerful protector. Rules of right and proper behavior	Therapist as authority: to please, to obey or to rebel. Rights and wrongs of you/they/me/it	Therapist as scapegoat. Sabotage of therapist. Power struggle. *Coup d'état*
Group focus	Concern with how to please therapist, conviction that as long as therapist is there all is right with group, untested assumptions about magical cure, individual concerns about inclusion	Preoccupation with impossibility of pleasing therapist, concern with how group should be controlled, concern with confidentiality, application of norms (like socializing outside group)	Preoccupation with power and authority. Dissatisfaction with therapists' behavior, token issues raised with therapist as manifestation of struggle for power and control

	Inclusion	Control	Power
Content themes	Discussion of symptoms, complaints about world and life, failures of other therapists, focus on past and non-group present, away from interpersonal group issues	Discussions of deficiencies of members' behavior, of failure of group to help members, of what is wrong with group, each other and everything. Indirect complaints about therapist	Discussion of ineffectiveness of therapist in group; either because of malevolence, benevolence, ineptitude, incompetence
Group activity	Idiosyncratic, stereotypic dependency solutions, denial of aggression, defensive pairing in flight, stereotypic social behavior, repetition of family roles, self-fulfilling prophecy	Passive-aggressive fighting in aggressive dependent and counter-dependent sub-groups. Sadomasochistic acting out, scapegoating, in-fighting, power struggles, use of group norms to manipulate members	Confrontation of authority. Positive and negative transference manifestations in repetition compulsion. Sabotage of decision-making by (1) token decisions or (2) refusal to engage in decision-making or (3) group 'decision' as triumph over therapist. Demand for guidelines, solutions, answers. Questions to therapist not for information but for control; therapist responses used as proof of therapist inadequacy, incompetence, manipulation, or sadism. Pairing for solidarity against therapist
Individual defenses	Anxiety, intellectualization, passivity, compliance, denial, projection, regression, masochism	Obsessive-compulsive rationalization, denial, reaction-formation, passive-aggressive obstinacy, projection, sadism	Denial, projection, displacement, splitting
Membership concerns	Inclusion	Control	Power

Table 5.1 (cont.)
Stage two: separation-individuation: interdependence

	Phase four: overpersonal enchantment	Phase five: counterpersonal disenchantment	Phase six: interdependence work
Implicit group goal	Symbiosis	Separation	Working alliance for therapy
Group organization	Whole group organizes around group as homogeneous entity	Fragmentation of group into individuals. Reactive individuation of individual members	Group-as-a-whole organizes around group goals
Group role	Overpersonal merging roles	Counterpersonal, alienating, paranoid, anomie roles	Interdependent problem-solving and decision-making roles
Voice of group	'Come closer'. Sub-group heroes representing group symbiosis; deification of group	'Too close'. Sub-groups and individual members representing voice for separation; denigration of group	'Work and love'. Sub-groups and individual members representing task and maintenance; interdependence for group goals
Group theme	Group as Messiah. Utopia	Group as disappointing object. All problems attributed to group. Fantasies of disintegration, death and/or suicide of group	Activation of self-leadership. Individual and group responsibility for progress and development
Group focus	Group conviction that the group is greater than the individual; salvation through membership in the group; creation of utopian ideals. Enchantment with group and self	Disappointment; rage and grief at loss of fantasy. Narcissistic pain; anxiety; sibling rivalry; distrust; suspiciousness; paranoia; homosexual panic. Rapprochement issues; separation-individuation issues; identity crises. Individual members regress to primitive defenses against dependency, revival of symptoms	Concern with therapeutic goals, each other and group. Testing expectations. Explorations of projections and transference manifestations against group reality testing mechanisms. Consensual validation. Inter-member support

Content themes	Triumphant jokes and heroic group tales. Discussion of group history, group as 'family', as 'nurturing parent', as corrective emotional experience. Focus on positive aspects of relationships. Self-disclosure	Bitter complaints and disappointment in group. Bitter sarcasm, denigration of group and previous relationships. Bitter 'I told you so's'. Complaints about group as *cause* of problems. Prolonged silence	Discussion of interdependent group roles. Use of group for insight into individual. Interpreting 'voice' of group, 'scapegoating' on individual and group level. Understanding of responsibility, accountability, authority and self-leadership issues in relationship to group and generalized to outside work and relationships
Group activity	Symbiotic pairing, over-estimation of group, symbiotic euphoria, pseudo group independence based on denial of ambivalence. Denial of depression and anxiety. Triumph conceals guilt. Eroticized pairing, strong tendency to act out; illicit meetings 'outside' group	Reactive independence, individuation, isolation, alienation, anomie, fear of fusion. Withdrawal and rejection of group and members. Narcissistic injury and feelings of shame and guilt result in group paranoia and/or passive aggressive immobilization of group: lateness, absenteeism, or disintegration of group. Identity crisis for individual members	Interdependent role relationships and sub-groups for work. Analysis of transference and resistance, related to both individual and group developmental themes. Working through of all 6 phases of development in cyclical recurrence with differing depth and emphasis as determined by group and member needs
Individual defenses	Denial, regression to omnipotence, fusion, grandiosity, euphoria, manic defense against depression, splitting, reaction formation	Denial, pessimism, depression, regression to narcissism, projection, displacement, splitting, reaction formation	Sublimation and all ego defense mechanisms as a function of autonomous ego: reality testing. Self and social validation
Membership concerns	Affection	Distrust	Trust

Chapter 6
Three levels of group process

We define the goal of membership in a psychotherapy group as 'participation in the development of a group that provides an environment that is therapeutic for each individual member. Each member must both help to develop and help to maintain the group as a relevant therapeutic environment'.

The selection of members for any given group needs to be made with this purpose in mind. If the members of the group are to bring into the group the raw material that the group needs to reach the goal, then the group members must be chosen carefully so that they possess the requisite resources.

In a sense, then, patients are selected for the group in which there is a goodness of 'fit' between the therapeutic needs of the person and the potential therapeutic environment within which these needs can best be met. In this chapter we will describe three different therapeutic environmental types, which we have called levels of group process. These three levels of group emerge from the combination of the members who join the group, and from the way the therapist influences the group. The therapist's influence is determined in part by the deliberate choice of intervention behaviors that are designed to serve as driving forces toward the goal that is appropriate to the group level desired.

It is sometimes questioned whether a therapist's behavior can be so precisely controlled as to choose interventions that influence the group's movement in relation to goal, and, if so, whether it is desirable to do so. We wish to answer yes, to both questions. We will start with the second point. Whether or not it is desirable to put into practice such understanding is only questioned, we think, when the understanding is either so precise that it destroys the 'art' of therapy, or is so rigid that it denies the possibility of integration into the therapist's pre-conscious and thus competes with his free-floating attention.

We have been as precise as possible in our explanation of group but we do not suggest that this explanation is a rigid set of rules. Rather, it is a carefully defined set of constructs which, when understood and mastered, may serve the function of increasing the range of therapeutic influence.

The first point was whether or not a therapist's behavior can be so precisely controlled. We take it for granted that all therapists' behavior is controlled at the unconscious level. The disciplined therapist controls his behavior at the conscious level by requiring himself to conform to the discipline in which he was trained. That this is possible at a very specific behavioral level is shown by the classic study by Lewin, Lippitt and White (1939) which demonstrated the effect of deliberate change of leadership behaviors on group morale, style of membership behavior and ability to work.

Three levels of group process are described in this chapter. Each level of group process presents an explicit, therapeutic goal for the group, an explicit therapist behavioral style which is designed to serve as a driving force toward this goal, and a selection of members that will potentiate the creation of a therapeutic environment in which the therapeutic goals can be met.

Other variables are considered in describing group levels. These variables include: expected phases of development and their manifest differences; symptoms of fixation; leadership style; training requirements; intervention focus, membership criteria; group orientation in time and space; and criteria for group viability.

The framework offered here distinguishes three levels of sophistication within each of the above variables, corresponding to the three levels of group. For example, the goals of a Level One group are to induce basic socialization skills and to help its members to individual identity. These goals distinguish the Level One group from the Level Two group, in which the goals are to induce social interaction and work adjustment; both are different from a Level Three group, in which the goals are to induce problem-solving interpersonal interaction.

Thus a description of each level of group provides the therapist with a cognitive map for both patient disposition and the direction of group development. One practical implication of this model is that many patients who have been judged 'unsuitable' for group therapy can be more correctly described as unsuitable to the particular level of group that was available; in fact the therapist may only conceive of one kind (level) of group. These same patients could very well be suitable for a different level of group whose goals are appropriate to the particular patient's needs.

Level One group

Group goal: level I

The objectives of a Level One group are to induce basic socialization skills and help the patient to an individual identity.

Operational objectives: level I

Operational objectives of the group are to help people interact with each other, learn acceptable social interaction skills, separate themselves as individual identities, and move toward productivity in their homes, in a job, or in retirement. The behaviors that are emphasized are those that help the patient to make the bridge from ruminative monologues that are self-validating and 'symptom validating' toward entering into a dialogue with others. A dialogue between people entails the mechanisms of social validation, discrimination between I and not-I: re-personalization of de-personalized communication, and differentiation between the phenomena of *feeling, thinking,* and *doing,* are such basic mechanisms.

Expected phases of group development: level I

Resolution of the flight and fight phases are set as a developmental goal, together with the interpersonal development that can result from this resolution. It is not to be expected that the authority issue (with the need to resolve the deep archaic, negative and positive anaclitic and narcissistic transferences) will be resolved. However, socially acceptable and individually rewarding behavior can be learned by identification with and imitation of the leader and the healthiest group members; this is then generalized to outside living.

Symptoms of fixation: level I

Tendencies to fixation are at the flight level (particularly with untrained leaders), or at the fight level (especially in groups where members are encouraged to act out aggression on inanimate objects, like pillows). Acting out aggression, as in gestalt groups for example, where people are encouraged to scream and roar, to beat on pillows or even to beat each other with foam rubber clubs, certainly provides a cathartic outlet. However, catharsis is only one aspect of the work of therapy - and unless methods for verbally working through this aggression are also built into the process, insight does not occur. For some members, the more they act out aggression, the more they experience it, and this becomes increasingly repetitious. We have direct reports from several members of one group where screaming, crying, and roaring were the established method for 'getting out' their anger; each reported experiencing anger more frequently and with greater intensity. There was an increase in violent dreams, awakening in the middle of the night in objectless rage, and more frequent use of activities like descending into their basements, taking solitary walks, or driving alone, to provide opportunities to curse and roar. Fixations at the flight and fight level prevent individual members from learning interpersonal skills; group may still help them learn methods for more adaptively handling their withdrawals and aggressions.

Leadership style and training requirements: level I

Leader behavior should be reality oriented, limit-setting, directionally goal-specific. Training designs for basic interpersonal skills can be used as well as models for understanding, like communication training, goal-specific gestalt exercises, and transactional analysis. Professional training in clinical psychotherapy and laboratory education are essential. These skills are needed for designing directed group experience, in the same way that laboratory workshops are designed, so that there is a group resolution of the issues that are aroused and containment of individual responses within the session, and for understanding the impact of different training designs on individual patient dynamics.

Driving forces: level I

The therapist actively discourages idiosyncratic, bizarre, and autistic behaviors, as well as talk about symptoms and blameful narratives that serve to excuse existing pathological and maladaptive life styles. He actively encourages the group to develop standards of rewarding behavior; these include *looking* at, and *listening* to other members when they talk, *responding* to another's topic, and *checking out* perceptions, projections and assumptions about what is currently happening. The group norm of dealing with what is *happening in the group now* allows patients to learn to deal with the immediate situation and react to each other in the present, as distinct from interpreting experiences in terms of fears from the past or fears of the future.

Membership criteria: level I

The people appropriate for this group are those with profound disturbances in separating self and object and in regulating aggression; i.e. those presenting severe difficulties with interpersonal relationships. Lack of social skills, difficulties in ability to apply cause and effect relationships, poor grasp of time/space concepts, low frustration tolerance and poor goal orientation are aspects of the problem. These people are frequently 'professional patients' who learn to relate successfully only in the role of patient, with their interpersonal behaviors organized around their symptoms.

Diagnostic guide: level I

This diagnostic guide is *not* the same as the criteria for membership. Rather, it indicates diagnostic categories which may be appropriate for the patient population, without in any way implying exclusivity. Members of Level One groups tend to be classified as chronic psychotics; either in remission or with intermittent episodes; inadequate passive-dependent personalities, chronic neurotics, severe obsessive compulsives, hypochondriacs, severe hysterics with conversions and disassociative reactions, low level borderlines, and severe narcissistic personalities.

Criteria for viability: level I

Signs of resolution of this level are the ability of members to respond to each other appropriately and to confront flight and fight behavior.

Structure: level I

A Level One population is not a stable population. Therefore, on an outpatient basis an overall membership of twenty people will probably provide a reliable attendance of between four to seven. Meetings of an hour to an hour and a half, once or twice a week, provide an operational framework for outpatients. Patients in partial or complete hospitalization can benefit from a daily group of five to eight members, lasting an hour.

Level Two group

Group goal: level II

The objectives of a Level Two group are to induce mature social interaction and work adjustment and help the patient develop the skills of self-determination and the feeling of a social identity.

Operational objectives: level II

The goals of this group are to consolidate the kind of basic interaction between people that allows satisfaction in relationships, to encourage the breaking down of a 'problem' into component 'problems' that can be dealt with practically, and to encourage the behavior, attitudes, and responsibility that permit adjustment to work or retirement in outside life and facilitate both individuation and interdependent decision-making within the group life. The process always involves generalizing insights and new behaviors gained in the group setting to situations in the outside world.

Expected phases of group development: level II

Resolution of flight, and fight phases, with partial resolution of the personal and counter-personal phases of the authority issue can be expected. Because of the population of this group, it is not expected that the group-as-a-whole will successfully work through the authority issue, although one or two members may, using the group milieu. When individuals are able to work with and through the authority issue, transfer to a Level Three group should be considered for their continuing work with object relations and separation individuation issues.

Symptoms of fixation: level II

Tendencies to fixation are in the acting-out of the fight phase, in which the 'hot seat' becomes an object of both fear and desire, and surviving the hot seat provides a path to the role of 'group hero'. This fixation co-ordinates with sadomasochism and anal ambivalence at the individual level. Another form of fixation emerges in the form of a partial resolution of the authority issue as achieved by splitting away from one leader and re-forming under another leader. The new leader may emerge from the group members themselves. Sometimes the new leader is a co-therapist, who, ignorant of the dynamics of the authority issue, acts out those dynamics in collusion with the group, leads a *coup d'état*, and sets up the group under his own leadership. This pathological solution leads inevitably to repetition when the 'new' group is again confronted with its authority issue. Typically, the group will again turn on its leader or disband.

Leadership style and training requirements: level II

A mixture of directive and non-directive tactics is required for effective leadership. Directive techniques are appropriate to group norms and goals. Confrontative and limit-setting behaviors are used to further socialization goals. Group problem-solving goals are facilitated by non-directive leadership. Professional training needed includes training in individual psychotherapy and clinical group psychotherapy and the equivalent of laboratory education and group dynamics. The latter should include specific training as a group leader by the T-group method so that work with group authority dynamics as well as individual transference resolution can be facilitated.

Driving forces: level II

The therapist's overall behavior is less directive than it is in a Level One group. This supports the increased emphasis put upon group responsibility. Monologue, self-defensive, hostile, blameful, evaluative, and scapegoating behaviors by members are discouraged; and self-affirmation, confrontation, openness, directness and feedback are encouraged. Norms of support and responsibility in the group are developed, along with standards that encourage open sharing of thoughts and feelings.

Thoughts and feelings are treated as information that helps diagnose issues in both the group and its members and therefore their expression is encouraged. Feedback is given about how members are perceived by other members in a group, and new, more socially adaptive behaviors and solutions are tried out. Role playing of alternative solutions to actual problems can be used. Certain major decisions that affect the group are made by the group. (A full discussion of decisions appropriate for the group or for the therapist is found in chapter 8.)

Membership criteria: level II

Some of the people who form this group may function in many ways that are similar to a Level One population. However, the crucial difference is that people appropriate for the Level Two group must have some insight into their maladaptive life styles and be motivated to change. Other Level Two members may superficially appear to be more appropriate for a Level Three group, but their inability to internalize insight as is the case with many borderlines is the determining factor in assigning them to a Level Two group.

Diagnostic guide: level II

Diagnostically, these are people who tend to fall into the clinical categories of adolescent, young adult, and adult adjustment reaction; psychosis, residual and latent; schizoid, paranoid, obsessive-compulsive, hysterical, and passive-aggressive personality disorder; selected borderline conditions, sexual deviation and certain drug dependencies.

Criteria for viability: level II

Signs of resolution of each of the three levels of group are the ability of members to verbalize insight and demonstrate struggle with the conflicts inherent in the issues of group development. Although it is not expected that a Level Two group will resolve each of the phases of development and therefore reach the goals of a Level Three group, this could theoretically happen if sufficient time and energy were devoted to group development. It is expected that certain individual members would resolve the authority issue and become qualified for a move into a Level Three group in which they could resolve issues in personal and counterpersonal relationships.

Structure: level II

A Level Two population should be required to attend every session as an important part of a therapeutic consistency. One to one and a half hour meetings, held once or twice a week, provide a time frame which can sufficiently involve all the members. Six to ten members is an optimal number: below six, the interpersonal confrontation potential is too intense and tends to arouse defenses; more than ten encourages the formation of active and passive sub-groups which then contribute to group fixation.

Level Three group

Group goal: level III

The objectives of the Level Three group are to induce problem-solving, interpersonal interaction, using the group as a microcosm of society. In this micro-society each person finds his social and individual role.

Operational objectives: level III

The goal of this group is to help people to use their interpersonal relationships with each other and to learn how to resolve the problems of everyday living. Group members and therapists are the social models here. The behavioral emphasis is on interpersonal sensitivity and resolution of the conflicts that arise during the phases of group development. These phases serve as a series of experimental situations fostering the acquisition, and practice, of problem-solving skills which can resolve group conflicts and which can then be generalized to outside social conflicts.

Expected phases of group development: level III

Resolution of all phases of group development is the goal for a Level

Three group. Whereas in a Level Two group it is not expected that every member in the group will reach that goal (even though the group-as-a-whole can function at that level), in a Level Three group it is expected that both individual members and the group-as-a-whole will achieve Level Three group goals. It is true that certain individual members will only intermittently reach the goals and then only in the context of the group, and not necessarily in a manner which is generalizable to their outside lives. For Level Two members who have worked through Level Two issues, a Level Three group is the indicated placement, and for Level Three members, continuation with a Level Three group is the treatment of choice.

Symptoms of fixation: level III

Tendencies to fixation in a Level Three group include all those found at the flight and fight phases in Levels One and Two, with the additional style of fixation in which phases are repeated with apparent insight but without real changes. Another and unique kind of fixation occurs in a Level Three group. The pleasure from membership support can become a goal in itself and be maintained at the expense of problem-solving and task accomplishment. More will be said about this under cohesion in special problems, chapter 8.

Leadership style and training requirements: level III

At this level leaders need the ability to be non-directive and facilitative. Professional training in individual psychotherapy, clinical group psychotherapy, and group dynamics with specific training as a 'consultant' group leader are necessary. The theoretical and practical sections in this book are intended to discuss in full the issues relevant to training Level Three group therapists.

Driving forces: level III

Therapist behavior is focused on increasing the group feeling of responsibility for what happens in the group, and discouraging dependence upon the therapist for what happens in group. Insight into how an individual's behavior in group affects both himself and others and insight into individual life style trends as they appear in the group, is the basic learning material. Group members are encouraged to experiment with alternative or new behavior responses in the supportive environment provided by the group, where they can obtain feedback on the effects of new behaviors. Co-operative and collaborative setting of group goals and solving of group problems, understanding the mechanics of problem-solving, and the experience of making and implementing decisions are the achievement criteria for people at this level.

Membership criteria: level III

The people appropriate for this group are those whose functioning include those required at Levels One and Two, who are currently self-supporting, and whose problems include dissatisfaction with their experience of psychic suffering and/or repetitive, self-defeating patterns in interpersonal relations or work.

Diagnostic guide: level III

Diagnostically these are people who cover the spectrum of clinical categories, including psychosis, but whose pathology is sufficiently contained to allow them to function in society. These people are able to internalize insight and work through conflicts.

Criteria for viability: level III

Signs of resolution at this level are the ability of members to verbalize insight, demonstrate insight into their behavior, and use the skills of consensual validation in the task of understanding their own and group level problems.

Structure: level III

Level Three groups tend to work with two concurrent major themes. A one-hour meeting appears too short to allow the limit emergence of both themes, while three hours appears to cross the fatigue threshold causing work to deteriorate and become difficult to integrate. Once or twice a week for one and a half to two or maybe two and a half hours appears to be a useful Level Three time frame. Six to ten members are able to work together at this level. Regular attendance is usually required of members by the group.

Coordinating the selection of members to the setting of group goals

Members

The developmental process of any given psychotherapy group generates the potential for a therapeutic environment that is tailor-made by, and tailor-made for, the individual group members who contribute to it.

The group process is needed to produce stimulation for therapeutic change, and that process can be facilitated by the informed directing of the leader. Group members' behaviors are the raw material for group development: discouraging maladaptive repetitive patterns of behavior at both the individual *and* the group level is one of the major functions of a group therapist. Without such informed direction, the goals that emerge are likely to be in the service of group survival at all costs, on the one hand, and group or individual gratification, through acting out of impulses, on the other.

The goal of a therapy group is to become a therapeutic environment and to maintain itself as a therapeutic environment. The selection of members for any given group is made with this goal in mind. If the members of the group are to bring into the group the raw material that the group needs to reach its goal, then group members must be chosen for possession of the requisite resources. Individuals whose ego restrictions and defensive needs would give them no choice but to block group development would be inappropriate.

Mismatch between the level of the group process and the ego strength of group members results in fixation in developmental phases, and the formation of specious therapeutic goals leading to acting out and repetition rather than insight and change.

The formation of groups based on either random or diagnostic criteria provides no reliable or predictable group development. In fact, for groups that survive past the initial phase, a natural selection appears to take place in which the group appears to 'form itself' from those members that come and stay. Dynamically what happens is that, instead of the therapist predetermining group goals and establishing the group with goal-appropriate criteria, the members themselves form a group from which an implicit goal emerges. This emerging goal may or may not be therapeutic and is more likely to be self-protective and regressive.

The selection of group members, therefore, is made in terms of the existing characteristics of a particular existing group. If the group is a new one, members should be selected with the projected developmental goal in mind. This selection process is different from the more traditional one in which the major criteria for developing a treatment plan that includes disposition to group psychotherapy are pathological symptoms and diagnosis. Selection of group members based on their pathology is only appropriate for that style of therapy in which the diagnosis determines the therapeutic goals. Disposition to groups using our level of group goal criteria demands different diagnostic and analytic criteria from those required by individual therapy (whether that individual therapy be carried out alone in a room with the patient, or whether it is carried out in front of other people as happens when individual therapy is done in a collective 'group' setting).

For example, dependency is a dynamic that will manifest itself differently in various people. The dependency of the 'passive-aggressive' is manifested and treated differently from the dependency of an alcoholic or schizophrenic. For those who make group psychotherapy dispositions on the basis of diagnosis, the need for therapeutic work with dependency may well be sufficient criteria for disposition to group psychotherapy. However, when disposition is made in terms of the resources of the patient, the particular behavioral manifestations of dependency will be seen as a resource or a liability depending upon the particular balance of dependent and counterdependent forces within the group, and the potential for resolution of group dependency resulting from the interplay of those forces. Thus, a patient with needs for treatment of passive dependency might well be a resource to a group whose balance was counterdependent, and a liability in a group where the balance was already overdependent.

Although dependency needs in an individual do become manifest in issues in group dependency, confusion can easily arise if terms like dependency, that properly apply to individual dynamics, are confused with similar terms in group dynamics like dependent and counter-dependent forces that emerge as group roles. It is important to understand that *the group dynamics of dependence and counterdependence are directly related to specific phases of group development, and specific sub-goals in group dynamics*; and they are independent of any *single* group member's individual dynamics.

Goals

Co-ordinating the selection of members to the setting of group goals entails having a framework for looking at groups that permits the identification of different levels of the same general goal, and having different goals that can function as necessary steps along the way to the overall goal.

Different goals, more properly termed sub-goals, perform a ladderlike function for the achievement of the major goal of a given level of group, which in turn is related to different phases of group development. Achieving the goal of working through each developmental phase provides the opportunity for each individual member of the group to work with the specific kinds of dynamics that are relevant to each of these phases, together with the development or consolidation of adaptive defenses that permit the working through of those dynamics in the social, group setting.

The three levels of group goal we described at the beginning of this chapter vary from the most sophisticated of the objectives, which is to induce problem-solving interaction using the group as a microcosm of society, to the least sophisticated, in which the objective is to induce the socialization skills that are basic to a social identity. Discriminations between different groups are made for the purpose of making a good match of members. A good match between group and members causes certain synergistic potential to become operational. When mismatches are made, the synergistic potential of the group is limited; for the individual member the group either fails to become a therapeutic tool or becomes one that is less than maximally effective.

For example, a sophisticated (Level Three) group provides the stimulus of a healthy society. This society requires individual members to respond adaptively, and thus to gain insight into the dynamics and behavioral manifestations of the conflicts that dispose them to respond maladaptively. In the process of reaching this goal (a therapeutic environment), the individual members are confronted with their own fixations in their own psychological developmental phases; this occurs in synchronicity with the developmental phases of the group.

Having passed through the initial dependent and counterdependent group phases and thus gained greater mastery of aspects of individuation, the group members can use their consequently strengthened egos for working through the more difficult and threatening resistances and repressions attached to earlier material. They can also master the annihilation anxiety that accompanies working with introjects, basic trust, omnipotence, narcissism and oral ambivalence, all of which will be evoked in the later phases. However, for patients whose basic need is a therapeutic tool that will help them build necessary functional ego and body ego defenses, the exacting requirements of sophisticated (Level Three) groups would prove traumatic and decompensatory rather than therapeutic. These patients need a group with a different therapeutic style and level of sophistication and do better at Level Two or Level One.

Defining three levels of group sophistication required that we discriminate between three kinds of group goals, and that we co-ordinate the selection of members to the appropriate group goal. As we have said, one of the most important skills for group psychotherapists is that of selecting members so that the group environment will be: (1) maximally therapeutic, and (2) one to which the members can contribute most. For those who are more familiar with the economy of group dynamics, it will come as no surprise that these two factors are reciprocal; that the kind of environment to which a person can contribute most is also the kind of environment and experience from which a person can gain most.

The following episodes illustrate how individual members' pathologies were de-emphasized, and how individual resources or ego strengths were mobilized, by the group of which they were a member. In each of these examples, the important point is that the group was able to provide a therapeutic response, where needed, as a function of the available group resources. In each case, it was predictable that the issue would be resolved by the group, because the resources were available for the phase of development of the group. However, what was *not* predictable was how the issue would be solved, or who would solve it.

In a group of medium sophistication, with a Level Two goal, Angel (diagnosed as chronic ambulatory schizophrenic) was hallucinating. Her hallucinations were known in the group language as 'going to the movies'. Group response to her hallucinatory episodes were to remind her, 'we can't see them, Angel, therefore they are not group business and we can't join you. Join us.' Each time, Angel did.

In an unsophisticated group with a Level One goal, Betty, a new member, monopolized in a droning, intellectualized monologue, counting the window panes as she talked. In membership negotiation with the group, it was agreed that Betty should either choose to talk or to count window panes – but not to do both at the same time. Betty made her choice, with the group's support, and took the first step toward learning dialogue and working with ambivalence. Betty had been diagnosed obsessive-compulsive character disorder.

An obsessive-compulsive disorder, like Betty, could, according to the selection-by-diagnosis method, be expected to be placed in a group with a higher-order (more sophisticated) therapeutic goal than Angel, a chronic ambulatory schizophrenic. However, selection based on life styles and job performance made a Level One group appropriate for Betty who, though better organized, was less socialized; and a Level Two group appropriate for Angel, who had adaptive social behaviors available to her despite her regressive psychotic functioning. When influenced by group norms, Angel was able to function at a higher level than Betty and to achieve ego growth thereby.

A patient shifting to a higher functioning group does best in a group that has already developed goal-appropriate norms that the new member can first mimic and then internalize. An example of this is Debra, diagnosed as chronic ambulatory schizophrenic, who had worked in a clinic Level One group for two years and 'graduated' to an ongoing Level Two group. In the early phases of group development many of her defensive maneuvers were highly therapeutic to the group. It was Debra's inputs that were frequently cited by the therapist as 'the voice of the group, which no one wants to hear'. The process entailed for the group and Debra in 'owning' the issues that she was raising, and her acts of resolving the defensive reactions at both an individual and group level, yielded therapeutic growth for both the group and its members. At a later phase, however, Debra's more regressive contributions became repetitive and non-productive. In an explosion of rage, expressed in a mixture of 'schizophrenese' and destructive threats, Debra accused the group of leaving her behind. Silence followed. The therapist judged that the group-as-a-whole had the resources to provide the necessary therapeutic environment for Debra, and waited through the silence, during which many of the other group members withdrew, some regressed into previous symptomatology like rocking or counting. As the silence continued and the pressure mounted, so did the possibility of violent acting out. It was difficult to judge where the group resources would come from. For the therapist to intervene would be to undermine the group's confidence in their own ability to resolve group issues. Yet, as a 'member' of the group, it may be that it was the specific resources of the therapist that the group needed. (The therapist 'as member' needs to be understood in terms of roles; the therapist's role is a specialized set of resources.) Finally, a member spoke: 'You're too sick for this group', he said. There was a group gasp of shock and horror. Again there was a long silence. It was Debra herself who finally broke the silence, passionately and intelligibly, claiming her right to membership in the group, her right to bring in *all* of herself, even the 'bad' part. She did not have to be rejected because she wanted to remain a child, but was given a chance to grow up. The locus of the group resource, in this case, was the patient herself. This incident appears to us to be prototypic in that it has recurred in recognizable form as part of the membership issue for each patient who makes the transition from a Level One to a Level Two group. It probably indicates the transition from mimicry to membership.

It is probable that the support and structure of a Level One group would neither have elicited Debra's explosion of rage, nor given her the conditions she needed to grow, i.e., to accept it in herself. In groups based on diagnosis alone, with her history of violent outbursts, Debra would probably not have been placed with the population that made up the Level Two group, and so might have lost a major opportunity for growth.

Another important consideration for group psychotherapy is the self-selection of members. We have said that formation of groups based on diagnostic criteria provide no reliable or predictable group development. For those 'diagnostically selected groups' that survive past the initial phase, a further natural selection appears to take place, with the results that the group appears to 'form itself' from those members that come and stay. Thus, instead of the therapist determining the group goal, and establishing the group with goal-appropriate criteria, the members themselves have formed a group from which an implicit goal has emerged. The emergent goal may be therapeutic. When it is, this accounts for those 'good' groups in which therapeutic changes happen to the patients for reasons that the therapist is often at a loss to account for.

Given the intense, regressive wishes of patients, the implicit goal of self-formed groups is likely to emerge as non-therapeutic. As Bion noted (1959), basic assumption groups compete successfully against the work group in patient groups. Therapeutic exchange itself rarely happens by accident; nearly always it requires informed direction by a leader.

Levels of group and phases of group development

For group psychotherapy to take place in each of the three types of group, the therapist needs two sets of skills: (1) the skills of intervening at the individual level in such a way that individual group members gain insight into themselves as they relate to the events in the group life, and (2) the skills of intervening at the group level in a way which permits the group to develop as a therapeutic milieu with norms of behavior that are conducive to individual insight and growth.

The therapist achieves this goal of helping group development by selecting different aspects of group activity to encourage or discourage. The kinds of things that a therapist will encourage or discourage at any one time will depend upon the therapist's overall goals for the group, the state of the group at that time, the level of group process that the therapist is working with, the present phase of group development, and the specific individual and group issues that are relevant to the moment.

The reason for emphasizing the importance of the group therapist being primarily concerned with guiding group development is that each particular phase of group development provides specific and discrete opportunities for insight and growth for each individual member. This is analogous to the psychoanalyst basically devoting himself to maintaining the analytic frame within which all else happens. As a group moves from one phase of development to another, so individual members are involved in a process that stimulates certain psychodynamic responses in themselves. Thus, the working through and mastering of group level developmental phases induces the working through and mastering of individual level developmental phases.

Group development phases have been described at length in chapter 5. Parenthetically, however, it is worth reminding the reader that the phases of group development do not emerge in the same sequence as the maturational phases of individual development. Rather, group development requires some resolution of anal ambivalence and phallic competition before oral dependence and basic trust can be worked through. Social defenses are required of a person in group – and it is the socialized defenses that are the first-level defenses for new group members. The advantage of this is that it permits group members to analyze resistances appropriate to the ego mastery necessary for individuation (with its concomitant separation anxiety). The working through of therapeutic issues in anal ambivalence and phallic competition is less evocative of ego decompensation than is the annihilation anxiety that accompanies threats to the defenses of earlier oral development phases and issues.

In working through the early phases of group development, the individual member strengthens his self-esteem and hones up his observing and adaptive ego. In addition, the interdependent aspect of group development provides each individual member with a level of group support that serves as an auxiliary ego that can be called upon in times of stress, or when the individual feeling is overwhelmed.

Access to the full range of defense mechanisms, as well as to the observing ego and to an available auxiliary ego (as provided by the group and/or the leader), are all necessary for the individual members as their negative and positive transference reactions become more primitive under the controlled regression that the conditions of a developing group provide.

What is not always well understood in the field of group psychotherapy is the importance of working through group phases in sequence. If the developing group does not master the first two phases of group development (the flight and fight aspects of the dependent/counterdependent issues) then the group does not have available the kind of mastery that is needed for the working through of the final two phases (the enchantment and disenchantment aspects of intimacy). Further, the group will not possess the group-level, interdependent strength that is needed for resolution of the negative and positive transference, achieved through the repeated working through of the authority issue.

The authority issue recurs cyclically in group life (as it does in 'real' life), and it is through repeated and ever more sophisticated resolutions of this issue that continuing group growth occurs. Such continued group growth results in a therapeutic group environment that provides an ever increasingly mature stimulus to individual growth at the personal level.

The dimensions of the authority issue and its potential for insight and resolution are very much a function of the level of the group, the sophistication of the group, and the experience of the leader.

A Level One group cannot tolerate the primitive, sadistic fantasies that are generated by the authority issue. This is not so much because the oedipal level is aroused, but because of the basic trust issues that are focused around the primal pathogenic introject. Whereas in groups where members have more ego strength it is precisely the potential for working with the pathogenic introject that makes the authority issue the most powerful stimulus in group life, in Level One groups whose members have weak or brittle egos, and where developmental mastery rests upon partial object relationships, the authority issue is too overwhelming.

A Level Two group will continually confront the transference aspects of the authority issue and, at each confrontation, interdependent membership work will be done and new aspects of group maturity will develop. However, whereas this development may be strong enough to support analysis and insight into the positive transference, group support tends to fragment during analysis of the negative transference; hence insight is more likely to occur at the individual rather than at the group level.

A Level Two group has the potential for insight into anal ambivalence, but not enough strength to confront the annihilation anxiety that accompanies insight into early splitting and the primitive rage associated with the pathogenic introject. This task is difficult enough for a Level Three group, and is only achieved in an ongoing Level Three group which has been in existence long enough for the necessary maturity to develop.

The authority issue is precipitated around any issue in which the locus of responsibility is in question. For example, when faced with the decision about when it is ready to take in new members, a group will go through certain predictable vicissitudes. The group will doubt that it really has a say; hence it gives verbal assent to the *therapist's* bringing in the new member. This is dependency resistance and leaves the locus of responsibility with the therapist, while the group gives token assent without committing itself to the consequences of the decision because it feels no real part in making it. This is frequently a fixation point.

The dependent/counterdependent struggle arises when the passive dependent sub-group members attempt to please the therapist by agreeing to the new member as soon as is convenient for the therapist, while the aggressive dependent sub-group attempt to please the therapist's unspoken wish by insisting that the group take responsibility for the decision. During this, the counterdependent sub-group refuse to work on the decision as originally stated at all, and insist on changing the subject matter of the decision to some other version, like *whether* the group will have new members at all.

The unrelieved tensions of the authority issue belong only in a Level Three group, where the conflict that is generated among the members, and between the members and the leader, can be resolved and insight for both the group and individual members obtained.

A Level Three group can be expected to work through the transference confrontations at a group level of sufficient depth so that the analysis of transference responses becomes available to the observing ego. The decision-making tasks of a mature group extend to every issue that affects group life: when and where to meet, assessing group readiness for a new member, setting termination and working through separation with a member, changing time or day of meeting to accommodate the schedule of an individual member, and (for groups of long duration) the raising of group fees and confronting the reality relationship between individual budgets, group leaders' fees and duration and/or frequency of group meetings. All reality issues of group life raise the need for group decisions, which in turn raise issues in dependence-independence, which in turn catalyze transference phenomena.

What is important to recognize as an issue of technique is that the behavioral precipitators of the authority issue (any issue on locus of power) will happen in every group, no matter whether the group is Level One, Level Two, or Level Three. It is entirely the therapist's monitoring of the group process that determines the degree of intensity with which the power struggle will be manifested. The therapist can reduce the intensity of the power struggle by reducing ambiguity, making group rules, specifying clearly what aspects of the group life the members can have influence over, and what aspects they cannot. The therapist can, conversely, set the stage for accelerating and increasing intensity by remaining silent, by not monitoring the projections with feedback or response, and by tacitly encouraging the development of a full-blown group paranoid reaction which will manifest with the intensity of the transference psychosis.

Fixations

Group decisions are a function of total group work, and involve the working through of individual transference for the therapists. A group may well spend from three to twelve months making a decision, and working through the different related issues that must be resolved at both an individual and a group level before a decision can be made that reflects the level of maturity that the group has reached. One group even wryly 'celebrated its first annual anniversary' of the particularly difficult issue of raising fees. This process demands frustration tolerance and working through for the therapist as the group decision also reflects the appropriate level of group leadership maturity. The difference is that, whereas the group members confront their acting out in the group, the therapists need to analyze counter-transference reactions between group sessions. This is where the co-therapy relationship offers a greater potential than either supervision or collegial consultation.

Unless the therapist has been trained to be aware of the specific range of counter-transferential responses that group therapists are vulnerable to, it is at best unlikely, and at worst impossible, for the group not to become fixated around a non-therapeutic goal. The characteristics of the way in which the group develops the pre-conscious or unconscious goal of survival and/or acting out will almost certainly reflect the therapist's own pre-conscious or unconscious conflicts, i.e., his counter-transference.

Thus, when the therapist's unresolved conflicts are in the area of oral omnipotence, his style will probably reflect conditional, benevolent, paternal nurturance and the group will respond with safe, passive, dependent confirming (and fixating) behaviors. When the therapist's conflict is in the area of adolescent rebellion (frequently manifested in a permissive, laissez-faire style of leadership), the group will respond with counterdependent, rebellious acting-out behavior against the therapist's own authority figures; such as the clinic setting, or the (therapist's) supervisor, or the police, etc. When the therapist's conflict is in the area of anal ambivalence, the group will respond with scape-goating behaviors. Those therapists who are unaware of their wish for the group to act out vicariously for them their own forbidden impulses, and those therapists who themselves wish to act out within the group setting, will tend to lead groups whose acting out results in compelling, repetitive expressions of infantile or sexualized behaviors and in gratifying but pathological interactive syndromes. Co-therapy reduces this potential for therapist acting out.

In the plethora of group movements which have characterized the innovative and explorative phases of the phenomenon of group, some of these maladaptive group goals have generated ritualized and socially sanctioned movements.

It should be noted that there do not yet seem to be clear criteria in the field that discriminate between those groups (whatever the movement they belong to) whose goals fixate them in repetitive patterns of behavior, and those groups whose apparently repetitive or regressed behavior is the manifestation of transient developmental problems.

It is of major importance that the therapist understand that group interventions – either verbally or by suggestions for an activity – are *tools* or means to the resolution of specific problems in specific phases that are part of a progression of development (as we have illustrated in the design techniques appropriate to Level One and Level Two groups). Interventions must become neither ends in themselves nor ritualized means of gratification.

The following examples suggest criteria for diagnosing fixation problems in groups by the quality of repetition, or the character of acting out.

Repetition, rather than the working through, of infantile impulses, is manifested in those so-called 'touchy-feely' groups where members provide mutual nurturance to regressive expressions of feeling and behavior; the group members and the group remain fixated at this stage, rather than working through it as a step in maturational development.

Sexualized acting out is manifested in those groups where social and sexual intercourse are encouraged between group members outside, and sometimes inside, the group. The members of such groups are not required to analyze the transferential nature of their behavior. Fixation in both individual therapy and in the group development inevitably results from acting out which, by its very nature, bypasses ego mastery and precludes any working through of the infantile issues from which the acting out arises.

Gratification of certain pleasurable but pathological interpersonal syndromes are manifested in those groups whose goal is characterized by stereotypic and repetitive behavior. An excellent example is provided by those groups that are fixated at the 'hot seat' phase of development. In such groups, membership status is acquired through surviving the hot seat; the entire group collaborates in a continuing sadomasochistic acting out, which gratifies the members at an infantile level and fixates the group development. Because of the severity of the initiation rites, member loyalty to these groups is high, group pressure is extreme and decompensation casualties for both leaders and members are great. Group pressure to conform exists in the groups themselves and in the societies or sub-cultures that develop around the group environment. Away from these group pressures members typically revert to their prior symptoms – unless the destruction of their defenses has resulted in chronic decompensation.

Summary

It is our intention to make it clear that unless a group therapist systematically influences group development according to some internally consistent set of therapeutic constructs, the group goal that emerges will at best provide neutral or benign pressures upon the individual and, at worst, will exert pressures toward fixation or decompensation. In order for a group therapist to facilitate the development of a group that in and of itself provides the major therapeutic influence, the therapist must understand the phases of group development (chapter 5), and must understand how to select the group goal that is relevant to the group members and the group members that are relevant to the goal.

Co-ordinating the selection of members to the setting of group goals entails a framework for looking at groups that permits the identification of (1) different levels of the same general goal, and (2) different sub-goals that perform the function of being steps along the way to the overall goal.

Identifying different levels of the same goal depends upon understanding that the therapist sets the character of the therapeutic goal by taking into account the social and circumstantial realities of the population available, the population needs, the potential time frame in terms of duration of meetings, frequency of meetings and life expectancy of the group, and the organizational setting that the group will take a part in.

Different goals or sub-goals that perform a ladder-like function for the achievement of the major group goal can be identified in different phases of group development. Achieving the goal of working through each phase provides the opportunity for each individual member of the group to work with the specific kinds of dynamics that are relevant to each of these phases, together with the development or consolidation of adaptive defenses that permit the working through of those dynamics in the group social microcosm.

The summary table that follows serves several purposes. First, it discriminates among each of the three levels of group process. Second, it provides a set of variables which serve to define each type of group process functionally. Third, it provides criteria for distinguishing three types of sophistication within each variable. These variables are: group goals and objectives, expected phases of group development, criteria for goal achievement and group viability; therapist's reinforcement behavior, symptoms of group fixation, membership criteria, and guide for group structure.

Table 6.1 Functional definitions of three levels of group process

	Group goals	Operational objectives	Expected phases of development	Achievement criteria
Group level I	Induce basic socialization skills; help patient to an individual identity	Help people interact with each other; learn acceptable social interaction skills; separate themselves as individual identities and social identities	Resolution of flight and fight phases for some group members	Recognition of difference between self and others; ability to decide approximately when to delay 'own need' gratification and when to require it
Group level II	Induce social interaction and work on retirement adjustment; help patient to skills of self-determination and feeling of social identity	Consolidate basic interaction skills; encourage breaking down of 'problem' into 'problems' that can be dealt with; encourage behavior, attitude and responsibility permitting adjustment to work or retirement	Group resolution of flight and fight phases; resolution of authority issue for some group members	All major decisions affecting the group are made by the group
Group level III	Induce problem-solving interpersonal interaction using group as microcosm of society in which each individual finds social and individual role	Help people use interpersonal relationships; to learn how to resolve problems of everyday living, using group and therapists as social models	Resolution of all phases for both individual members and group	Co-operative, collaborative determination of group goals and solving of group problems; understanding of mechanics of problem-solving, decision-making, and implementation of decisions

Table 6.1 (cont.)

	Criteria for group viability	Behavioral emphasis	Therapist discourages	Therapist encourages
Group level I	Members demonstrate ability to interact with other and confront flight	Those behaviors that help patients make the bridge between self- and symptom-validating monologues to dialogue with others; discrimination between I and not-I; differentiation between feeling, thinking, doing	Idiosyncratic, bizarre, autistic behavior; talk about symptoms; blameful narratives which serve to excuse pathological and maladaptive life styles	Establishing standards of rewarding behavior (looking at and listening to other members, etc.). Patients learn to deal with immediate situation apart from past and future fears
Group level II	Members confront dependent and counter-dependent issues in decision-making	Group responsibility. Therapist less directive than in level I	Monologue, self-defensive, hostile, blameful, evaluative, scapegoating behaviors	Self-affirmation, confrontation, openness, directness, feedback; development of norms of support and responsibility; open sharing of thoughts and feelings as *information*, diagnosing group conditions and members' response to them
Group level III	Members gain insight into group and individual issues of interdependence and intimacy through consensual validation	Interpersonal sensitivity; resolution of conflicts arising in phases of group development	Dependence upon therapist; unrealistic goals	Increased group feeling of responsibility for the group; insight into individual behavior and life style trends as they affect the group; experimentation with alternative new behavioral responses

Table 6.1 (cont.)

Group level	Symptoms of fixation	Membership criteria	Diagnostic guide	Group structure
Group level I	Chronic rationalization leads to fixation in flight; chronic passive-aggressive responses lead to fixation in fight	Severe difficulties with interpersonal relationships; poor socialization; difficulties in applying time/space concepts; low frustration tolerance; poor goal orientation	Chronic psychotics; passive-dependent personalities; chronic neurotics; severe obsessive-compulsives; hypochondriacs; hysterics with conversions and dissociative reactions	Membership of twenty provides attendance of four to seven; meeting for one hour to one and a half hours, up to seven times in an open-ended group. Structure adjusted to particular group population
Group level II	Scapegoating; division into competing sub-groups; conformity to hero-leader; repetitive rebellion without resolution	Those who can function at level I, and have some insight and are motivated to change	Adolescent and young adult reactions; residual and latent psychotics; selected borderlines; personality disorders; sexual deviants and selected drug dependents	Six to ten members optimal, meeting for one to three hours, once or twice a week in an open-ended group
Group level III	Solving individual problems as a defense against solving group problems; group problem-solving as a defense against interpersonal intimacy; intimacy as a defense against individual and group problem-solving	People capable of functioning at levels I and II; self-supporting; problems are dissatisfaction with themselves and psychic suffering	May cover the spectrum of clinical categories, including psychosis, but pathology is sufficiently contained to allow them to function in society	Six to eight members optimal, one and a half to two hours, once or twice a week, in an open-ended group

Group practice

Richard Peters with Yvonne Agazarian

Chapter 7
Interviewing and preparing a patient for group psychotherapy

The goal of an interview with prospective psychotherapy patients is to determine whether or not therapy is relevant to the patient's problem. The psychotherapist can be helpful in one of three ways. The psychotherapist can be directly helpful through some form of psychotherapy that he performs. He can be indirectly helpful by referring the individual to some appropriate person or agency where help might be obtained. He can be helpful by suggesting to the person that his problem seems to stem from the actual life situation in which he finds himself so that a solution might best come entirely from his own resources: i.e. he does not need psychotherapy or other outside help.

In order to arrive at one of the above determinations the therapist forms tentative conclusions about the nature and source of the distress as the person understands and experiences it. At the same time the therapist must also arrive at a tentative hypothesis about the source and nature of the problem. The therapist must also assess the motivation of the sufferer to invest emotionally and financially in the appropriate form of psychotherapy.

In the interview, treatment goals of a prospective patient are thoroughly explored, whether they are explicit or implicit. These goals may be realistic or unrealistic; by which we mean that he may explicitly desire changes that can be reasonably expected to occur as a result of the currently available psychotherapeutic techniques to be proposed to him, or he may expect transformations that are improbable or impossible in the light of present psychotherapeutic expertise. These latter, unrealistic goals need to be modified if grounds for a proper psychotherapeutic contract are to be arrived at. Such a contract, or set of explicit, mutually agreed-upon goals, can be referred to later by either party in order to assess the progress or possible approaching termination of the psychotherapy. (For a thorough description of psychotherapeutic contracts in psychoanalysis, see Menninger and Holzman, 1973.)

The above discussion refers to explicitly verbalized goals only. It is well for the beginning psychotherapist to remember that the patient will always have implicit goals, of which he may or may not be conscious, which are not realistic, but rather are archaic, magical, and grandiose.

Finally the degree of ego strength, amount of available healthy narcissism, and level of object relations attained are carefully assessed, for it is in those three areas that the ultimate treatability of a prospective patient is determined.

Although we speak here of an initial interview, it is our custom to extend the evaluation for as long as we judge it to be necessary to reach conclusions of sufficient probable validity to justify making preliminary recommendations about treatment.

It is only after following the above diagnostic and evaluative procedure that one can talk about interviews whose object is the disposition of a patient to a psychotherapy group, if appropriate. The present authors ordinarily combine the recommendation with the final diagnostic interview. This is, in our experience, frequently the fourth interview. The patient is told that psychotherapy might lead to better understanding of just what troubles him and that his procedure might best be carried out in a psychotherapy group. The patient is encouraged to communicate all questions, concerns, and doubts relative to psychotherapy, particularly those aroused by the specific group modality recommended. Those doubts, and associations connected with them, are explored and the issues underlying them are either clarified by additional information or are demonstrated to be related to the emotional issues for which psychotherapy was recommended in the first place. Approximate date and time for beginning, fee, and other technical arrangements are agreed upon and psychotherapy is ready to begin. In the case of a referral to an established group, the date may have to be deferred until the group itself can discuss it as a therapeutic issue; this information is shared with the prospective member.

But why group psychotherapy and not another psychotherapeutic modality? We have said above (chapter 5) that diagnostic category is not by itself a useful way to discriminate between the three functional levels of groups or around which to build a group. Nor is diagnosis necessarily a good indicator of whether or not group treatment is desirable. It is likely true that some particular group is appropriate for any patient, excepting only those who are simply too afraid of people to be able to tolerate the tension engendered by entering into and remaining within a group. Such patients will, in any case, rarely accept a group placement and should not be pressured to do so.

In chapter 6 it was explained that a given person might be quite right for one group and inappropriate for another. Since correct disposition is specifically a placement problem it does not answer questions about the general suitability of group psychotherapy for a given patient. Once general suitability for group psychotherapy has been determined, placement in the appropriate group is in order. However, potential for correct placement must be considered before making the *recommendation* to the patient that he enter group psychotherapy. No such recommendation should be made if an appropriate group is not available either immediately or within a relatively short period of time, such as six months. A patient does not have the criteria he would need to go out and find the 'right' group for himself, and there is no therapeutic purpose in giving a prescription that cannot be filled.

It was indicated above that, potentially, most patients could be treated in a group setting. That does not mean that most *should* be so treated. In practical terms there are advantages to group treatment: it is relatively inexpensive and groups usually meet once a week, making the investment in time and money small as compared to other forms of psychotherapy. For some people money may be an overriding factor, they simply cannot afford two or three individual treatment visits a week over one or more years, with all the motivation in the world. Group psychotherapy is relatively affordable!

Where symptoms are most clearly expressed in interpersonal areas, where the individual finds difficulty in dealing with other people, and particularly where he is not aware of how his own behaviors and attitudes contribute to this difficulty, group psychotherapy can be uniquely helpful. This is because in a group precisely those inappropriate behaviors and attitudes that need to be changed will emerge, and, eventually, in their full range. In contrast, because of transference elements and the technical stance (neutrality) of the analyst, many crucial interpersonal behaviors may not emerge in one-to-one therapy. The analyst only hears the patient's version of interpersonal events; this version may be quite inaccurate because of denial, confusion, intellectualization, repression, and other typical distortions. While he will suspect or know that the patient is providing highly distorted information, still he does not witness the real event. In the live group setting, however, the patient's attempts at distorting group history and the difference between the aims and his methods will be confronted regularly by group members. Many times this produces an additional bonus in that the therapist does not have to confront touchy patients himself and can therefore be more easily retained by such patients as a 'good' object, i.e., an understanding individual who does not often injure their self-esteem, for instance by backing them up against a wall. To sum up, acting out behavior, super-ego pathology, character defenses, and narcissistic manipulation are likely to be identified, and to become available as topics for explicit therapeutic discussion, in a relatively short time when group therapy is the modality.

Following directly from the above, ego-syntonic pathology can be detached from its state of personal acceptability much more easily under the pressure, and with the support, of a group. Merely hearing others discuss similar behaviors as problems, or seeing how self-destructive these behaviors are for other group members, creates doubts, causes self-examination, and confronts the patients in a very gradual and effective way.

Above we have discussed the general way in which a psychoanalytic psychotherapist approaches a prospective patient and comes to a decision about treatment or disposition. Some factors that argue in favor of group psychotherapy as the modality of choice were presented. A discussion of the specifics of preparing the patient for the therapy group is now in order.

The patient, depending on his particular personality, will probably want to know, at some point or another following the recommendation to group therapy, why this particular modality has been suggested. A summary of the kinds of interpersonal difficulties that he has described during his evaluation sessions, of his inability to form and maintain gratifying relationships with others (Yalom, 1970), is a helpful orienting method. He is told that the group provides a setting in which he can explore his interpersonal relationships with others, and receive and give honest feedback. This information is tailored to fit the specific kinds of difficulties in love, social, or work relationships that he and the therapist had previously discussed. He is told that he will have the opportunity to learn about the difficulties and anxieties experienced by others and how they attempt to cope with them, and that this can enrich his understanding of himself. It is also explained that the giving and getting of honest personal opinions and accurate feedback enables the group to be a learning experience in which old behaviors are examined and new behaviors can be tried out, and that this is potentially quite different from the repeated frustrations that the patient has been experiencing in his interpersonal relations to date.

Preparation of the prospective group member has three major goals.

One is to provide the information that the patient needs for initial placement of the group within his life space in the most fundamental terms, such as where, when, how often, how long, how much, etc.; the second is to sufficiently allay the patient's initial anxieties concerning a therapy group, so that he is able and willing to tentatively commit himself to such a course of treatment; the third goal is that of beginning to shape group norms in the direction of a therapeutic group environment.

It needs to be said here that there is no exact order in which the various kinds of information to be described below should be given to the prospective group member; this is because the therapist is attempting to respond to the flow of the interviewee's questions and associations, and these will vary quite a bit from person to person. The sensitivity and empathy of the psychotherapist will determine when and how each bit of necessary information is introduced into the preparation.

Initial placement in life space

This information is usually given for the purpose of orienting the new member to the group.

1   Day and hour of group meetings;
2   address of group meeting room;
3   length of time each session lasts;
4   frequency with which group meetings are held;
5   fee and payment schedule;
6   number of members presently in group;
7   length of time this group has been in existence.

Some of the above topics need no explanation; the day and hour of the meeting and the address at which it is held are set at the discretion of the therapist and are subject to the availability of the patients.

Through personal experience and familiarity with the group literature the psychotherapist learns how long a group should run in order to progress as far as it can in one day, taking into account the therapeutic goals of the group as defined by its level of functioning (I, II, or III) and the contract made with the individual members of the group. In a level III, insight-oriented group an hour and a half (Foulkes and Anthony, 1973) has been most generally found to be optimal. Obviously with a level I, hospitalized group, with goals of minimal, appropriate interpersonal contact, flexible adjustment of the time period and frequency to the particular population is made and appropriateness to group goal is more important than a set length of time.

Like length of sessions, number of sessions per week is a matter of proper dosage. In a matter exactly analogous to individual psychotherapy there is a treatment intensity that is optimal and which is heavily influenced by the frequency and duration of the sessions. Members of groups meeting more than once weekly will experience greater transference pressures and a stronger pull to regress. There will, in addition, be increased demands on their time and money, which, while realistic, also tend to increase each person's internal level of tension. Therefore, as in individual psychoanalytic psychotherapy, ego-strength, motivation, and amenability to psychological insight are the major factors to be considered in deciding on the proper number of sessions per week. Most level III groups meet once a week; hospital groups may meet daily.

It is not useful or beneficial to see a patient or a group more frequently than is optimal, and it is unfair if not actually damaging to their financial position.

The fee is partly determined by the psychotherapist's fee structure but must take into account the financial realities of the patient population from which the new group member comes. The payment schedule is of some importance to private groups in that lateness of payment or non-payment are group issues and are discussed in the group setting. The familiar issue of payment for missed sessions is included under this rubric, although it could be discussed separately. We favor a monthly charge, payable on the first meeting date of the month. Although group discussions about whether a patient is liable for a given missed session or not is grist for the decision-making mill, the reality of financial policy is the therapist's decision, not the group's. Therefore we explain that payments are made on a twelve-month basis regardless of vacation time, missed sessions, therapist absence, or whatever.

The number of members who will be encountered by the prospective patient is a piece of reality and is given to the patient if asked for. This issue will be further discussed under the heading of shaping norms. The same can be said about the length of time the group has been in existence; this information is given if asked for, and more will be said about it below in the discussion on shaping norms.

Allayment of initial anxiety about group therapy

Certain topics are commonly raised by prospective members. While an exhaustive list of these topics is not provided here, what follows is illustrative of fears that may be stimulated by the recommendation to group:

1   Confidentiality of personal information;
2   rejection by the group;
3   embarrassment over revealing intimate information to strangers (group members);
4   pathology of others.

Prospective group patients often worry that information presented in group sessions will 'leak' and get back to someone who knows them in the outside world. They can be assured that this has not proved the case in the past and that such an event is not expected to occur in the future. If time permits associations to this worry can be explored with the patient. Most important is to encourage the patient to raise this concern *with the group,* where it is always a therapeutically productive issue.

Worries about rejection by group members are best dealt with by helping the worrier to link up his present fear with painful experiences in the past via his associations. Again, the patient should be reminded that this may well be a useful group-related issue for him to discuss with the group.

Fear of being embarrassed in front of group members should be handled in much the same way as fear of rejection. In addition, the information already given about the way a group operates through sharing and honest feedback is helpful in letting the person know that he will not be alone in revealing his intimate thoughts and feelings.

Fears concerning the imagined pathology of as-yet-unseen fellow group members are quite likely to be projections, the defensive nature of which is not conscious to the patient. Such fears may be expressed as fear of mental contamination (Foulkes and Anthony, 1973) or as doubts about what 'a bunch of sickies' can do for the patient. Exploration of free associations is one avenue of relieving this kind of concern. Another is by telling the patient that these are people like himself who share many of his anxieties and concerns; such information helps him to approach the projective nature of his fears.

Beginning the shaping of norms

The following topics are not laid down as *rules* for reasons to be discussed below, but are suggested as ways in which the therapeutic potential of the group experience can be maximized. The group itself will perform the function of setting actual working norms for its members:

1   Punctuality;
2   regular attendance;
3   rule of free association;
4   honesty in feedback;
5   socializing outside group with members;
6   eating, drinking, gum-chewing and smoking in group;
7   drinking or sedating before group.

As would be the case if individual psychotherapy were recommended, the prospective group member is told, tactfully, that punctuality and regular attendance are important for the optimal functioning of psychotherapy.

It is useful to encourage the uncensored verbalization of thoughts and emotions in all groups above the lowest level (where toleration of tension is the issue). For this reason the request is made to each prospective group member that he set up free association as a goal to strive for. The same can be said of the giving of honest feedback to other group members; it is presented as a goal rather than as a rule.

As Foulkes and Anthony (1973) and others have pointed out, meetings, visits, and the formation of intimate relationships outside of group sessions all bring unnecessary difficulties to the therapy; this is because the group members are not privy to these interactions and cannot confront the members involved with their distortions and repetitions (irreality). Another problem arising from outside relationships is that such contacts lead to the formation of sub-groups within the group, which share non-therapeutic norms of secrecy and indulge in extra-group processing of guilt feelings arising from their outside activities.

The only preparation for such potential difficulty the group therapist can give to the new member is the suggestion that outside contacts are not beneficial to group psychotherapy.

All of the above issues, punctuality, regular attendance, free association, honesty in group, and socializing outside of group, have one characteristic in common: they cannot be enforced by the therapist. This fact alone would require that they should not be presented as rules to prospective patients. The aim of presenting them even as suggestions is purely that of providing a potentially useful piece of information that can be made into a new norm or fitted into an existing one.

Two other topics fall under the shaping of norms heading:

8   Agreement to work for six months before making a decision to leave the group; this provides both the group and the patient a sufficient opportunity to work together.
9   Agreement to spend at least six weeks in separation from the group; this is to ensure that important issues in termination and separation can be worked through by both the patient and the group.

These agreements are as unenforceable as the other suggested behaviors discussed above. They differ from other topics under this heading in that they are verbal agreements that the patient enters into with the therapist rather than behavioral goals he subscribes to. They, too, have only the purpose of informing the prospective patient about potential behavioral norms of group therapy. The norms implied by these agreements are: toleration of tension while exploring the meaning and source of that tension, that is, not responding to pain and ambiguity by flight. Change takes place slowly and requires time and effort to achieve it.

Some further discussion of attributes and needs of psychotherapists and group members will put the whole issue of preparing patients for group therapy in a clearer light.

The behaviors of psychotherapists in regard to the group can be looked at in the following way. Such behaviors arise from two sources: those that might well be called idiosyncratic and those which involve the expertise presumed to be residing in the therapist because of his training and experience. Idiosyncratic needs of the therapist influence arrangements such as day and hour of meeting; location; initial group fee; and the furnishing and equipment of the group room. These arrangements, then, are called idiosyncratic in that they arise from the needs of a psychotherapist to order his time, his surroundings, to put a monetary value on his work, to please his aesthetics (décor), and so on, in such ways as best suit himself or best suit the organization that employs him. The second order of behaviors, those arising from the theoretical model by which data generated by the group are to be understood and interpreted, are designed to meet the therapeutic needs of the patient. The therapeutic needs of the patient, then, determine how the group must ultimately behave if the patient is to change interpersonal behaviors in the direction of reality and thus achieve more success and gratification from them. Technical considerations, then, lead to therapist behaviors designed to facilitate verbalization of impulses and fantasies in the group and to reduce acting out. When a member (or several members) of the group is reliving unconscious wishes and fantasies with a strong sense of immediacy and without any notion of the source and repetitive character of the behavior, it is termed acting out; such behavior is often impulsive, bypasses the ego, and is frequently accompanied by a refusal to recognize its displacement or projective origin.

If acting out involves physical contact, especially of an aggressive or sadistic nature, it cannot be tolerated in the group setting and must be discouraged by the group therapist. Whether the goal of the treatment be *insight* with the replacement of regressed or primary process expression of drive and conflict by reality-oriented, secondary process dominated functioning, or *structure building* with replacement of archaic, developmentally arrested ego functioning with ego autonomy, the major vehicle for such change is the verbally-mediated, secondary process. Verbalization involves symbolization, delay, interposing thought between impulse and action, object-directed behavior, logical processes; in short a complex set of ego functions. And the therapist's task, whether in group or individual psychotherapy, is *always* that of keeping impulses out of the motor sphere and in the psychic sphere during the therapeutic process. Whether the therapist announces no physical contact as a group rule, or whether he encourages the group to explore the issue and to develop for itself an explicit norm, is a matter of the method that the therapist chooses.

Nowhere else can the difference between psychoanalytic psychotherapies and other therapies be better demonstrated than on this point, in regard to this rule. Psychoanalytic group psychotherapy, like psychoanalysis proper, is a verbal form of treatment and does not willingly promote physical or other regressive forms of discharge.

It follows from the above that therapist behaviors in the preparation of patients for group that promote the development of the kind of group we have just described are technically correct, and those therapist behaviors which would interfere with the development of such a group are technically incorrect.

It is also, however, clear to the sophisticated psychotherapist that he cannot put himself in the position of interfering with every acting out behavior that he recognizes as such, whether within the group or without the group. If he were to do so he would become a real, parental, super-ego figure whose value as the promotor of ego growth and insight in the group would decrease at a rapid rate. Furthermore, the group's ability to work includes the freedom and obligation to recognize the behavior of its members for what it is; this means the toleration of much of the acting out of individuals, both as themselves and as parts of, and voices for, the group. Gradually the acting out will become ego-alien and its sources will be understood by the group and by its members (keeping in mind the different theoretical levels at which we work). Therefore anything that the group therapist does in the process of preparing a patient for group that prevents him from being a real resource to the group by setting himself up as an authoritarian super-ego is technically incorrect.

In summary, this chapter has presented an outline for the conducting of initial interviews with potential group psychotherapy patients (and other patients as well) by psychoanalytically oriented psychotherapists, has advanced the necessity for accurate assessment of pathology, ego strength development, and motivation, and has argued for the importance of making an explicit therapeutic contract with the patient.

The preparation of patients for group psychotherapy was discussed, and three specific goals were cited: placement of the group in the patient's individual life space; allayment of his anxieties about group psychotherapy; and the initial shaping of norms.

Idiosyncratic and technical sources of therapist behaviors in preparing group patients, and the technical needs of the group for its proper development, were discussed. Aspects of group that should be kept in mind from the very beginning, and, thus, should influence patient preparation, were presented.

Chapter 8
Specific problems

Introduction

Once a group has developed structure and thus can be viewed as a working group rather than as a group in formation, certain problems arise which are of a repetitive and predictable nature. These problems are difficult to resolve and reappear in many guises. This chapter provides a discussion of such problems and their causes, and makes technical suggestions for their resolution.

The most common and persistent problem in psychotherapy groups is the issue with authority, in which parental transference is cycled and recycled at different depths and different intensities. The scope of this problem contains the issues in adolescent resolution, with the ambivalent conflicts between fantasy and reality; dependence and independence; passivity and activity, and responsibility and irresponsibility down the continuum of the developmental scale to the early splitting of the object into good and bad and the projection of the pathogenic introject. For the therapists, these phases require the most skill in resolution, and the most analysis of their counter-transference, as well as the greatest stress on the co-therapy relationship. The resolution of these authority phases are also, in our opinion, the single most therapeutic experience for each and every group member in psychotherapy groups which develop in the style that we are describing and explaining in this book. We have dealt with this at some length in chapter 5.

We wish to emphasize this point again here. In our opinion the resolution of different phases of the authority issue constitutes the major therapeutic task for the group, comparable to the working through of the negative and positive transferences in psychoanalysis. Even more seriously do we point out that the ensuing work around issues of intimacy, which require resolution of difficulties with object relations involving non-parental figures and the formation of satisfactory peer relationships and love relationships, can only be developed within the parameters of the scale and depth that the resolution of the authority issue has reached. In other words, libidinal cathexis of other real people in the life of the patient is qualitatively and quantitatively determined by the degree of success or failure previously achieved in bondage, regressive or fixated, to the combined parent imago and its superego derivatives.

The most catalytic agents for the group 'authority issue' are issues in decision-making. Facilitating the development of the group's decision-making skills, and supporting the group while those skills are exercised, is another major area in which both the maturity and the skills of the group psychotherapist are crucial.

Difficulties experienced by group therapists in helping the group through issues that arise in the decision-making process derive from one of two sources. The first source, at which this book is aimed, is that of lack of proper understanding of the group dynamics of decision-making, and/or failure to appreciate the crucial nature of the task. Counter-transference is the second cause of difficulty. Unresolved authority issues within the therapist, especially as manifest in an archaic superego structure, tend to make him either intolerant of the protracted ambivalence and the lack of clarity of authority boundaries, or unconsciously manipulative in leading the group to a premature resolution. The great ambivalence within the group as to whether they can really possess the authority and the means to make a decision, or want to use it if they do have it, is precisely mirrored in the psychotherapist who does not trust the group's right or ability because he does not trust his own.

Some special problems that arise in the process of group psychotherapy, and are more general to the field, follow. Many of these problems can and do occur in individual psychotherapy and, as such, will not be unfamiliar to the individual psychoanalytic practitioner. However, these problems are often viewed by unsophisticated (from our point of view) group therapists as individual problems, i.e., problems manifesting individual dynamics, and are dealt with as such. We present such problems as group problems, and see their resolution as being at, and arising from, the group dynamic level.

The following specific issues in group psychotherapy are discussed below: decision-making; acting out and the many meanings of acting out; socializing between members; members leaving: terminating therapy and dropping out; new members; taking over another therapist's group; boundary behavior in groups; group size; silence.

Decision-making

Mature decision-making skills and resolution of the specific problems that the group must confront and make decisions about rests largely upon the therapist's ability to distinguish what decisions are appropriate. In other words, the level and the kind of decisions that a group makes for itself must remain within the aegis of the therapist.

Let us first make clear what decisions it is *not* appropriate for a group to make. Broadly speaking, any decision that is properly the responsibility of the therapist, and which cannot be properly handled by the group unless they have the therapist's training or resources, cannot be appropriately delegated to the group. In other words, all decisions that have to do with the patient management. Patient disposition, treatment plans and medication, for example, are obviously not appropriate for group decision-making, although in some cases the group can, and does, make appropriate input.

Less obviously, all group decisions should remain under the aegis of the therapist until a group is able to make a decision. The purpose of group decision-making is to facilitate group development. To face a group with decisions that it does not have the skills to make, or to face a group with a decision at a time when it is not in any condition to make the decision, is to defeat the purpose of group decision-making in a therapy group.

There is one other serious limitation which should be applied by every therapist to the question of whether or not to delegate a decision to the group, and that is whether the therapist really wants the group to have an experience in decision-making. It is important to discriminate between the two because, for a group to understand that it is making a decision which has real consequences in group life and to discover that, after all, the rules have been changed and it was just a decision-making exercise, is to repeat developmental trauma rather than to facilitate group development. This is an important issue because putting into practice the belief that decision-making is a crucial therapeutic tool makes serious demands upon the therapist's power and control.

We suggest that *all* decisions that affect *group* life are appropriate potential decision-making material for the group. And, by implication, all decisions that have to do directly with an individual remain the property of the therapist. Thus all group rules can potentially be the responsibility of the group to make and to modify. In the case of group rules, it is the therapist's job to decide which rules to start with but leave for the group to modify, and which rules to leave for the group to build through their experience as the group develops. Other group factors like termination time of a member, the bringing in of new members, the day, time, duration and fees of a group are also potential decision-making material for the group.

For example, one group spent sixteen months deciding whether or not to raise group fees. The current fee, unchanged for five years, represented the lowest end of the fee schedule for a one-therapist group, and this group had two therapists. The process and the subject matter was rich in stimulating insight into resistances and defenses for the group members. It also taxed to the utmost the therapists' commitment to their group model, their counter-transference to the group and occasionally their counter-transference to each other as well. All therapists are used to owning a great deal of referred power. Although therapists are frequently confronted with issues in treatment that are frustrating and sometimes feel overwhelming, these are part of the job. Not every therapist experiences feelings of helplessness that come from having 'given away' his *real* power over decisions that will affect him in his personal life: affect his calendar (if the group decides to change the time or day to accommodate a member); or his money (if the group spends many months deciding on an appropriate raise in the negotiated fee). It is true that the therapist is a member of the group and, as such, no consensual decision can be made without his commitment to it. However, the consensual decision-making process, while exceptionally effective when successful, is also exceptionally frustrating, and often arouses within the participants the urge to regress to dependence on authoritarian rule. The therapist, who espouses the group psychotherapy model that includes consensual decision-making, is no exception.

It surprises some of our colleagues that rules like 'whether or not to socialize' are a matter of group decision at all, and are not just automatic group rules that the therapists set. The first and weightiest reason that we don't, is that we think it unwise to make a group rule that we cannot enforce. To do so is to make it more difficult for patients to talk about their experience in breaking (or keeping!) rules. This therefore makes it less likely that they will get insight into their acting-out, or that the group will get insight into the group dynamics that any patient's acting out is usually a part of, particularly in the rule about socializing outside the group (see 'Socializing Between Members' below). One of us, for example, had a marriage result between two members who met regularly after a clinic group where the clinic had strictly imposed a rule (unenforceable) against fraternizing outside. When the marriage ended in divorce, one of the partners joined one of our Level Two groups. This group coincidentally was in the process of deciding about socializing outside group. Again the member began dating one of the other group members – but this time the issue was analyzed in group. This resulted in the patient gaining insight and the group becoming clearer about the issues in their socializing decision. The same one of us also observed the process of a relationship growing between two people in group, analyzed at a group process level and in individual therapy, which ended in a marriage (after termination of therapy). This marriage has been rewarding to both for more than ten years. Therefore, it is not the *fact* that group members meet, become attracted to each other, have affairs or marry, that is the problem in and of itself. It is how these things occur, and whether they are a part of individual resistance to therapy, and/or acting out of group conflicts, or whether it is part of a process in making a mature relationship.

The major question becomes whether or not leaving certain crucial decisions under the aegis of the group increases the risk of acting out, or decreases it. We are convinced that helping the group to learn how to make decisions that affect group life, at an ever increasing level of sophistication, increases the therapeutic potential of the group environment, decreases acting out, and increases the potential for working through the conflicts that are acted out.

For a group to develop the level of sophistication needed to make successful consensual decisions requires that the therapist makes any judgments along the course of the group's development. Making this kind of judgment is difficult for the experienced, let alone the inexperienced, therapist. While it is true that experience is one of the major assets for making this kind of discrimination, understanding group dynamics and applying that understanding to deciding on readiness is an avenue that is available to the inexperienced therapist.

Each group can only make the decisions that it *can* make, and can only make them *when* it is ready. At the end of chapter 6 there is a summary table of the three levels of group, their goal and function, and the group behavior that is available to each type of group for decision-making. For the Level Two group, being able to make certain appropriate decisions is, in fact, the suggested 'success' criteria for this group's function.

Different kinds of decisions are appropriate to each of the three group levels and decisions appropriate to one level are often grossly inappropriate for another. For example, whereas it is appropriate for a Level One group to *discuss* any of the issues that affect their group life should they wish, so that things don't 'just happen to them', it is usually enough to raise the issues for discussion, and rarely appropriate to expect the group to be able to, or even wish to be able to, decide about many group issues. However, it is important to note that a Level One group is capable of functioning periodically at a Level Two level, and then the alert therapist can build on group issues and can provide a decision-making experience for the group. A Christmas party, for example, can be a real decision-making triumph for a hospitalized, regressed Level One group. It is particularly important that a Level One group have a success experience with decision-making, and equally important that the therapist, in the wish to promote a success experience, does not do the decision-making himself and then give the group the credit. Just as players know when someone 'lets them win', so a group, at whatever level of functioning, is rarely fooled by their therapist.

Judging which decisions are appropriate to a Level Two or Three group entails knowing the group's decision-making history and being able to gauge how far they have progressed along the hierarchy of decision-making skills. The summary tables at the end of chapters 5 and 6 may facilitate this diagnosis.

We have treated decision-making at some length as it seems to us that it is a 'special problem' in group that we have, to some extent, helped to create. Worse, when we offer it as a model that in fact provides conditions for therapy which are less therapeutic without it, we are offering the group psychotherapy field a problem to share. This is particularly so in relation to the problem of acting out, as will be discussed in the sections following on 'acting out' and 'socializing between members'.

Acting out

Psychoanalysis has made an important contribution in bringing the phenomena of specific impulsive behaviors into relation with the dynamics of treatment, particularly as they reflect the transference. Freud proposed that patients often *act out* impulses aroused during the treatment hours, *after* the sessions, *outside* of the treatment room.

He suggested that there is less possibility of the patient becoming aware of the repetitive nature of such acts since he is not in a position to be interfered with via interpretation; hence he is more likely to gratify his repressed urges rather than to examine them. The implications for treatment are extremely clear.

Group offers a different situation from that of individual treatment in many ways, and particularly as regards the handling of acting out outside the group, We see two sorts of acting out behaviors that take place outside of the group sessions.

The first category of acting out follows the same model that is familiar in individual psychotherapy. The patient acts out impulses aroused in the group sessions with some non-group connected people or situations. For example, the group is approaching rebellious feelings toward the therapist's authority, and during the intervening week a patient gets into a power struggle with a boss, or a spouse, or a bus driver, or some other person who represents authority to him. As in individual psychotherapy, this material does not become available for analysis until the patient brings it into the session. Sometimes the acting out in the intervening weeks is in fact idiosyncratic to the group member, but, much more frequently, what the individual member experienced as a personal issue that had made the week difficult turns out to be just one example in the group of other similar experiences, and sometimes all of the members will take their turn sharing examples of the same kind of difficulty. These coincidences can be used powerfully toward group insight, particularly in groups who are familiar with the tendency for members to act out the group issue, and can therefore use the information to surface the group issue.

The second category of acting out occurs at the level of the group. Just as the individual patient can relive unconscious wishes and fantasies with intense urgency while refusing to recognize either their source or their repetitive character, so too can the group. This behavior at the group level can take the typical form of scapegoating; a group pattern of missing sessions or coming late; interaction between members outside of the group setting (discussed below as a separate problem); social chatter in lieu of work during group; supporting tantrums that actually preclude the group's ability to work; and so on. Different ways of acting out would make an exhaustive list. Group therapists must learn to recognize acting out in terms of the dynamics of the immediate group situation, not just in terms of some individual specific behaviors. One of the outstanding contributions of depth psychology has been the recognition that given behaviors can only be understood in terms of the total picture, which includes unconscious levels of meaning as well as ego compromises and cultural availabilities; hence any behavior could and does at different times have different meanings for the same person or the same group.

What is important for the diagnosis of group acting out is that the group is discharging its energies in the pursuit of repetitive, regressive goals with satisfaction occurring at the regressive level instead of being expressed in a form that lends itself to interpretation, understanding, and growth - i.e. lends itself to the therapeutic process. The requirement of the psychoanalytic psychotherapies is that drive and ego energies should (1) not be gratified in the hypercathected and regressed form in which they emerge in illnesses; (2) not evade the scrutiny of the therapeutic process altogether; and (3) emerge in the verbal form, which brings them eventually under the sway of the reality-ego and into the mainstream of present-day psychic life. Acting out violates all of these requirements.

At the level of group, the evasions are the same as those of psychoanalysis; the group gets satisfaction out of repetitive, regressive behaviors at the expense of verbalizing the conflicts and pursuing the phase-appropraite group task that was being worked on or was about to be undertaken. A single example will suffice: the sadistic and masochistic gratification that is experienced when the group persistently scapegoats a member for some alleged dereliction of duty or other, if not interpreted, can destroy the group's ability to get analytic work accomplished.

The solution to acting out is almost always direct interpretation. In its broadest sense, acting out functions not only as a repetition, but as a resistance also. Effective interpretation would take the resistance value into account as well as pointing toward the gratification of unconsicous wishes being experienced by the group. An interpretation might then be expressed in the form of a question, such as: 'what needs of the group are being met by scapegoating member so-and-so?' or 'what dilemma is the group attempting to resolve by behaving as if member so-and-so has the problem, instead of everyone?'

It may be appropriate at times that an interpretation of acting out be made on the individual level, in which case it is made in the manner proper to individual intervention; even there, at the first convenient point, its function for the group needs to be brought into focus also.

In the form of group psychotherapy that we propose, where the group is responsible for the rules that affect that group as soon as the group is able to take the responsibility, the handling of acting out is not as simple as it is in individual therapy. In individual therapy we can say to the patient that when acting out starts, therapy stops, or we can ask the patient to abstain from a particular behavior which is serving to act out dynamics important to a particular phase in treatment. In a group, however, where the development of therapeutic norms for the group emerge as a function of the therapeutic needs of the group, the therapist sails between Scylla and Charybdis in this matter. Acting out can occur which will be dangerous to the ultimate success of the therapy and could lead to group fixation at some phase; acting out can lead to truly important insights that move group and individual along at an accelerated pace. No one sails between Scylla and Charybdis without being of two minds! Our resolution is to attempt to give such acting out an ego-alien character by *suggesting* that it is not a good idea, while leaving the group to wrestle with the problem of whether or not to make it a rule. Most important, however, is the therapeutic climate of a properly led group, a climate which consists of a set of norms which include empathetic understanding, open communication, generic reconstruction on the group and individual levels, and non-punishment.

Outside interaction and socializing between members is a particularly significant aspect of acting out in groups. Because of its importance we discuss it separately in the section following.

The many meanings of acting out

Whereas in individual therapy it is always appropriate to interpret acting out in terms of individual dynamics, this is not so in group. The therapist must make the decision whether interpretation of the individual dynamics is the appropriate intervention for the individual member and for the group. The complexity and challenge of this decision is illustrated in the example below.

In a group that was still ambivalent about whether or not to meet outside, Dick and Jane had been meeting regularly to play racquet ball. In this particular session, Jane was expressing disappointment that Dick did not want to meet after group that evening. Dick was responding wearily that it was not that he did not want to, but that he was tired and wanted to go straight home. Jane, a woman who tended to present herself as a tough, independent jock, let down her guard and explained that she wanted love, that she was lonely, that in the outside world she was always too involved, and that, somehow, in group it felt that relationships could be different. Dick, responding to her sincerity, then told her how he had wrestled with the decision about whether or not to ask her to his party, and had decided not to because it seemed to make group more difficult, and besides, he wanted to keep the therapist's rules. Jane interrupted immediately with a protesting 'What rules?'

Let us look at this episode from the many meanings of acting out, for Dick, Jane and the group.

Dick, the son of a rigid and demanding father who inhibited Dick's dating during his adolescence, had compromised by excelling in athletics, becoming a football hero, partying after the games with the cheerleaders and the team and not dating any 'steady' girl. He was still unmarried. Underlying the history of his adolescent dating were his oedipal dynamics, where his wish for his mother had been overwhelmed by his fear of his father, with whom he had identified as the aggressor. His incestuous, ambivalent wishes for his father and for his mother were bound within his present life style. His *macho* athletic life brought him the admiration of women, whom he rejected because of the exigencies of his training demands, and the locker rooms providing a ritualized defense against his unconscious homosexuality.

Jane, an unusually tall girl, had reached her full height at eleven when her peers had not yet started their growth spurt. During her junior and senior years, she had not dated. She compensated by excelling in athletics and currently, in her late thirties, was divorced, and playing on a rugger team, where she frequently became injured sufficiently badly to be 'carried' off and nurtured. The daughter of a flighty, feminine, uncertain mother, she had adored her father. During Jane's oedipal and pre-oedipal years, he held her frequently on his lap, tucked her into bed, called her 'his girl'. Her mother encouraged their inter-actions calling them 'lovers', and calling Jane 'lovey' as a nickname. Jane experienced increasing restlessness when her father held her on his lap, and became known as a child who was always on the go, always running and jumping about. Her parents had her tested for hyper-activity. They were advised to channel her energy into sports. Her sexual energy was still channelled into sports.

Dick and Jane's mutual acting out repeated for each of them problems in their individual dynamics. For either or both, individual interpretations timed and phrased appropriately might well contribute to their gaining insight. However, as we have said, acting out performs a function for the group as well as for the individuals involved in it. Let us continue to explore the meaning of this acting out in terms of the dynamics of the group.

It has been mentioned that the group is in the process of developing norms. Issues in the development of norms differ according to the different phase of development that the group is in. This group is at the point of emerging from the dependent flight phase into the beginnings of the power struggle of the fight phase. At this point, norms are very often used by the group to represent both the dependent need for rules of 'right and proper behavior' and the counterdependent need to have rules against which to rebel. Thus the issue of norms is often the bone of contention over which the group fights.

A second aspect of the dynamics of group that are important in understanding and interpreting the acting out of these two members is the issue of pairing. Pairing is another group phenomenon that happens in different ways for different purposes at different times in the group. Probably the most dramatic form is the group-induced pseudo-sexualized 'partnering' of two group members who are unconsciously expected to give birth to the solution to the group's problems. The pairing dynamics of this particular case give an excellent example of how the group dynamics are expressed through those members whose individual dynamics are served by breaking the group rules.

A third aspect of the dynamics of group that are relevant to this issue are the dynamics of the authority issue. The therapist of this group was in supervision with one of us. In the weeks before this particular session he had been working hard in supervision on the fixation of his group in the dependency phase and in encouraging the group to explore and make decisions on issues that affected the group life. This shift in his technique had resulted in more energy becoming available in the group for work, an increase in the morale of the members, and also an increase in anxiety. The group was basically highly ambivalent about the less directive role that their therapist was taking, as was the therapist himself. But whereas the therapist was conscious of his ambivalence, the group denied theirs. Thus some of the members of the group heard their therapist 'telling' them not to meet outside, some of the members heard him suggesting that they explore the group and individual meanings of their meeting outside, and still others of the group did not hear their therapist making 'any rules at all'. Thus, the acting out of the two members fulfilled many group purposes. Some of these are summarized below:

Dick and Jane acted out the dependent flight forces in the group by allocating issues of love, sexuality and relationships to the 'outside' of the group. They 'repeated' at the group level for the group life what Dick and Jane repeated at the individual level for their individual lives;

and that is the expression of a frustration in such a way that no resolution is possible.

Dick and Jane's roles represented both the counterdependent, rebellious forces and the dependent, compliant forces in the group. Dick and Jane were a voice for the ambivalence in the group. One side of the ambivalence was represented by the wish to 'disobey' the therapists' unspoken (but 'heard') message that the group would not socialize outside. The other side of the ambivalence was represented by the wish to please the therapist and obey him and gain his approval and support by conforming to his will.

The goal of the group was met by Dick and Jane by 'having someone else do it while we watch'. This enabled the group members to act out voyeuristically while keeping the oedipal and negative oedipal dynamics unconscious. This permitted individuals to retain in fantasy issues that they did not want to discuss in the group, and permitted the group-as-a-whole to regress to an earlier mode of behavior.

This earlier behavior enabled the group to divorce itself from any problem that any member brought up in group by sitting back and giving advice to the 'working member', intellectualizing, working 'on' the pair instead of on themselves, and keeping their individual eyes on the therapist for approval and support. This individualized mode of work maintained a series of dyadic relationships with the therapist and served the resistance of the members to working in a group, and maintained the individual fantasies of 'being special' to the therapist.

Socializing between members

It is impossible to prevent group members from interacting outside the session. They meet in the waiting room; they meet on the street outside the office when coming and going, they ride up or down the elevator together; they park their cars in the same parking lot; and so on. And in these more or less chance encounters they interact and have feelings about the character of the interaction. What is important here is whether or not the experience as the members perceive it comes into the treatment to be discussed and interpreted, or whether it is suppressed. What is suppressed becomes sooner or later a hidden agenda at the group level, and behaviors arising from it are hard to understand when the rest of the group does not have the information that might clarify them.

Chance meetings, as described above, occurring as unavoidable consequences of the logistics of group therapy, are of no major concern other than as regards the necessity of bringing them into the sessions. Meetings that are either non-chance or in which chance is exploited for acting out purposes are a major concern. It is also impossible to prevent this kind of phenomenon. What is important for technique is the need to make it possible to bring the information about such encounters into the treatment situation. One method for encouraging the group to bring outside interactions back into the group is to question and interpret.

During the early phases of norm setting, whether or not to meet outside the group is always a major issue. It involves the group giving up an individual freedom at a time when they are not yet convinced that what they get in return from the group is worth it. It is at this time that we raise the question of 'what are the issues in the group that are being handled by meeting outside the group', or offer an opinion 'that the group might consider how meetings outside can bring more into the group than they take out'; or interpet the group process by pointing out, for example, that the group, by making friendships outside, are defusing the conflicts inside the group. Usually a group will make the choice not to meet; either because they see the common sense of the rule, or because they intuit that we basically hold a traditional view, and we would prefer to either take the rule for granted or to encourage the group to make it. Be that as it may, in the interests of observing 'what happens' rather than imposing a judgment that may have been inappropriately transferred from individual therapy, we have most often not overtly interfered with the group's handling of their outside contacts, other than in the ways mentioned above.

One of us has observed, without actively interfering, five years of a group's life whose members socialized regularly, meeting after group for drinks and sandwiches, visiting each other over holidays, and calling each other up for support. This was a Level Two group, the one we have referred to in chapter 6 as the 'closet decision-makers'. There is little doubt that for some of the members, the meeting outside provided a significant experience of belonging, and that some fruitful gains in the ability to make object relations took place; there is no way, of course, to know whether these same gains would have taken place without the socializing. There is equally little question that for some of the members the outside meetings were costly in terms of their therapy. Conflicts that were potentially useful between members in group were acted out outside group: one young man, whose resentment towards his father started to manifest in transference reactions to another member, lost all insight potential for that time, when, rather than confront the issue in group, it was 'settled outside' by his going to work for the other, and from then on experiencing him as 'the good father' both in group and out. We have already mentioned the inappropriate marriage that arose from another group. In both these cases, the material that was acted out at one time did come into group for analysis and insight later. But it is certain that much potentially important material does not. It is also interesting that the 'socializing' group, as it grew in sophistication and maturity, changed the rules. This was not done by group decision in the group, but by a change in the socializing patterns. Some six months after members had ceased to meet outside, they discussed the pros and cons of meeting outside and the effects it had had on the group process.

The example above shows how one of us, watching the effects on the group process and on the patients' therapy of a group policy of meeting outside, relied on the underlying conviction that, if the group process is basically healthy, its members will not make irretrievable decisions that will harm each other or the group. The example following shows in contrast how one of us broke our own rule and intervened, interrupting the early phases of group development by requesting the group not to meet outside group during the week, not to meet before group, and not to have a drink before group the following week. The effect of this intervention on the subsequent development of the group is something that we continue to discuss, and still leaves us in two minds as to whether or not it was a group-appropriate intervention.

The group was a Level Three group, whose members were young professionals. It was in the early stages of development, and had had a significantly difficult early history. First, its co-therapists had never worked together before. The new co-therapist had long experience in psychoanalytically oriented individual therapy, and some experience (but no formal training) in a psychoanalytically oriented group. He had no experience with the model of psychotherapy that we are presenting in this book. Second, originally designed for eight members, the group started with six, and one of them dropped out after the first few months. An additional shock occurred when a new member arrived, attended his first session and never returned.

Because of its size, and because of some of its early trauma, the intensity of the process between members increased, and was responded to by close pairing and more than usual fluctuations of attendance. The close pairing reflected, not only a defense against the work of the group, but also the covert group goal of entering into an individual

therapy relationship with the new co-therapist because of his considerable reputation.

The group had met after each session and had paid little more than
lip service to the question of what group issues were being so dealt
with. Pairing intensified, and although their problems with sexual
attraction were discussed in the group, it became more and more
obvious that sexual acting out was imminent.

Then the co-therapist was absent for a session. Throughout the
session I, the one who remained, wrestled with whether to set limits
on the group, or whether to trust the process. You will know from the
introduction how the decision was made. The group was asked not to
meet between sessions, to leave separately, to return to group
separately, and not to drink before they came. The immediate
consequence of the request was that the sexual acting out did not
occur. The long-term effects on the group are still not clear at the time
of this writing. It is certainly true that the group had much unfinished
business from the early meetings outside, and did not in fact begin the
work on confidentiality and trust until, nearly two years later, some of
the mistrust that had been engendered in the early outside meetings had
been worked through. It is also true that the group used the mistrust
issue to block accepting new members. Interpretations about displacement of distrust of the therapists on the one hand and revenge on the
therapists on the other fell on deaf ears. The group itself often referred
to the 'request' and remained ambivalent about it. It is hard to tell,
looking back, what consequences on the development of the group the
interference with its process had. Perhaps, as in the Level Two group,
it would have been better to have worked with the group while it
gained its own equilibrium: perhaps intervening at that point set a
crucial boundary without which the group would not have survived.
The fact that we cannot, at this point, be definite about our opinion
underlies how important this issue is to us. We are still exploring the
nature of the boundaries to set up in starting a group, that will
contribute to its developmental potential without undermining its
potential autonomy. Too loose, and the group chaos threatens group
disintegration; too tight, and the rigidity threatens to smother the
group process.

For those therapists who prefer to make a statement about the
boundaries that are most likely to benefit members of a group, we
are glad to offer the following structure that we have developed,
although we have not yet used it in starting a group, and therefore
have not yet had the opportunity to observe its consequences. As

you will see from the following, we have delineated time, place, duration and fee; procedure for termination, and suggested boundaries for meeting outside. The advantage of such introductory guidelines is that the members will have on paper, to which they can refer, the suggested boundaries of their group life. We are interested to see whether this advantage is not also a disadvantage, in that, in our experience, both individual members and groups go through periods in which they suffer a strange amnesia for the group's procedures and rules. Frequently, this amnesia precedes an important process of restructuring. It remains for us to see how groups (infinitely creative) use an initial guidelines statement.

Guidelines for group psychotherapy

A psychotherapy group is in many ways different from any other kind of experience. The following comments and guidelines have emerged as helpful from other people's experience in groups.

Pay attention to your initial reactions to your group. You may well find that you learn a lot about the way you respond in everyday life.

The work of the group is best done within the group setting. Meetings outside tend to diffuse this work. Discussing in group all chance meeting between members reduces the risk of interfering with the conditions for group work.

All who join group are asked to make a minimum commitment to six months of group experience, within which time many of the work issues usually become clear.

When leaving group, members are urged to negotiate a termination phase of not less than six weeks so that they, and the group, can work through issues of separation.

Group sessions last for one and a half hours. Time boundaries are observed and groups stop and start on time.

The group fee is calculated on a monthly basis and is due on the first group session of each month.

Conflicts over money should be talked about in group, not 'acted out' in late or skipped payments.

Members are urged not to miss any group sessions.

To summarize: when we say we are of two minds about outside interaction between members we mean that we would like to prevent such acting out in the interest of a clean, clear technique of group psychotherapy, which would be uncluttered with the subterranean effects of unknown behaviors. We also recognize that we have no power to prevent it. Serendipitously, the eventual identification and analysis of outside acting out between members can often be extremely rewarding in terms of the insights it produces. Only if a group climate exists which makes it impossible ever to discuss the outside interactions of members does this benefit fail to occur. A group that makes its own rules owns them, which contributes both to following them and to analyzing impulses and events that impinge on them.

Members leaving

Termination

The time comes when a member has finished psychotherapy. Suffice it to say that termination is appropriate at the time when a person believes that he has fulfilled, to his satisfaction, his therapeutic contract, and the therapist does not disagree.

The actual event begins, however, with the patient, or occasionally the therapist, raising the issue of termination during a group session. When the group begins to grasp that this is a serious proposal rather than simply the sort of wish that has been expressed by one member or another off and on throughout the life of the group, the impact is enormous, whether covert or overt. At first the group may refuse to countenance the idea and will become angry and/or depressed, depending on its particular character. There is likely to be a great deal of group pressure on the sudden 'deviant'. (And how the member handles the pressure is an excellent index of his real readiness to terminate.)

What has happened is that trauma on a number of different levels has overtaken the group. The individual dynamics around object loss, separation, loss of love, castration anxiety and narcissistic loss of self-esteem are hypercathected in various ways and combinations, and to different degrees. At the group dynamic level the whole structure of the group is threatened, the obverse of the threat posed by a new member. Since the functions of the group must continue to be performed and the roles appropriate to their performance must be occupied, the question of who will now be and do must be fought out, negotiated, experienced painfully or anxiously, all over again. New patterns of intimacy, influence, and communication must be discovered. In an experienced group the threat of a new member may also fuel the tension almost from the beginning.

The technical handling of termination is relatively straightforward. In our groups, a six-week period is ordinarily already a group norm, or at least exists as a contract between individuals and the therapist, and this is usually adhered to. With a person who is terminating because he has indeed 'finished', honoring the six weeks' convention is rarely a problem, since he understands the importance of working through separation for himself and for the others.

Six weeks usually provides sufficient time for the group levels to be worked into full awareness (they will not really restructure until the terminating member is gone), and the issues of individual loss *et al.* to be re-experienced and reinterpreted in terms of loss, past losses, and the transference elements bridging the two. Narcissistic pain resulting from the sense that 'I am not finished', as well as oedipal rivalry, are also significant areas to be examined in the six weeks, and after. And then, he is gone.

Dropping out: resolving loss

The loss of a member through termination, while traumatic, and requiring hard work to properly digest, is at the same time a very positive experience, since the members experience and can identify with success.

Not so when a member drops out. The group either learns about this through direct communication or through the failure of the member to return over a period of time. In either case, the effect is traumatic. All of the group structural and individual dynamic levels discussed above are aroused in the same manner.

Another painful affect accompanies all of the others; this is comprised of guilt, shame, and sense of failure. The group feels that it has failed to meet the needs of the member who has left. It questions its ability to perform its therapeutic task. To the degree that the member consistently aroused anger, the group will experience guilty fear of itself as dangerously omnipotent. A sense of having been the victim of sadistic impulses will arouse a sense of impotent rage. Finally the group's trust in the therapist will be tested; at the group level the incompetent leader or the malevolent leader or each in turn; at the individual level the inadequate, uncaring, or 'bad' imagos.

If all of the above issues do not appear to arise overtly, most or all of them will be there as hidden agendas for the group and negative transference for the individuals. A careful and prolonged exploration and working though is required if the group is to avoid fixation and a therapeutic impasse.

In summary, the group will see termination as the logical and desirable outcome of completed developmental tasks and achievement of autonomy. The pain experienced as a result of termination is the pain of separation and grief, but not of loss. The resolution is a 'good' pain that accompanies growth, increased ability to experience appropriate affect and a deepening readiness for intimacy for the member. It is a group event, scored much like a well-played goal, that heralds the end of one game and the beginning of another one. Members who leave group because they are ready remind each member that, in time, their turn will come, and represent the achievement of the group goal.

Dropping out, in contrast, is an experience of frustration for the group. It is frequently experienced as a group failure, a repetition of narcissistic hurt, an ambivalent affect. Too often the group feels guilty, and too often their need to externalize the guilt and blame the therapist re-opens issues in trust. The working through process is often long and difficult. However, if the group can come to terms with failures as well as successes, it takes a step towards an increased maturity.

New members

Introducing a new member into an ongoing group is one of the most important experiences in group life. From the perspective of group dynamics, a new member will affect the group norms, its cohesiveness, its communication patterns, and the working methods it has developed to reach its goals. Integrating a new member into group requires regression in group function to allow for the de-differentiation of established patterns to permit the forming of new patterns that include the new member's resources. This regression is a 'regression in the service of the group ego'. Some groups are more reluctant than others to enter and work through this process.

In this sense, even a member who has been absent for a period of time while the group has been working and growing will require some of the same membership work that a new member requires before being reintegrated into the group. The most dramatic example of this occurs in the moving narrative of a small group of concentration camp babies who grew up without a constant mother figure. These children, who were about three years old, were brought to England and kept together as a group. One, however, was quarantined first. When she returned to the group some ten days later, the group-as-a-whole regressed, losing all the skills, including the security, that they had acquired during her absence. Having regressed to her level, the entire group then redeveloped together.

The dynamic issues entailed in bringing a new member into group are one of the major reasons that the group needs a period of preparation for a new member. Therapists who are not aware of the group dynamic issues may well be perplexed when the group appears to function much the same, but somehow their work no longer gets done. Therapists who are either unaware, 'forget' or ignore the fact that introducing a new member into an ongoing group will arouse primitive envies and jealousies that have their roots in the trauma of the birth of a brother or sister in every single member with siblings – as well as the envies and jealousies related to the oedipal triangle – will be ill prepared to facilitate the new member's entrance, or to help the group get insight into, and to work through, important therapeutic aspects of these primitive responses.

Each group therapist will have his own policy for introducing members into their groups. Our policy is clearly defined. Members in our groups know that we have set a 'full' membership at eight, and that when the number falls below that, either because a member terminates, or drops out, then the group can expect a new member. The group, however, can and does function with less than eight while it goes through the process of preparing for a new member.

There are several phases in preparing for a new member. The first phase is explicitly recognizing that a decision about *when* the member should come must be made. The second phase is resistance:

1 the resistance to making the decision,
2 the overt or covert resistance to having a new member at all,
3 the subordination of the new member issue to whatever the major phase issue is for the group,
4 the use of the new member as ammunition in the particular aspect of the power and intimacy struggle that is current in the group,
5 the meaning that taking in a new member has for the individual members,
6 the group reluctance to take in a new and 'foreign' element to the existing group structure,
7 the analysis of the many fantasies about what new member means to the group.

This process is seldom fast, particularly as the decision about new members is usually catalytic to much work, important at all levels, to both the group and to the individual members. The work of preparing for a new member is hard, and making the decision of when the new member should arrive is an ambivalent experience at best, and an exigent experience at worst. It is also a demanding and expensive issue for the therapist. We have already mentioned that therapists who are not willing to commit themselves to group decision-making as a therapeutic method are wise not to engage in it, and particularly wise not to include the group on the 'new member' decision. Not only is it a process that demands much frustration tolerance as well as experience and skill in facilitating, it is also a process that keeps both the group chair and the therapist's pocket empty for the length of time that the decision takes.

It is important to separate out those aspects of deciding to take in a new member that are different from the general difficulties in decision-making that groups experience. There are, however, certain predictable problems that seem *always* to happen when we ask a group to set the date when they feel that they will be prepared to take in a new member.

It took us many years to understand why, when a group is asked *when* it will be prepared to take in new members, it responds with *whether* to take them in at all. At first we interpreted this as a general resistance to making decisions. But it is not true that groups change the parameters of all the decisions that they make, although it is true that all groups do have problems with decision-making.

With this particular issue, however, it is clear that the question cannot be heard. There is a predictable lapse of time between the phrasing of the question and the 'hearing' of the request that the group set aside a period of time to *prepare* itself to take on a new member. From the therapist's point of view, this is a request that the group focus on the issue, and explore what it means to the group as a whole in the light of the work that it is currently doing, and that individual members explore what bringing in a member means to them, both generally and also at this particular time. Only thus can a new member, in fact, be accepted by the group.

From the group's point of view, there is the experience that they have been asked to take part in something, like the birth of a sibling, over which they have no power at all. They are also being asked to share the therapist when they already feel that there is not enough to go round. Therefore at a deep unconscious level the group is not merely resistant, it is immobilized, frustrated and angry. This is most typically manifested in one of several ways.

Denial is one response in which the group behaves as if there has been no question. Sometimes the group will continue with their work until their guilt grinds them to a halt, and they reluctantly raise the issue. Other times they are capable of continuing 'innocently' for as long as it takes for the therapist to raise the issue again, victims of a total group amnesia. In this case the group is saying: 'decision? what decision? there is no decision!' And of course, from one perspective, as always the group is right. Until the group can 'hear' the decision, there is no decision. Until the group can understand what it means to prepare, they are being asked to do the impossible. In fact, for many members in psychotherapy 'preparation' has no meaning because learning conditions were impaired for them in growing up. 'I've never prepared for anything, I just did the best I could when something came along.' 'How could I prepare? I don't know what it means.' At a deeper level the group is talking about survival. 'It's like swimming. Each time I jumped in I was sure I'd drown and I survived somehow. I never "learnt" to swim. Nobody taught me. I still can't swim. I just jump in and survive.'

Another response is over-compliance, in which the group quickly agrees and depersonalizes. In this case, over-compliance is not the simple ploy of making a quick decision as a solution to the problem of making a decision, but the compliance of despair. As one member put it: 'I can't make a decision about what I want, because all I want is to do something to please you. So I'll say yes. But when I say yes, then I get a new member to share you with. And how do I know that afterwards you will be pleased and it will have been worth it?'

Stubborn, overt, angry resistance is the third type of response to the request for a new member. If this is not a group manifestation of the authority issue, and it most frequently is, then the underlying dynamics are very similar to those underlying compliance. 'How can I do anything but resist you when I don't want to share you? How do I know I will still be special?'

The issue of introducing a new member is particularly useful in providing conditions for insight into issues of power, control and authority. Some members feel angry because they feel that they are being asked to take part in a decision that they feel the therapist should make, unable to recognize that the therapist cannot make a decision about 'when' the group is prepared until the group is willing to prepare. Others use the issue to take revenge on authority by thwarting it, as they feel authority thwarted them. 'Now it's my turn - and I won't let you.'

As we have mentioned, the translation of the question of *when* to, *whether* to bring in a new member is the most predictable, and also, perhaps, the most surprising event that occurs over the new member issue. We have experienced the *when-whether* shift in all groups, as soon as the group is able to deal with the decision as a 'real' decision at all. This includes even our most experienced and sophisticated groups, who have been through the same issue time and time again. As one of our more seasoned members exclaimed: 'I know that you have the authority to bring in new members. But all I can think of is no, you can't. I will resist you and resist you. I can't think about the issue of "preparing" or of "when", because all I can do is resist.'

When the group is finally ready to 'hear' the issue and do the work of preparation, the worst is over. The therapist then knows that the date for a new member will be set in line with the reality needs of the group, rather than as a function of unresolved dynamic issues. The kinds of reality needs of the group will be events like: a member absence that has to be taken into account; a particular issue that requires working through; the termination phase of a particular member or an impending date that has psychological significance for a particular member, like a death anniversary, that the member wishes to work through with the 'old' group. Most of the deeper dynamic content, like issues with power and authority, sibling rivalry and oedipal jealousy are usually near completion by the time that the group-as-a-whole is able to 'hear' and work with the question.

There are two major factors in the entrance of a new member into group. Preparation is the first, and we have dealt with preparation of the group at length above. Preparation of the patient is also a very important factor, and we have dealt with that in chapter 7, 'preparing a patient for group'. However well prepared the group and the patient are, inevitably there is still the impact on the patient who has been told that group therapy is available, but that the group will decide the date of joining. This will have a specific significance to each and every new member, and is an issue that should be worked with early in group, if the member is not to act out in group the dynamic meaning of having been kept waiting, sometimes for months.

The second major factor is matching the group and the patient. We have dealt with this from most aspects in chapter 6, where we explore the factors in assigning patients appropriately to a group whose goals and style of function are compatible with the patient's needs. There is one aspect of 'matching' that has not been explored in that chapter and needs some mention here. However appropriate the patient may be psychodynamically to a particular group, there is the factor of experience. The naive patient may find it absolutely impossible to tolerate the experience of group, not because of being dynamically unsuited, but because the group's behavioral norms are too discrepant. Thus, we have had a new member enter group on a day when one member told the group that her father had just been killed. Although the member herself felt supported by the group, the new member never came back, shocked that the group had not physcially held and comforted the woman in her grief. In this case, the group rule that all impulses should be expressed in words and not in actions was intolerable. Another example of discrepant norms was that of a new member who, though he had been in analysis for many years and was aware of the difficulty he experienced in expressing his feelings, left group after his first session because he became too anxious in its climate of intimacy.

Another aspect of 'matching' which presents a serious problem is matching the experience of the patient with the experience of the group. We prefer (and so do our groups who often request it as an admission criteria) to place patients with prior therapy experience in groups who have been working for some length of time together, and to place patients without previous therapy experience either in a 'new' group, or in a Level Two group as preparatory experience to a move into the more appropriate Level Three.

In one sense, of course, it is impossible to prepare a patient for group. Group is a new experience for a patient, however much therapy the patient has had, and however much previous group experience. In another sense, it is impossible for us as therapists to predict what will happen when the new patient and the group get together. Thus in one group, for example, a new patient was attacked unmercifully for weeks, and defended herself with great skill and self-control. The group and she immediately entered into a reciprocal role relationship in which the group acted 'mother' for her, and she acted 'scapegoat' for the group's repudiation of their own competence. We had expected a smooth transition in that the group had worked particularly hard on their preparation; and the new member was well along in her therapy. Looking back, the weeks of attack were more difficult for us as therapists than for the group, who in fact were in the process of working through role issues that were relevant and important to every member of the group, while we were struggling with our own needs to intervene in the scapegoating.

The above episode characterizes one final point that we wish to make before ending this chapter, and that is that, for a new member, initial experience with group, although apparently a social experience, is also a repetition of early object relationships. Therefore, for those therapists who have patients in both individual therapy and in group therapy it is useful to be prepared to hear the patient's response to group as a response to a parent or sibling. Thus one patient, who wanted to leave group because she could not endure the anxiety of waiting for the attack that she was sure would come, was relieved of the anxiety when she got the insight into her expectation that the group would behave like her mother.

Taking over another therapist's group

Taking over another therapist's group is rather like being a baby-sitter or a stepmother. The way the group behaves will depend largely upon four factors. The first will be the relative compatibility or incompatibility of your leadership style and the group's own therapist's. The second will be the phase of development that the group is in. The third will be the level of group. The fourth will be the character of the group in terms of how active or passive its general behavioral tendencies are. These four factors may also relate to a fifth: environment.

For those groups which are a part of a larger system, the way the group behaves will also be influenced by how acceptable the substitution of therapists is to the larger system. At the end of this section we will illustrate this environmental aspect of the issue.

Taking over a group when the therapist is absent is less likely to elicit extreme reactions from the group than taking over the group permanently. The major and immediate issue is the group's reaction to having a 'substitute' therapist which will reflect the basic relationship of the group to their own therapist, their response to his absence, and the meaning to the group of the reason for his absense: vacation, illness or a competing commitment. A Level One group may not admit this as an issue at all, and supporting the group through the feelings of abandonment, and reassuring the group that the therapist will return, will probably be the major task of the substituting therapist. In both Level Two and Level Three groups, however, the dynamics are more complicated. If the group is either a passive group, or in the flight phase, their response will probably be to be very 'nice' and they will tend to remain in platitudinous flight for the period through which they have to survive until their own therapist returns. If the group is an active group, they will probably respond to their therapist's absence within the characteristic issues of the phase of development that they are in. Thus, a group in the fight phase might well attack the 'baby-sitter'; in the enchantment phase, ignore him; and in the disenchantment phase use him to underline their general disappointment. A group in the phase of the authority issue may well use the experience of the replacement therapist as an excuse for their barometric event, proving to themselves that they do not need a replacement and can do very well without any therapist at all (see chapter 5).

In all the above modes the work of the substituting therapist is the same. First, to work within the group's existing norms. Second, to help the group work through their reactions to their therapist's absence and to get insight into the issues that his absence raises for individuals and for the group. Third, to facilitate expression of grief, rage and its concomitant guilt. The major mistake that a substituting therapist may be tempted to make is to attempt to give the group an experience of what an alternative (or better?) form of therapy is like. If the norms of the group for which he is substituting violate either his beliefs or his professional ethics, the time to respond to this violation is *before* he substitutes. Once he has accepted the role of substitute therapist, then the boundaries of his performance need to remain within the norms of the group. After his responsibilities as substitute are over, he may well take issue with the group's therapist. To act out differences or competition with the group's therapist in the group cannot be an acceptable alternative.

Taking over another therapist's group permanently is a more complex issue. How the group behaves initially will relate much more to their issues with the leadership style of their accustomed therapist than it will to that of the new therapist. Lewin, Lippitt and White (1939) did an important study on styles of leadership and the consequence upon group behavior of following one particular leadership style with another. The three leadership styles were autocratic, democratic, and laissez-faire. Autocratic leadership can be translated into any therapeutic style where the rules of the group, the group process and the activities in the group are mainly a function of the therapist's decision. Thus, for example, a transactional analysis group, a gestalt group, and any other group where the members engage in a series of prescribed activities fulfill the criteria for a group where the responsibility for what happens is the therapist's and the predictability of what happens is high. Laissez-faire behavior, on the other hand, can be translated into the therapeutic style where 'anything goes' in the group, and the therapist encourages any member of the group to explore any issue in any desired way. These will be the 'permissive' groups. The democratic style can be translated into the therapeutic style where the group is encouraged to take responsibility for its own growth and development, and the therapist acts as a facilitator to the process rather than as a legislator of it. According to our schema of group levels, Level One is characterized more by autocratic or directive leadership; Level Three is characterized more by democratic facilitative leadership; and Level Two is characterized predominantly by democratic leadership with incidents of autocratic directive and laissez-faire or permissive styles.

An important aspect of the Lewin, Lippitt and White study is the aspect of the group response to the new leader that is a function, not of the new leadership style *per se*, but of the inherent compatibilities and incompatibilities of the new leader's style with the old. This is an aspect that is not often understood by therapists as they take over another therapist's group. They may be well aware of the situation that we have discussed in the issues of substitution; facilitating the group's responses to the loss of their therapist. However, the need to pay attention to the transition in terms of therapist style of leading will probably be a new idea for many of our readers. The following is a simplified guide to the predictable results of leadership style changes.

Following an autocratic or highly structuring leadership style with a permissive style will almost certainly cause great anxiety, to which the group will respond with either exaggerated fight or flight defenses. Should the group regress to dependency and flight, then the continuing ambiguity of the laissez-faire and democratic style will almost certainly result in overwhelming anxiety to which the members will respond by dropping out of the group. Should the group respond with fight, the continuing ambiguity will almost certainly precipitate bitter scapegoating, with the loss of the scapegoated members, or reactive guilt and despair and depression together with the wish for another leader. This search for a new leader may remain within the group if the group is cohesive, or it may be acted out by members searching for outside leaders to follow.

In those cases when the autocratic structure has been particularly inflexible, the response will be powered with the same kind of energy that occurs when a lid is taken off a pressure cooker. In this case the new leader may be actively scapegoated in a premature authority issue for which the group has not had the opportunity of doing adequate preparation work. The therapist needs to treat this as a group emergency, emphatically and succinctly repeating the specific group dynamic that the group is acting out until the group can take it in and work with it. In this particular case it is unlikely that the group can work through the authority issue, and most probable that they need to resolve issues in the flight and fight phases in preparation for their barometric event.

Following the autocratic style with any other style except directive is the sequence that is most likely to get the therapist into serious trouble and that may jeopardize the existence of the group.

It is important that the new 'democratic' therapist provide a transitional structure which the group can use while they work with their response to the loss of their leader, their relationship with the new leader, and the resumption of the work of the group. The transitional structure will provide a flight-oriented group with boundaries for their anxiety and a focus for the analysis of their dependency wishes and fears; a fight-oriented group with a clear target against which to rebel, and perhaps also as a motivation toward work with power and authority.

However, there are other transitions which present some predictable difficulty. When a democratic style of leadership replaces a laissez-faire style of leadership, there is a stronger possibility that the group will act out whatever underlying dynamics existed under the group solution to the leadership style. The requirement that they put into words the underlying purpose of their behavior; that they examine and understand rather than act, may provide the group with great relief from the underlying group pressures that were manifested in acting out; or may challenge maladaptive but gratifying solutions that the group does not want to give up. In the first case, the group will most probably enter the flight phase. In the second case, the group will probably respond in fight.

An autocratic leader who follows a laissez-faire leader will probably provide the group with a structure that is sufficiently tight to prevent the group from acting out the underlying dynamics, and they will rather adapt their behavior in overt compliance to the new rules while they passively sabotage them. The major problem to be solved will be the resolution of passive aggression.

Whether an autocratic leader who follows a democratic leader will be accepted by the group will depend upon the phase of development that the group is in. In the flight phase, the autocrat will be welcomed as a savior; in the fight phase, he will be accepted as a focus for the dependent, aggressive-dependent and counterdependent forces in the group. It is unlikely that the group will be able to resolve the authority issue with an autocratic leader. Success for the new leadership will depend upon whether the resources that the leader possesses within his leadership style can be utilized by the group in their ongoing work, or whether the change in leadership will stimulate the group to regress and fixate, either in flight or fight.

The laissez-faire leader who follows a democrat may expect the group to scapegoat him or ignore him according to the developmental phase they are in. Acceptance of his leadership will depend upon the group's ability to generate experiences that are meaningful to them.

Problems in taking over the leadership of a group are not confined to the transitions that need to be made from one leadership style to another. As we mentioned in our opening paragraph, the leadership transition may well affect not only the group itself, but also the environment of which the group is a part. We close this section with the following narrative to illustrate issues that relate not only to the group, but to the milieu of which the group was a part. The successful transition of the therapist depended upon making a transition from the existing group norms to group norms more compatible with her own leadership style, as well as making that transition in such a manner that the impact that the group changes had on the group's environment could be accepted and supported.

Transition House was a live-in rehabilitation center for young adult alcoholics and drug abusers. It was staffed entirely by graduates from its program with the exception of a psychologist, a social worker and a part-time psychiatrist. The program functioned in a milieu therapy model with a one and a half hour gestalt therapy group three times a week. Due to the success of the program, the psychologist took on full-time administration duties, and brought in a group therapist, trained in our model, to replace her in group.

The group experienced predictable transition pains from the active, directive, gestalt model to the group-as-a-whole model. Particularly difficult for the group was the shift from the warm, self-disclosing, responsive gestalt therapist to the objective, non-reactive, group and individual responsibility focus of their new therapist.

The group began with the not unusual boundary incidents of lateness in arriving, bringing with them impediments from the outside world into group, like magazines, cups of coffee, cookies, cigarettes. The therapist, recognizing that the transition was going to be difficult for the group and concerned with the acting out that too much group ambiguity might precipitate, formalized some clear rules against which the group could focus its anger. These were the rules of no smoking, eating or drinking in group. The group retaliated by legislating a 'cigarette break', and, like the elevator group (see section on 'boundary behavior in groups'), proceeded to develop two groups: the therapy group and the cigarette-break group, each with different norms and goals.

The staff of Transition House also experienced difficulty with the new group therapy structure in that the new group therapist was not a member of the team, did not take part in the general life of the house, and did not encourage discussions about the individual group members' performance in the therapy group with the staff.

Different members of the staff would 'coincidentally' arrive during the group's cigarette break, to chat with them about group. It became clear to the group therapist that 'group psychotherapy' was on the way to becoming the scapegoat for problems in the milieu. Clearly it was important that the staff of Transition House should understand enough of the group method and its purpose to support it. Her first move was to get an invitation to a staff meeting to explain the group method. She explained that this method was designed to help group members confront their dependency and their issues with authority; that this was particularly appropriate with a drug-dependent population, and that it could be expected that the staff would be approached both covertly and overtly to sabotage this goal. She suggested that the staff should not schedule any competing activities for the group members during group time (which had been occurring), and that problems that began in group should be worked out between members in group, rather than be 'talked over' with staff members outside group. The staff agreed to support the boundaries between group business and not-group business.

However willing the staff were, the fact remained that the norms that were developing in the group were highly discrepant with the norms that had existed before in the group, and that continued to exist in the milieu. There was thus an ongoing tension between the group and the milieu. Specifically in the group, the therapist continued to encourage the exploration of blurred boundaries, unclear role relationships, and the purposes that obscuring served. The therapist consistently pointed out that rules that the group made for the group needed to be enforced by the group, and that when the group blurred the rules, they no longer had working means to achieve their goals. For example, the cigarette break served a purpose and function provided the group rules were kept. The break was taken when the whole group felt ready, and the whole group returned from the break together so that group work could continue. Thus 'rules' around the cigarette break were applied consistently to every member.

In contrast, in Transition House rules were frequently modified for individuals, and each individual was more or less successful in gaining special privileges without those privileges being clearly related to a therapeutic purpose or to the needs of the milieu. The milieu of Transition House contained much inter-member manipulation between all levels. For example, one group member was given individual therapy with the psychologist, even though individual psychotherapy was not part of the milieu therapy plan; sanctions were imposed for infractions of the law, and not carried out, members of the milieu had the responsibility of 'informing' on each other for infractions, and tended to 'inform' only on the unpopular members, while the staff tended to punish only the unpopular members and turn a blind eye to infractions of the more popular.

As the group progressed through the flight and into the fight phase of development, these issues surfaced in the group and were carried into the milieu. The group started to impose norms on its members which extended past the group and into the general milieu. When people were treated differentially by the staff, the differential treatment was raised as an issue in the weekly general meeting. The staff experienced themselves under pressure from the patients to set clearer and more consistent boundaries. Thus, when the group entered the developmental phase of issues with authority and power, they found ready support from their staff. The staff and patients drew up a petition for a more active, more educative, more directly 'useful' form of group psychotherapy, and requested a transactional analysis group model to be brought in. This petition was brought into group.

In confronting the therapist with the petition, the group precipitated its barometric event (see chapter 5). In their 'cigarette break' group, they shifted into the phase of enchantment, and returned for the last half of the group like conquering heroes. They were no longer in the least interested in substituting some other group model for 'their' group. The staff was left in the exposed position of championing a cause that had clearly more to do with their reaction to the therapist than the group's.

During the following week the group therapist again met with the staff to discuss the form of group therapy that she was using, and to explain the different phases that group could be expected to go through, as well as the different pressures that these phases would create on the staff to 'act out' for the group.

The above illustrates very well how, when the norms of a group are discrepant from the milieu in which the group functions, the therapist must be prepared to act as a facilitator and publicity agent for the group with the group's environment, if the environment is not to ally itself with the acting out of the group members. In this case the pressure to clarify boundaries and roles, to take responsibility for behavior and its consequences, and to refrain from escaping into ambiguity when confronted with issues in dependency threatened the entire milieu, of which the group members were one sub-group and the staff another. Through the changes in the group members, and through the careful management of the relationship between the group and the milieu, the norms of both the group and the milieu were modified in a therapeutic direction.

Boundary behavior in groups

It is not always appreciated what an important phenomenon boundary behavior is, and how much group process can get irretrievably lost when incidents that happen across the boundaries are not brought into group. The boundary of the group is the dividing line between 'group' and 'not-group'; 'in group' and 'out of group'. The major boundaries that serve as a demarcation between the group and the group's environment are time and space. Boundary behaviors are the incidents that occur as the thresholds of group time and group space are crossed.

Group therapists are frequently not alert to boundary behavior. This may well be because group therapists are not always good at keeping boundaries themselves. The group therapist who does not start and stop his group on time is blurring group time boundaries. The therapist who sits chatting with his group members before the group starts, or walks out with his group at the end, continuing to comment on the group interaction, is blurring group boundaries of time and space.

We have mentioned elsewhere that probably the best training experiences available to group therapists in group process are the Tavistock conferences (England) or A. K. Rice conferences (United States) that focus on issues of power and authority. At these conferences, time boundaries are maintained to the second. Some measure of the importance to group process that time boundaries can serve is illustrated by the following: at an A. K. Rice conference in Philadelphia attended by over eighty people, where boundary behavior had a major focus, the staff and two conference members arrived on time at the final meeting. Every other member of the conference arrived between one and three minutes late! In the discussion that followed it became clear that this breaching of the time boundary had been an unconscious acting out of the whole group.

The above example illustrates another important issue in boundary behavior, and that is that boundary incidents are not necessarily explained adequately in terms of individual dynamics, and are most often an important source of information about the dynamics of the group. This is not, of course, to say that understanding boundary incidents from the perspective of individual dynamics is not an important source of understanding. It is to say, however, that although boundary incidents may appear individualistic, they are always also closely related to the dynamics of the group, and a rich source of information about the group process. For example, in the case of one member who frequently managed to 'catch' one or the other of the co-therapists either before or after group in an attempt to 'gossip' about the therapists' outside life, the temptation was to interpret her behavior in terms of her strong need to have privileged information in order to maintain her feelings of self-worth.

When it surfaced in the group that the group membership as a whole were pairing and gossiping on the way in and out of group, as a defense against intimacy in group, all 'gossip' stopped, including hers. Thus the one member's individual need for 'privileged' information accounted for her particular manifestation of the whole group's resistance to intimacy through the distancing behavior of gossip.

The most interesting boundary phenomenon that we have witnessed occurs in what we call the 'elevator group'. There is only one single large elevator from the office where group is held to the ground floor. One group in particular have developed a strong 'elevator' group that has different norms from their 'therapy' group. The elevator group waits until all the group members have come aboard, stay together as a group until they reach the front door, and then maintain the group rule of 'no socializing outside group'.

There appears to be a selectivity of what elevator-group information is relevant to the therapy group and what is not. By and large, as far as we can tell without formally inquiring, it appears that all interpersonal incidents that contain either therapy group content or strong feeling are brought back into group, and all social chatter is exempt. Boundary incidents that occur on the way into the elevator and on the way out of the elevator are brought into group and discussed with the same attention and importance that issues within the group are given.

Seven different groups use the same elevator facilities. Only this group, however, indicates a clear elevator-group structure with all group properties including boundary incidents. It is perhaps no accident that this particular group struggled long and hard to develop the norm of not socializing outside. Their greatest area of ambivalence in their decision-making was whether or not they lost or gained more for the therapy group by the socializing incidents that occurred outside. It is possible that the elevator group provides them with the best of both worlds.

The group's careful attention to boundary incidents between the therapy group and the elevator group was an important aspect that ensured that the different goals of the two groups remained compatible with the overall therapy goals, if not within the strictest interpretation of the therapy group norms. Boundary incidents contain important information for the therapist. In the case of the elevator group, the group-that-formed-in-the-boundary appeared to represent a creative solution to channelling outside social material back into the group. However, it is important to analyze boundary incidents with care, as they are often symptoms of dynamic material that has not yet surfaced in the group and is being either 'taken' outside or acted out.

Boundary incidents can be divided into two kinds. First, there are those incidents which are primarily acting out behaviors which occur at the boundary of the group. For example, lateness is a boundary acting out phenomenon, as is leaving group in the middle of a session.

Second, a different and equally important aspect of boundary phenomena are those incidents in which information is transmitted (acts which in fact transmit information) from the group to the environment, and from the environment to the group. The clearest teaching example of this is the 'fishbowl' technique, in which a small group works in the center of the room, with an observing group sitting in a circle around it. During this exercise, there nearly always occur boundary incidents, in which members of the 'outside' group break their observing role, and enter into the work of the members of the 'inside' group. Members of the 'inside' group have two predominant responses. When the 'inside' group is engrossed in work, it will often continue to work without any conscious awareness that the outside group is attempting to get in. Other times the inside group will respond to the outside group, or will initiate the contact itself. This exercise illustrates clearly the relationship between the crossing of boundaries and other aspects of group process, like cohesiveness, norms, goal orientation and roles. The more cohesive the group, the less permeable are the boundaries (i.e. the less receptive it is to information). The more functional the norms, the sharper are the acceptable and non-acceptable behaviors at the boundaries.

The 'fishbowl' example above generalizes well to the real life boundary issues that occur when a group is subject to influence from its environment. We have discussed the importance in paying attention to the relationships between the group and its environment in the section 'taking over another therapist's group'.

This issue has also been discussed in this chapter in the light of the relationship between a therapy group and an in-patient unit.

From the aspect of boundaries, it is important to pay attention to maintaining clear boundaries that serve as a demarcation line between the group and the group's environment. Boundaries are the transition threshold which determine appropriate changes in behavior. Behavior that is appropriate in group is often not appropriate outside group, and vice versa. When people in the environment understand this principle they are then able explicitly to support and facilitate appropriate changes, and to differentiate between group members' behavior that is an acting out of issues in group from behavior that has a more general source. This is not to imply that inappropriate behavior should be condoned in the environment because of its relationship to the group, but rather that when the behavior is so related, environmental pressure can be brought to bear to encourage members to deal with the behavior in group, rather than acting it out inappropriately.

To summarize, when group boundaries are clear, even when a group appears to be a very strange phenomenon in the environment, there is a better chance that people in the environment can respect it. For example, group therapists take it for granted that a psychotherapy group will have the same room at the same time for the same duration each week. However, unless these boundaries are explicit to administrators and other workers in the environment, unwittingly there may be scheduling or priority conflicts within the environment that threaten to undermine the very existence of the group that the environment supports in principle.

Group size

We have come to prefer eight members in our groups, four men and four women. However, although this has emerged as our preference, we know of no theoretical grounds upon which to choose this particular number, and are aware that to some extent it is a matter of personal choice. Foulkes, for example, preferred seven.

We do know, however, the parameters below and above which the number of members in a group becomes a factor in the kinds of group dynamics that develop, and whether or not those dynamics serve the goal of therapy. If the group is either too large or too small, the number in and of itself makes for special problems.

The one-person, two-person, three-person and four-person too small group have characteristics that are similar, and also have some specific differences which make for specific problems in management.

The one-person group is particularly interesting from a theoretical point of view. It is, for example, perfectly possible to analyze an individual from a group frame of reference if the different identities within the person can become characterized as 'members' of himself. This is, in fact, done in transactional analysis groups and in gestalt group therapy with the multi-chair technique in which one person sets up chairs for his nurturing parent, critical parent, adult, adapted child, rebellious child, free child and little professor, and then proceeds to problem-solve his therapy issue, moving from one chair to another as he speaks in his different roles. Neither of us has observed this process with an eye for the group dynamics, but it is not facetious to suggest that they may well be in operation. However, for our purposes, the one-person group is a digression, as it will apply to group psychotherapy only when no members show up at all, and the therapist is left (just as in his worst anticipations) sitting alone in the group room being 'the group'.

The two-person group, or dyad, has in fact probably had more literature written about it than any other social science phenomenon. We refer, of course, to individual psychotherapy. It is fruitful, particularly in psychoanalysis and in psychoanalytically oriented psychotherapy, to analyze the treatment process from the framework of group dynamics. It is abundantly clear from this framework, for example, that psychoanalysis works because of the ambiguity of the analyst (group leader), and the concomitant regression on the part of the analysand (group member). It is also possible to listen to a psychotherapy patient's 'flight', 'fight' and 'pairing' free associations as resistances to the work of psychotherapy. For our purposes, however, the issue of a dyadic group is relevant to the specific case when only one patient turns up to group. The impulse for most group therapists is probably to call group off, as if 'the group is not here'. We do not do that. The 'group' *is* here. It exists within the designated boundaries of time and space. To the extent that one member can perform a role for the group, this member has, by coming. What is more, to the extent that one member can perform part of a role for a group, or be an expression of multiple roles, so this member can. We therefore hold group when 'only' one member turns up, whether we are serving singly as a group therapist, or in the co-therapy relationship. Group with one member can be very fruitful for the member. Typically it is a mastery experience, and tends to be part of the history of the group that the group refers to, and continues to learn from, long after the episode is over.

The one-member group does require some changes in technique by the therapists if the session is not to turn into a free-association session by the member. Thus we have found it appropriate to be more active in one-member groups, helping the member summarize his experience both in terms of himself and his own insight, and in terms of his membership in relationship to the other group members who, though absent physically, are present psychologically. (Indeed, groups do seem to have the phantom limb phenomenon, frequently keeping an empty chair for the absent member within the circle, and gesturing to it at the times when the member could appropriately join or benefit from the content.)

The three-member group in a psychotherapy group manifests much of the expected dynamics that have been explored, described and researched in group dynamics. A three-person group tends to break down into a 'pair and a spare'. The 'spare' is then relegated to audience, scapegoat or arbitrator, or is related to in a contending, competitive, co-operative, or combative way. When roles are stable, the predictability in the three-person group is high in terms of who will do and say what to whom. When roles are unstable, the communication pattern will be highly predictable, but who will play what part in it will not be.

The three-person group will provide excellent opportunities for the analysis of triangular relationships, including the most famous of all, the oedipal. We have found, however, that firm intervention on the part of the therapist is needed if the triangularity aspects of the dynamics are to be explored by the members. It seems that jealousy and rivalry toward one person by another is more easily analyzed in a larger group. In fact, when only three members arrive for group, because of vacation times, or other vicissitudes, the number is often quoted afterwards as ideal, in which great intimacy was experienced. It is probable that the denial of the threats inherent in the triangle relationship contributed to the 'good' experience.

The four-person group tends to stable relationships, frequently functioning as two sub-groups, one member of each sub-group carrying the work for the group. A four-person group can confront issues in group development.

A group of less than five, while often voiced as 'comfortable' by the members, tends in fact to intensify the merging and loss-of-identity fantasies to the point that most of the group dynamics can be explained in terms of defenses against closeness or regression to symbiosis. There is an immediate, observable issue in the normal course of cohesive development. In groups of four or less, and sometimes in groups of five where there is intensive pairing, cohesiveness either fails to develop past weak bonding (more usual in Level Two groups), or develops so strongly that the bonding serves to contribute to the group resistance (more usual in Level Three groups).

In the first case, where cohesiveness does not develop, the group will manifest much flight behavior, spurts of vicious fight behavior and a tendency to outside pairing. The authority issue, if it occurs at all, is more a manifestation of member fight or pairing than it is a group issue. These groups usually do not survive. The obvious response to the problem of an uncohesive small group is to introduce new members. The difficulty is to introduce new members in such a way that the group can integrate them. It is also difficult for a member to 'join' an uncohesive group. Nearly always the efficient response will be to disband the group and start again, with a group of five, six or more members. Members of the disbanded group are not inappropriate for this new group formation. The new group experience may very well become a good one for them.

In the second case, where the too small group supports its members in resistance, several characteristic and different kinds of phenomenon become manifest. First of all, because of its cohesive nature, whatever the group decides to do, it does with considerable hard-headedness. This includes developing maladaptive norms, absenteeism, fixation, repetition, any and all of the ills that psychotherapy groups suffer from. Absenteeism in the small, cohesive group is of a different nature from absenteeism in the cohesive group. In the non-cohesive group, absenteeism is listless, members forget the group night, are chronically late. In the cohesive small group, however, each absence will probably be surrounded by 'good' excuses. Members will phone and express their regrets, warn the group ahead of time, talk about their absence in the following group. Lateness also usually has a 'good reason', and lateness and absences become subject matter for the group; not in the sense of norm setting, as it is in developing groups, but in a repetitive way in which discussion serves fixation instead of change. The too small group tends to talk much and do little. It will discuss at length about what is good for the group, but tend to come to no conclusions that can be applied for the good of the group. Again, the solution is to add members. In the too small cohesive group, however, there is great resistance, usually well rationalized, to new members. Whereas the bonding in the non-cohesive too small group is so weak that there is little energy available for group work, in the cohesive too small group it is so strong that energy is locked too tightly in the bonding to be free for work. Thus, the group is characteristically repetitive, stereotyped, and very predictable.

An interesting and moving experience occurred when a strongly cohesive, too small group that had become reduced to three members agreed to take in three new members at once.

The group had spent many sessions coming to an agreement to accept new members at all, and many more sessions preparing for their coming. With great diligence the group attempted to anticipate all the problems that might arise both for themselves and for the new members, and to find ways that would both facilitate the comfortable entry of the new members as well as ways to communicate the specialness of the group's being.

The crucial session arrived. Three new members arrived. Only one of the three old members arrived. With great responsibility the token member carried out the group plan, welcoming the new members and presenting to them the 'rules' in an attempt to maintain the cohesiveness and structure. The new members were not interested in the 'old' group's rules. 'All that is, is now, and that is us,' they said. '*You* have an old group. We have this group, and we will make its rules.' In the sessions that followed the new group did. We do not know whether all groups of three who receive three new members would meld so successfully, or learn so much from the 'death' and 'birth' of a group. Nor whether, in all cases, the 'new' group would develop significantly faster than new groups do, with 'new' members being integrated significantly faster than new members usually are. We do know that in this one instance the hard, conscientious and somewhat painful work of the 'old' group, and the honest, confronting and supportive work of the 'new' members, formed a satisfying and hard-working new group.

Silence

Silence has many meanings. The first problem with group silence is to understand its meaning. The pause between experiences or emotions, the hiatus that follows a completed piece of work, or the quiet of preparation are not a group problem. These are working silences.

When a group uses silence as a specific behavior, however, there may be a group problem. The first diagnostic clue to a silence problem is the discomfort of the therapist. Particularly for the therapist new to therapy, or new to group therapy, silence in group can be experienced as a pressure to 'do' something. There is a basic question to be asked by the therapist of himself when the group is in silence and he feels pressure to 'do', and that is 'who owns the silence?' The answer is always: 'the group owns the silence'. This is a helpful question in that it reminds the therapist that his therapeutic task is not to make himself more comfortable but first to diagnose and then to decide whether or not to give voice to the silence or to sit with the group until the group can. For some therapists, silence is more difficult to endure than for others. Therefore, beginning the work of diagnosis may mean a difficult analysis, not only of his counter-transference, but also his own particular wishes and fears. Silence is a strong ambiguous stimulus to projection, and the therapist will experience the same pressure to defend himself against it that the other group members will be experiencing. By analyzing his own projections, the therapist may get his first clue as to what the silence is about.

The first fear for most therapists is that the silence will last for ever - or at least throughout the whole period of group. In reality, it is appropriate for the therapist to prepare himself to sit the whole group in silence if he diagnoses this as a useful therapeutic response. In the silences that we have experienced, we have, at times, not only been prepared to do this, but even expected that that was what we would have to do. An hour and a half is a long time to prepare oneself to sit with a silent group, particularly when one's own fantasy material should not be used as a relief from the pressure but as material for counter-transferential analysis. We have found it helpful to remind ourselves at this time that during the hundreds and hundreds of times that we have sat in silence, wondering if *this* is the group that will sit for the whole period without talking, the longest silence rarely persisted for more than twenty minutes to half an hour. In all our group experience, separately and together, we have never had a group that stayed in silence for the entire period.

The second useful fact about silence is one that therapists sometimes forget. However uncomfortable the therapist is through the silence, his discomfort will most probably not be as intense as the other group members' discomfort. This in fact is an important diagnostic question. If the therapist is in fact more uncomfortable than the other group members, the silence is probably directly related to him, probably related to aggressive or sexual wishes towards him, and most likely of all, those wishes will be related to the group authority issue. This first diagnostic question is relatively easy to answer for himself by observing the group. People betray the degree of their discomfort in their non-verbal behavior. Mild discomfort usually manifests interpersonally, and there will be covert glances and half smiles or shrugs or sighs, or a deliberate looking away from each other. These silences do not usually last long as group energy is still mobilized and available, and group content is usually just below the surface.

The preliminary sign of withdrawal is a shift of attention from people to things. There will be prolonged gazing out of the window, attempts to read the title of someone's book, preoccupation with fingernails, fiddling with jewelry or clothes, abstracted expressions and fidgeting. This kind of silence usually involves slightly more threatening material which is being defended against by displacement behaviors. This kind also is typically a short-term silence. However, occasionally this silence can be followed by a more complete withdrawal. This will happen when the material that the group is defending against has archaic elements, strong transferential elements, or content that has not been worked with in the group before.

There is no mistaking a withdrawn silence. Group members sit still as well as silent. There is little movement, and no eye contact. Clues to the content of the silence are subtler. When the group is in fantasy, the facial expressions are abstracted, but not frozen, and the group atmosphere is light. One of us experiences it as vaporous, rather like sitting in an early morning or late evening mist. Both of us experience strong pulls to drift into our own fantasies without analyzing them for their counter-transference content, as well as a tendency to 'forget' to monitor the non-verbal material of the group.

There is a different feeling to a group of people sitting silent with their own individual fantasies when the group is a Level One group. In these groups the atmosphere is not so much light as empty. We are not predominantly dealing with psychotic group silence in this section, because, from our framework, leadership of a psychotic group is geared to promoting interpersonal interaction and to discouraging fantasy, delusion and hallucination (see summary chart at end of chapter 4). However, in the discussion of a seriously withdrawn group that follows, the experience of sitting with the silence is not unlike that of sitting with a severely withdrawn, psychotic group. In a psychotic group the shift from the empty atmosphere of a fantasy withdrawal to a more regressed withdrawal will probably be experienced by the therapist as heavy, leaden, dense and impermeable. This same experience of density and impermeability also characterizes the withdrawn Level Two or Level Three group when the resistance is strong and the material against which the group is resisting is deep.

The source of diagnostic information about the silence in a group that has regressed to a deeply resistant withdrawal is: the group non-verbal behavior; the atmosphere in the group; and one's own counter-transferential response, in that order. We find that each type of silence stimulates, for each of us, different resistances in ourselves. It goes without saying that the most difficult counter-transferential reaction is to the deeply withdrawn group, because the counter-transference response is predominantly affective and not verbal. We each experience the same kind of reluctance when we need to reduce our resistance to deeply regressed patients in individual therapy in order to become available to them for a working alliance. This experience, difficult as it can be in individual therapy, is more difficult in group. Strong counter-transferential affective responses can be experienced like almost overwhelming fear or grief or rage, together with cognitive confusion, an uncertainty as to whether the fear or rage is an identifi-cation with the group's fear or rage, or whether it is a personal response to some other group dynamic that the group is expressing in their silence, like stubborn reactive resistance, murderous impulses, annihilation anxiety, intolerable abandonment.

These are the silences that are the most difficult to endure, the hardest to understand, and which stimulate the greatest impulse to intervene on the one hand with the least idea of how to intervene usefully on the other. These are also the silences from which it is probably most important to permit a group to emerge themselves. More likely than not the group will break the silence in a way which :s most appropriate to the group's ability to work with the threatening material. So often we have sat through a silence that is experienced almost as life threatening, only to find that the group, when it did break the silence, initiated work with such a trivial or light-hearted comment, discrepant to the experience that we ourselves had just endured, that our first thought was that *we* were crazy. Occasionally, however, a silence of this nature is shattered by an explosive reaction from one patient, unable to endure the pressure, who acts out the group issue rather than 'voicing' it. This can take the form of a scream of fear, a cry of pain, a precipitous rush from the room, or even an explosion of rage in which an object is broken. When one patient expresses the group issue in this way, shocking as it may be, it is again most often best to refrain from 'handling it' provided the group has developed a working potential.

The silence is a group property and so is the expression of that silence. At this point it is important to underline that it is best to refrain from intervening and to let the group regain its own equilibrium *provided the group has developed a working potential.* Just as with decision-making, where it is important to pace the nature of the decision to the level of decision-making ability that the group has reached, so this principle of readiness applies to all group-autonomous responsibility. Here, we underline the second principle of assessing group readiness: *the therapist is part of the group.* If the therapist is not ready in himself to permit the group to solve its problem, then the therapist should act unilaterally as 'leader', even if it means a regressive experience for the group that the group will subsequently have to work through. Therefore, it is only appropriate for the group to work through a group trauma without the active intervention of the therapist if the group has the working potential and if the therapist can support them in using it. This speaks to the issue of whether or not someone can get hurt in these deeply regressed silences that have the potential for ending traumatically. In our own experience, no one ever has. In our own judgement, on those rare occasions when we have heard reports that people have been injured in group, it has either been because the group was prematurely given responsibility for its own structure, without the preparatory group development work, or acting out was already a part of the group structure.

Two main approaches are open to the therapist once a decision is made to interrupt a group silence. The first is to ask a question, and the second is to make an interpretation. Questions are basically different formulations of the major issue: 'what is the problem that the group is attempting to solve through silence?' Interpretations can be of three kinds. There is the interpretation that 'reminds' the group of the group rules, the rule that group members are required to put into words what they are experiencing. This 'reminder' can be given as a super-ego comment 'the group is not giving voice to what is going on', or as an ego-supportive suggestion: 'one way of understanding the content and implications of this silence would be to share the fantasies that are going on at the moment'. Finally an interpretation can be given as an interpretation: 'the group wishes to withhold today'; 'the group, by saying nothing, is attempting to control the therapist'; 'the group has been struck dumb by their guilty thoughts'; 'the group's pleasure today is a silent secret', etc.

Which is better, silence, question, instruction, support or inter-pretation? The psychoanalytic approach is always that the therapist only intervenes if the patient is stuck, and intervenes only as much as is minimally necessary; the best most growth-producing work is always done by the patient himself. This principle applies particularly well at the group level. A request to consider the content of thought and fantasy is the more minimal approach; it appeals to the group level of the observing, co-operative ego, upon which analytic psycho-therapy depends. In contrast to the full interpretation, a request for psychic material, if successful, engages the group in the ongoing process of arriving on its own at the interpretation. Further, because of this approach the group therapist is in a position to help the group resolve the resistances against the content of the interpretation as the group moves toward it. This conforms to the proper sequence of analytic work, so thoroughly developed in the psychoanalytic theory of technique, i.e., analysis of resistance precedes analysis of under-lying content.

The silent member

Everything that we have said about group silence applies to the silent member. We have found that our impulse to personally intervene in a member's silence usually has more to do with our counter-transference than it does with the actual needs of the silent member. Through the years of our experience in groups, we have 'lost' two silent members. The first was predominantly passive, and had successfully resisted therapy of all kinds from her early teens. The second was vengefully, bitterly, angry. Even though he was able to talk and work and gain insight for short periods of time, his repetitive need to take revenge on the group and the therapists by a stubborn, resistive silence was greater than his ability to work through his pain.

Predominantly our experience with silent members is that a great deal of work has been going on during their silence. This is reflected by the following statement, made by a member who had been silent for eighteen months, to another, who talked a great deal. The talkative member had asked the group despairingly, 'how do I become a person?' The silent member replied: 'I'll tell you how to become a person. You sit silent for a long time. I stopped talking and sat silent for a long time and listened to my feelings, because when I talked, it was just a role I had played. What's the use of talking from a role? Now, when I'm not in touch with my feelings, I shut up, because what's the point of talking through the top of my head. There are two truths: the truth of your head and the truth of your feelings. And when the two meet, you give six weeks' notice.'

Chapter 9
Transference and counter-transference

This history of psychoanalysis can be said to have begun with Anna O.'s transference reaction to Breuer and Breuer's counter-transference response: immediate and total abandonment of the patient (and the field). While it required some years for psychoanalysis to fully appreciate the Breuer lesson, contemporary writers are quite aware of transference and counter-transference as they occur in individual psychotherapy, e.g. Giovacchini (1975), Langs (1978), Jacobs (1973), Khan (1973). We intend to describe in detail the importance of transference and counter-transference in group psychotherapy, following a brief discussion of their role in psychotherapy in general. Emphasis will be placed on those counter-transference issues which constituted a major theme in the preceding chapter. It is important to remind the reader that the purpose of this book is not to teach psychoanalysis but rather to describe its interfacing into group psychotherapy.

While it has not been the policy of the authors to define psychoanalytic terms in this book, the extraordinary importance of counter-transference requires that it be defined exactly, as it is used here and elsewhere in the book. Laplanche and Pontalis (1973) defined counter-transference as follows: 'the whole of the analyst's unconscious reactions to the individual analysand - especially to the analysand's own transference.' Following this line of thought it becomes clear that the personal analysis of the therapist is of crucial importance in first allowing him to have access to his own emotions and then permitting him to be aware of his own tendencies to distort and otherwise defend against stimuli provided by other people, especially patients.

It is the authors' opinion that the failure of psychotherapy, where it occurs, is largely due to two factors: ignorance on the part of the therapist (Kohut, 1971), which is correctable by further training, and failure to recognize and properly utilize counter-transference (Langs,

239

1978). At the latter's doorstep can be laid faulty selection of patients for psychotherapy by the therapist and choice of the wrong technical procedures as the treatment goes along. Counter-transference errors can be partially avoided by good supervision and/or a return to personal analysis for the therapist. Many psychoanalysts, in fact, regard proper clinical supervision as entirely devoted to analysis of counter-transference.

As in the case of counter-transference a clear definition of the term transference is in order, since its use constitutes a basic element of this book. Again quoting Laplanche and Pontalis (1973):

> For psychoanalysis, a process of actualization of unconscious wishes. Transference uses specific objects and operates in the framework of a specific relationship established with these objects. Its context *par excellence* is the analytic situation.
>
> In the transference, infantile prototypes re-emerge and are experienced with a strong sensation of immediacy.

Perhaps the element of this definition least explored has been the term 'relationship' and its interpersonal implications; in groups the opportunity for examining such interpersonal implications arises.

Following from the above definitions and discussion, the process of psychotherapy as understood and practiced by those who adhere to the psychoanalytic model takes place briefly as follows: the patient presents himself to a psychotherapist either on his own or another's recommendation. He is requested to explain in his own words and from his own point of view what troubles him and how he, the patient, might expect the psychotherapist to be of help in the matter. If treatment is mutually agreed upon after the period of evaluation, the sessions continue on a regular and more frequent basis. Because of the nature of the situation set up by the psychotherapist and the freedom of the patient to arrive at the material he discusses at his own pace and with as little censorship as he can manage, transference gradually takes place. The psychotherapist is more and more experienced by the patient, through displacement, not as he is, but as one or more stereotyped, infantile objects around whom the patient's unconscious conflicts revolve. Gradually the transference elements coalesce into the 'transference neurosis'. Unresolved conflicts have brought the patient into treatment and they are reduced or abolished through the interpretation and working through of transference and resistance.

Transference, as noted above, refers to the displacement of whole complexes of unconscious ideations and fantasies upon the person of the psychoanalyst. This process takes place just as readily in a group situation if the group is handled properly; it can be inhibited or watered-down in group psychotherapy by the same technical moves or errors that would deflect it or dilute it in individual psychotherapy.

The group situation sometimes changes not the *phenomenon* of the transference displacement but the *manner* in which it exhibits itself. In psychoanalysis the analyst gradually becomes the focus of all of the patient's transference phenomena: mother, father, siblings and significant others. In the group, especially where co-therapists are available, the various infantile objects and the whole complex of ideas attached to each do not have to be forced onto one individual; there are several people to choose among, and obviously some will have characteristics and behave in ways which make them more easily the object of specific parts of the patient's transference than others. While this poses some difficulty in the making of clear transference inter-pretations, because there are more actual resemblances between the original object and the transference object, these difficulties are minor. It also has some signal advantages. In psychoanalysis proper, the interpretation of transference and indeed the understanding by the analyst of what is happening, let alone interpreting it, can be made more difficult by the shifting nature of the transference. Is transference anger a derivative of anger directed at mother or father today, or grandmother? What imago is the souce of this or that superego attitude?

Where the transference is split among a number of objects within the therapy milieu, the nature of the patient's transference material can be very much easier to understand. This is because of the fact that the transference identity of several of the people in the group can be ascertained for each patient and that patient is highly likely to consistently project or displace onto a specific person that portion of the transference pertaining to a particular infantile object. In addition, these transference objects, in the form of other group members, are present simultaneously in the group milieu and are interacting. The patient, by observing these interactions, can gain access to material about the nature of the *relationship between his infantile objects* which is stirred up and made available as he is stimulated by and distorts the relationships and interactions between his transference objects in the group. Hence, a source of material not always readily available in psychoanalysis proper presents itself in a highly usable form to the group psychotherapist.

Furthermore, transference material is available at the group level as well as at the individual level described above. Because of the similarity of the emotional conflicts, frustrations, and disappointments experienced by patients, particularly where they are appropriately chosen for equivalence of ego level, it is possible for strong emotional experiences of a transference nature of one or two members to awaken those particular transference conflicts or disappointments in other group members as each individually experiences them – all variations on a theme, as it were.

The result is a group level issue, e.g., of oral dependency, castration anxiety, toilet training, etc. This easily observable phenomenon is, we believe, what the group analysis school would call 'resonance' (Foulkes and Anthony, 1965). Its interpretation on a group level can often take up one or more entire sessions, with the advantage that the group members get to experience a specific issue from many sides and often to work through more aspects of it at one time than could be accomplished in individual psychotherapy.

We now turn to transference as it relates to other group dimensions and themes. One or more theoretically different phenomena will occur simultaneously in a group, and the therapist must make a choice between which of them he will pay attention to, and which interpret, when the moment is propitious. The rule of thumb for making this choice is as follows: membership issues (group level) first, norms (group level) second, resistances (group level) third (often expressed as a norms issue), group level transference (resonance) fourth, partial group transference fifth, and individual dynamics only where the other levels are not competing. The order of intervention is not in any way to be viewed as rigid or ironclad. Should the therapist judge that the needs of an individual and the group would best be served by interpretation at the individual level, he must act thus.

Because of a complex array of defense mechanisms – character traits and attitudes, acting out behaviors, resistances, and non-verbal communications – it would be, at times, almost impossible to decipher the latent or hidden content of the patient's communications: this is where counter-transference comes in. By the process of free-floating attention, i.e., by listening to the patient while at the same time following his own associative train of thought, and experiencing the accompanying affect, the therapist comes to understand the unconscious messages being sent by the patient. A further quotation from Laplanche and Pontalis (1973) describes exactly what happens in the correct technical use of counter-transference:

To allow oneself to be guided, in the actual *interpretation*, by one's own counter-transference reactions, which in this perspective are often not distinguished from emotions felt. This approach is based on the tenet that resonance 'from unconscious to unconscious' constitutes the only authentically psychoanalytic form of communication.

The actual experience of this 'resonance', and its translation from phenomenological data to psychotherapeutic interpretation, was exquisitely described by Reik in his book *Listening with the Third Ear* (1948), and has probably not been improved upon since.

All of the above comes directly from the study of individual psychotherapy. Let us examine what happens in a therapeutic situation where there are nine or ten people instead of just two. At any given point in time, once group structure has been established and a group history exists, two things are occurring simultaneously within the group. A relationship exists between the group members and the therapists and this relationship is powerfully affected by developing and unfolding transference. This transference progresses from session to session almost as if there were no time intervals between sessions, and is exactly analogous to the emotional continuity of individual psychoanalytic psychotherapy sessions. At the same time, things are happening in the daily lives of the group members which stimulate elements in their unconscious psychodynamics and result in various derivative feelings about themselves and others. Such external events, and the affective states connected with them, may provide a good deal of the material (manifest content) discussed in group sessions, especially at the beginning of sessions. This, again, is very like a psychoanalytic session. Because of the particular transference state existing at a given time, external events may be reported in the context of expectations and unconscious fantasies based on the transference (latent content), i.e., the patient is expecting criticism, advice, indifference, sympathy, or whatever affective response the particular transference repetition (imago) he is experiencing would provide. The resulting 'resonance' from his unconscious is already somewhat in tune with the unconscious of the other members, since a group tends to experience its ongoing transference issues *as a group*, with each individual member sharing one or another level or aspect of that transference expectation. As the topic is discussed and responded to by the members the 'resonance' gets more and more congruent and both group authority and individual transference expectations become more specific.

The topic of discussion moves from the external events with which the session began, to the group itself. A strong affective mood (climate) develops and focuses increasingly on one or both of the authority figures who are also, simultaneously, parental transference objects (therapists). In a more defensive form it may displace to a group member. The power of this now greatly amplified 'resonance' cannot be overestimated as the example of the 'incompetent father' will illustrate (see pages 249–50). If an individual patient can provoke strong counter-transference feelings in a therapist, multiply that times eight for a minimal estimate of the counter-transference potential facing a group therapist. More realistically, consider that the pressures upon a deviant in a group are certainly not simply additive but are exponential. How easy it would be to get oneself off the hook by answering a simple question about why one did this or that or where one went on his or her vacation. 'The road to hell is paved with good intentions!' and the road leading to psychotherapeutic failure is most often paved with little erosions of the 'abstinence rule', or, in Langs' (1978) terms, little bends in the framework, i.e., unrecognized counter-transference.

As stated above, in psychoanalysis counter-transference is the resonance from the unconscious of the patient to the unconscious of the analyst. It needs to be clearly recognized that the unconscious of the group psychotherapist also 'resonates' in tune with all the other unconscious affects in the room. The special problem for him as for the psychoanalyst is the fact that he is almost always the object of powerful feelings, conscious and unconscious, on the part of the group members, which seek to influence his behavior in all sorts of therapeutic and anti-therapeutic directions for repetition or gratification. He is, however, the object of group pressure on authority figures at the same time as he is individually pressured by member transference expectations.

If there is a co-therapist, the therapist who is presently the object of group pressures is not a lonely deviant, but instead feels supported and can rely upon the other therapist to help the group to see the underlying transference elements via interpretation. The safeguard against counter-transference errors provided by such an arrangement, *when the co-therapists have a healthy working relationship,* is very effective.

The final step in resolving each particular group issue comes when the interpretation of group behavior, both verbal and non-verbal, is made by the group or to the group. Such an interpretation will of course be made many times in slightly altered forms; this is the 'working through process' so familiar to the psychoanalytic psychotherapist. Often the individual transference dynamics are then interpreted to as many individuals as are ready for that level of interpretation in the course of the same session.

Just as in the case of individual psychotherapy, often the only clues to the locus of unconscious conflicts being expressed by the group are the free associations of the psychotherapists. It should be made quite clear that in the absence of confirmatory verbal material from group members such data as the unsupported associations of the group therapist can provide a temptation for projective identification by the therapist onto the group or individual members. This is the other edge of the counter-transference sword: unrecognized and hence potentially destructive counter-transference.

Nevertheless, not only the free associations but the affective states connected with them, alert the psychotherapist, sometimes painfully, to the latent content of the group's behavior. This is the point at which recognized counter-transference is instrumental in the group's progressively uncovering and working through the members' pathogenic conflicts especially as they reveal themselves in transference. This is best done when the associations of the therapist then organize the previous confusing data into a meaningful context. This is also the point at which the therapist(s) can be seduced or frightened by counter-transference and proceeds to miss the point or, worse, to bungle the treatment entirely.

There is a group or systems level construct which we call role (see chapter 2) which is independent of the individual at either person or member level and which is a function of the group dynamics. The phenomenon co-ordinated to this construct is manifested in much the same way as counter-transference; in fact the group therapist who falls victim to it experiences it as an inexplicable counter-transference if he attempts to understand it from the individual perspective. It becomes meaningful only when viewed from the perspective of group. A part of the therapist that can be called his group part perceives directly or derivatively the latent content of the group behavior and makes interpretations of the group behavior on the basis of these inner experiences. To the degree to which these personal experiences can function as an organizer of previously confusing or misunderstood group behavior, the therapist can be confident in making an interpretation which is not based on his own distortions induced by group forces.

We have said above that counter-transference is the most valuable technical implement that the psychotherapist possesses, *if he knows how to use it*. We have also said that it is the cause of therapeutic error on the part of otherwise well-trained psychotherapists who would not be expected to err out of lack of training.

Just as in individual psychotherapy, where the transference may well begin when the patient first hears the therapist's name, and certainly when the patient makes the initial contact; so in group psychotherapy the transference begins before the patient enters group.

The following is an example of transference and counter-transference in individual therapy influenced by pending group placement:

Zoe, a 27-year-old unmarried woman, had been in intensive psychotherapy for several years. She presented many neurotic features, most of which had been worked through during the course of treatment. Because of some unresolved characterological problems which were not readily amenable to therapeutic intervention, her psychotherapist recommended group therapy in lieu of her regular individual sessions. It was carefully explained to her that honest feedback from her peers would be very useful in her attempts to understand her social frustrations and failures. She apparently readily accepted the new arrangements and the reasons for them.

During the two months' time which elapsed while she was waiting the expected opening in the group, some curious but not unusual things developed in her individual sessions. She began talking as if she no longer needed therapy, while at the same time describing more acting-out behaviors; there was nothing available to interpret, however. Two weeks before she was to join the group, she discussed with the therapist her inclination, which she had not carried out, to act out some regressive urges. The therapist found himself feeling angry and critical toward the patient; this attitude was somehow conveyed to the patient who then became defensive and uneasy. After the session, the therapist asked himself why he had allowed himself to behave as a punitive superego, instead of as a psychotherapist, but could not make anything of it.

During the next session nothing came out that clarified this therapeutic error. The following session was different, however, the patient discussed taking a friend to dinner. Again the therapist found himself feeling (and communicating) a punitive, angry attitude; this time in regard to taking people out to dinner when she was in financial straits and attempting to free herself from a long-term dependence on parental funds. The patient then proceeded nervously to make very clear that she was indeed handling her money extremely thriftily and well.

The therapist at this point said to himself that he had now been angry twice; each time he had acted out the counter-transference and then been informed by the patient that he was not accurate in his reading of the situation. She had made him angry at her and then foolish; she might well be angry at him, too. She recognized some feelings of guilt with perhaps a 'little' anger, but couldn't locate any reason for the anger. She was reminded, she said, that she was frightened about the coming group experience and had been having second thoughts about her need to continue in therapy.

She then recalled that it was the therapist's suggestion that she attend the group. Next she remembered that she had lately been frightened of group therapy because she imagined that her individual sessions would henceforth be taken up with what went on in the group. The therapist then reminded Zoe that one area they had never really discussed was the arrival of her only sister on the scene when she was three. She began to cry and became quite upset, saying she thought the therapist would be angry because she did not want to share him with the group; this was connected to a past conflict over sharing her parents with the new sister. She left feeling relieved and ready to face both the group therapy and unresolved elements of her intense sibling rivalry.

If the therapist had not followed up the counter-transference in the content of the group placement, and pointing the interpersonal consequences of it out to her along with her role in activating it, the transference fantasies relating to the birth of her sister would not have come to light, and she might have terminated psychotherapy rather than re-experience the traumatic situation with not one, but seven, new siblings. One such example should make it abundantly clear that patients do not come into group therapy lacking in already mobilized transference expectations. This example also points out the importance of a psychoanalytic training for group therapists.

The difficulty in reporting failure to recognize and utilize counter-transference becomes clear as soon as one thinks seriously about the problem. How can one report what one has failed to see? This simple fact probably accounts for the failure of psychoanalysis to fully appreciate the importance of this phenomenon despite Freud's recognition of it early this century (Freud, 1910). Realization that psychotherapy is an interpersonal process – a *relationship* – as well as the overwhemingly apparent emotional demands encountered in the psychoanalytic treatment of psychotics, changed all that. The experienced psychoanalytic psychotherapist can, in hindsight, discover his counter-transference errors, either because they were not grave enough to destroy the treatment and so came to light when he got a second change, or because he recognizes belatedly his failure to understand the crises which resulted in premature termination. An example of the latter kind has been selected. While this example is not in a group context it is clear-cut in pointing out the necessity for psychotherapists in any modality looking to counter-transference issues.

Gina, a 28-year-old unmarried woman, had been in treatment for something less than two years. She originally appeared to be fairly neurotic with some characterological features. At the point in time that concerns us here, she began telling the therapist anxiously that he wasn't there when she, from the couch, couldn't see him. The therapist, having previously misinterpreted some memories of night fears as oedipal, failed completely to understand what Gina was trying to convey in the transference and was not able to help her to resolve that anxiety. Things settled into a therapeutic stalemate, thereafter, and the patient left treatment. While many gains had been made in her Gina was clearly not finished. She had been attempting to verbalize early anxiety about object loss connected with her mother's habitual disappearance from the house when Gina was otherwise occupied and not in the same room with her mother. 'When I can't see you, you're not there.' The failure of the psychotherapist to understand because his own internal process was triggered resulted in incomplete success in treatment.

Before providing examples from group psychotherapy, a brief reminder seems to be in order. When we are talking about psychoanalysis or psychoanalytic psychotherapy we are describing transference and counter-transference in the usual way.

In the case of group psychotherapy, the problem becomes more complex. As we pointed out above there are two major theoretical perspectives in the therapy group:

1　the individual perspective which is called by us 'person' and 'member' and in which psychoanalytic constructs retain their appropriateness; and
2　the group perspective which is called by us 'role' and 'group', in which group process or systems constructs become more useful, which saves us from the necessity of redefining psychoanalytic terms to fit the group perspective - such a redefinition would only serve to confuse the reader.

Wherever below group phenomena are described in psychoanalytic terms, this automatically can be taken by the reader to refer to the individual perspective, whether person or member, and where other than psychoanalytic terms are used, it can be assumed that we are referring to role or group perspective. Thus psychoanalytic theory is used to describe the 'visible' group and group dynamics to describe the 'invisible' group.

Turning now to examples from group psychotherapy, it is necessary to keep in mind two characteristics of group situations which affect the group's reaction to leadership and the therapist's perception of group pressure. First and most important is the powerful quantitative increase in the force of emotions that can be directed toward *any* group member by a majority of the group. While the target of such behavior is most likely to be the therapist, the phenomenon is also well known in the group behavior called 'scapegoating' (see chapter 5). It is often intentionally used and directed at individual members by group leaders in 'instant intimacy' groups and other popular forms of group endeavor. Where such a group force is used to break down healthy or necessary defenses, it is highly questionable; this is most especially true in the group therapy of drug addicts wherein a variation legitimized by the term 'hot-seating' has often been the technique of choice. A psycho-analytic description of such behavior, by leaders and therapists, would say that powerful, sadistic and controlling counter-transference needs are being met at great expense to the victims of the group pressure to conform.

A second characteristic of therapy groups is the relative ease of understanding transference phenomena once they are manifest; this is especially the case where co-therapists are leading the group. Transference objects tend to be stable because there are many members and each can, and tends to, become individually associated with specific imagos.

A case of the successful use of counter-transference in the group follows. One afternoon the group was discussing parents and authority figures. Betty opened with a description of the telephone conversation that had taken place with her mother two days before. She angrily and bitterly recounted all the mistakes, errors, and failures her mother had inadvertently revealed during the course of their talk. A second member, Fred, was quick to take up the topic, citing examples of his own mother's misjudgment and her ability to disappoint him consistently. Joanna was angry at her work supervisor's failings and described how she had to make right his incompetent tactics of supervision in regard to her own unit. All of this was experienced as frustration, without accompanying insight. The theme continued with strong affect attached to almost all of the associations of all of the members.

After an hour or so of this (this group runs for one and a half hours) a curious and, from the therapists' points of view, painful and funny set of events took place. One therapist, noting that the late afternoon sun was shining in Betty's eyes, attempted to 'unobtrusively' pull the louvered blinds to a better angle for Betty. The blinds rattled and banged, the sun shone more brightly in Betty's eyes, and the group's attention was completely distracted from its topic. The more the by now quite embarrassed therapist tried to right things, the more noise there was and the worse the situation became; the blinds, although both simple to operate and thoroughly familiar to the beleaguered therapist, remained infuriatingly uncontrollable. The group focused its attention with contempt and disgust upon the struggling therapist and made several sarcastic comments which made it abundantly clear that the group thought the therapist was incompetent in every way.

The member beside the therapist seized the cords, whipped the blinds instantly into a desirable adjustment, and the group returned to its business. The therapist, slumped dejectedly in his chair, next attempted to lean his chin on his hand, a gesture he had managed several thousand times in the past. Not this time! His elbow slipped off the chair arm, and he slid sidewise, almost falling out of the chair. The group snickered derisively and pointedly ignored him from there on.

While this was going on, experienced like a piece from a nightmare by the offending therapist, the co-therapist was practically hysterical with suppressed mirth. The group members let it be known that they were not impressed with that therapist's behavior either.

Suddenly the meaning of his strange incompetence dawned on one of the therapists. The group was in a transference phase where the incompetent parents of adolescence were a source of both rage and pity. But *such was the force of the transference affect building and resonating through the group, that the therapists had acted out the group's wish.* The group wanted the therapists to be incompetent parental figures, as they had experienced their own parents to be during adolescence. This interpretation was quickly made at the first opportunity; immediately the group's belligerent and condescending attitude disappeared, to be replaced with linked-up affect and memory. The sense of inadequacy just as quickly vanished in the therapists. That most necessary step which provides for real ego growth and for potential behavioral change had been taken as a result of the trans-ference interpretation. Only thus can individuals understand the degree to which present functioning and experience are interfered with by unfinished business from the past; unconscious is made conscious. Parenthetically it must be noted that as in individual psychotherapy, no single interpretation is that powerful in and of itself; its effect was the result of consistent interpretations cumulating over a period of time.

An example of counter-transference not fully seen and understood during the session is next. Some introductory remarks are in order, however. Although the same marked responses to accurate transference interpretation are seen in group psychotherapy as in individual psychotherapy, the converse is not as likely to happen. Due to the network of libidinal ties that exist in a therapy group, the treatment of the individual member is not as likely to be fatally disrupted or prematurely terminated by unrecognized counter-transference. This is especially the case when there are co-therapists. In individual psychotherapy the necessary splitting of the ego into observing and experiencing parts is at times more difficult because everything of a transference nature revolves around the same person. In the group, the erring or non-empathic therapist does not completely or even to a major degree represent the whole of the therapy experience. Further, co-therapists functioning effectively as a team are better able to unmask and correct counter-transference failures. Some of the above elements figure in our example.

Phyllis opened the session with a series of events which began with an important social success followed by a description of how she had burnt herself seriously in a kitchen accident and had to be taken to the nearest hospital emergency ward by a neighbor; her husband was away at the time. She was angry that he failed to notice the bandage on her hand when he returned. She then added the description of an incident wherein he had turned off the light in the cellar while she was doing the laundry; this had occurred immediately at the end of a conversation in which she had criticized him over not changing the bath towels after he used them; 'he is too passive to change the smelly towels on his own', complained Phyllis.

Fred then informed the group that he was feeling good about his recent job successes and about a new girl friend. Next, he talked about a business venture someone was urging him to undertake, a venture which would call for extensive use of Fred's professional skills at no fee. Fred experienced some conflict about making a commitment to this scheme; typically for Fred, however, the compromise form in which this conflict was expressed was as criticism of himself for being 'afraid to get involved'.

During the discussion centering around Phyllis's distress and compaints the therapists were active to a degree that was unusual, pointing out things that the group was perfectly capable of seeing for itself.

In Fred's case, it was clear to the group that he was about to stifle his perceptions of potentially being exploited (the source of his conflict) in order to repeat a familiar pattern in which he again ends up thoroughly exploited and feeling bitter about it. Again, the therapists were busy doing things that were well within the capabilities of the group members.

One of the co-therapists, feeling uncomfortable about the excessive number of interventions they had made, pointed out to the group that the therapists seemed to be extraordinarily active during this particular session. The same therapist then experienced great difficulty in not continuing to make comments at the same rate as earlier in the session; it was a sensation like keeping one's feet braced against the current. The therapists were not able to fully resist the pressure to talk and because of that inability the group did not come to understand their need to receive 'help' from the therapists. As in individual psychotherapy gratification in group psychotherapy leads to fixation, not insight!

The value of the co-therapy method was never better demonstrated than in the post-group discussion that day. By sharing their subjective experiences, the power of the force toward activity generated subtly by the group's needs became really clear to both therapists, each was not left to wonder if it was simply his or her own need to be active unrelated to the group process of the day. Together they were able to arrive at the dynamics of the group itself. Although this recognition came too late to make an interpretation which would benefit group members that day it would be useful next time. The group was clearly demonstrating a need to withdraw from new and successful behaviors, which aroused unconscious anxiety, by regressive acting out of passivity and helplessness, e.g., Phyllis's burn and subsequent need for treatment, Fred's entering into an exploitive situation again; the transference element had been the regressive wish to be passive and be taken care of by parents (therapists) in order to put an end to the anxiety aroused by successful activity. For some members this anxiety was at the level of individuation versus fear of object loss, for others it was castration anxiety with a fear of loss of love. This example illustrates how the *group-level* conflict between passivity and activity, with the wish for the leaders to take over, can express member dynamics from different levels of *individual* pathology. Fred was re-experiencing a pre-oedipal level struggle with unfinished individuation-separation best described by Mahler's rapprochement conflict (Mahler, 1968); Phyllis a neurotic-level early oedipal position where success with others aroused fear of mother's jealousy, the other members of the group experienced the group conflict at that particular pathological level where each found himself or herself to be fixated in regards to activity versus passivity.

The co-therapists were also able to fruitfully examine their individual level counter-transference needs, which the group pressure aroused and successfully exploited to serve the forces of resistance rather than to foster therapeutic insight.

The next two clinical vignettes provide an interesting and instructive contrast between co-therapy as an immediately useful protection for the group against counter-transference, and co-therapy when the therapists are caught in mutual counter-transference which only serves to confirm the group in its repetitive distortions.

An important way in which counter-transference in the group differs from individual psychotherapy, is that it can be more difficult to identify counter-transference towards a single member. In the following example, where the therapist acted out counter-transference towards an individual member, the therapist was particularly vulnerable to the counter-transference because the group as a whole was working with narcissistic pain. Thus, in the following acting out of transference there is manifested both the counter-transference response to the individual, and the counter-transference response to the group. The group therapy room was heated from two sources, the steam heat radiator, and a supplemental space heater that could be controlled within the room. One member whose neurotic compromise took the form of chronic complaints, and who was particularly vulnerable to narcissistic hurt, had recently oscillated between intensified complaining and helpless pleading, stated that she felt cold. The therapist 'found' herself out of her chair, fumbling with the cord of the heater, attempting to disentangle it from around patients' chairs in an effort to connect the heater and turn it on. Suddenly 'coming to' she found herself the focus of an amused and bewildered group, and heard herself say in distress, 'Dick, what am I doing here?', thus scoring two 'firsts' in her ten-year-old role as co-psychotherapist in this particular group. It was the first time she had left her chair to 'fix' something and the first time she had directly cried out to her co-therapist for help. In counter-transference to the 'helpless' aspect of the patient, she was unable to 'withhold' the 'warmth' and 'nurturing' that the patient and the group 'needed'. Her behavior served as a basis for her co-therapist's intervention which redirected the group to exploration of its associations to this event.

The second example illustrates the power of counter-transference reaction to group that was acted out minimally in group and intensively in the debriefing, or processing, session afterward.

The group was in acute narcissistic pain, where anything less than experienced perfection was felt as a humiliating loss of face. Interventions were particularly difficult to make in the group, since they tended to be experienced as narcissistic wounds; and the therapists had spent considerable time discussing different ways of wording the interventions so that the group could experience empathy rather than injury. In this particular group session the group was blaming one therapist bitterly for being cold, unyielding, ungiving, frustrating, rejecting and uncaring: the 'dry tit' and worse – never satisfied, never praising, always expecting more however hard they worked, however much they did: voraciously demanding. The therapist, feeling the impact of the thrust much as one experiences a projective identification in individual therapy but with the magnitude increased by resonance, searched for the familiar non-verbal support of the co-therapist, while he did the familiar and expert work of 'mid-wifing' the attack and helping the group to verbalize the archaic version of their fantasies.

This team work, so familiar over the years that we have worked together, serves each of us as a source of comfort and strength; strength, because the group's work gets done more easily when one therapist sits as the object while the other therapist takes the role of facilitating the insight into the group conflict with the object; comfort, because of the knowledge of one's partner's empathy, expressed verbally in many debriefing sessions when the 'attacked' therapist restores ego equilibrium and massages the inevitable narcissistic hurts associated with psychoanalytic psychotherapy.

This time, however, as the beleaguered therapist looked for the non-verbal support, she found none. Instead, she experienced her co-therapist as 'joining' the group in the attack, 'heard' him not only empathizing with the group's feelings of deprivation, but reminding them that in fact they had a 'right' to their anger because they had suffered 'real' deprivation, from a truly depriving object. The attacked therapist experienced herself as being described as 'the castrating female'; and felt sadistic rage in response. Her version of the proper intervention would have been to interpret the projected oral sadism of the deprived infant, splitting the object into 'bad' therapist and tenuously experienced 'good-but-injured' group. However, falling back on technique she maintained her role of 'passive object' and did not act out towards her co-therapist or the group. She endured the long minutes to the debriefing session in order to work it through with her co-therapist.

At the debriefing session, she assailed her co-therapist with a barrage of questions which her co-therapist experienced as a sadistic attack. She experienced his responses as further accusations that she was in fact castrating. Although neither had insight into his or her counter-transference acting out, both knew that they were somehow acting out in roles for the group. Their meeting ended without resolution at that point. There are times when co-therapy results in more pain from the counter-transference experience in the short run; provided that the co-therapists are committed to resolving such problems, it is more successful in the long run.

The following week when they met over lunch they were able to work out all the complex dynamics and gain the extra insight into the process of the group. Two aspects of transference and counter-transference were in fact in play. The members' experience of deprivation towards the depriving 'mother' was compounded by the rage at the sadistic mother who castrates the father and thus renders him useless as an idealized object or an object for identification. The attacked therapist, taking comfort at first from the fact that her co-therapist could emphatically help the group explore their deprivation feelings, had been shocked when she heard him 'verify' the feelings, and felt him join in the attack. In the post-group session, she acted out the group's perception of her, while he in turn acted out the group's need for protection in their autonomy against the sadistic, rejecting mother. Once again we are in awe of the power of the group.

Parenthetically, a tendency to experience different aspects of the group dynamics is not unusual in co-therapists, and can well be a major asset of the co-therapy relationship. One source of the difference comes from the counter-transference reactions to a split of transference; the most obvious example being when one therapist is experienced by the members (and experiences himself) as good and the other is experienced, and experiences, being bad. The other source of difference is each co-therapist's psychodynamics, which tend to resonate to different themes. This tendency does not mean that the areas of understanding are not in fact frequently reversed, nor that patients, individually and at the group level, do not transfer all aspects of their dynamic conflicts onto both of us, separately and together. What it does mean is that in debriefing sessions, each therapist tends to rely upon the other as an expert in that particular area, while continuing to be surprised and to surprise by often possessing the insight themselves that they were expecting from the other. Indeed each therapist does feel more 'in tune' with the area he has specified as his own.

To final clincial example, above, indirectly points to these areas of competence considered by the authors to be necessary for the adequate performance of group psychotherapy.

It is clear that a person wishing to perform group therapy needs to be learned in the dynamics of groups-as-groups and thus thoroughly familiar with the manifest forms in which latent group affects are expressed. We hope that we have made it abundantly clear that the manifest content of group discussions is as likely to parallel the underlying latent concerns of the group as are the words of individuals likely to conceal latent regressive wishes, this is particularly true of individuals and groups in stressful situations such as psychotherapy. We hope that it is evident that the interpretation of group level contents and resistances must precede individual level, i.e., psychodynamic, interpretations, and that training for such intervention is a must for successful group psychotherapy.

The ultimate benefit for the individual patient in group psychotherapy as in individual psychotherapy is derived from working through his own psychodynamics. This can only be done where the therapist is able to help the patient in that process by coming to understand the patient's psychodynamics. At some point, the Freds must understand the separation–individuation level of their activity–passivity conflicts and the Phyllises must explore their oedipal anxieties. Therefore, group psychotherapists must understand the psychodynamics of individuals just as thoroughly as they understand group dynamics. Further, they need to know what individual psychodynamics are potentially expressed in various typical group conflicts and phases. And they must be as technically skilled in the interpretation of one as the other. They must also know when to make interventions on the level of group dynamics and when on the level of individual dynamics.

Group psychotherapists, in order to be able to consistently avoid counter-transference errors, must have worked through their own psychic conflicts and be thoroughly familiar with their own needs, this must be so at a group level as well as at an individual level. Hence, candidates should undergo psychoanalysis or intensive psychoanalytic psychotherapy, and should experience prolonged membership in a group whose function is to thoroughly explore the dynamics of the group. Both experiences should be thoroughly integrated with intellectual mastery of psychodynamics and group dynamics; hence group psychotherapists must have considerable formal training in the two disciplines. This is not a prescription that is easy or quick but it is more likely to result in adequate psychotherapeutic competence.

Chapter 10
The co-therapy issue

The recent literature on group psychotherapy has, on the whole, neither praised nor encouraged the use of co-therapists in the group. An amusing, and to us extraordinary, comment on co-therapy was made by an instructor in a graduate class on group therapy recently, who told the class that co-therapy was only practiced by those who were afraid of the group (personal communication). A second indicator of the trend to discourage co-therapy can be noted in the virtual absence of this topic from the program of the American Group Psychotherapy Association's 1976 convention; one workshop out of the entire program was devoted to co-therapy issues, and that single exception was an experiential assay into the specific interpersonal problems of specific pairs of co-therapists, not a discussion of the basic theoretical and practical issues of co-therapy, and in the 1979 convention even this topic had been dropped.

The present authors, in contrast, have found the technique of co-therapy very rewarding, and sometimes far more effective than individual group leadership. We, therefore, want to share our enchantment with the method in a systematic and comprehensive way with others in the field.

In this chapter we will describe the advantages and disadvantages of the modality and give our unsupported (and unsolicited) opinions as to the less publicized reasons that might motivate some group therapists to deprecate or avoid the rigors of a co-therapy experience.

The advantages that we find in the co-therapy mode will be presented first, followed by the disadvantages. Wherever there are two sides of the coin, i.e., wherever the potential advantage has an equally clear potential for mischief if the situation is allowed to develop in the wrong direction or is mishandled, the advantage and its alternative disadvantage will be presented together. An example of such a case is where mutual support between therapists is replaced by competition or conflict.

257

1   Diagnosis is greatly facilitated by the ongoing consultation of two diagnosticians whose separate points of view and necessarily different sensitivities can sometimes make for far more comprehensive clinical pictures of individuals and of the entire group. The mandatory post-group processing of the data by a pair of co-therapists not only leads to continuously correcting and more and more finely focusing and ongoing diagnostic picture, but provides something unique in psychotherapy – the opportunity for regular case conference after each and every session. Such a luxury is ordinarily only available during the supervision of a therapist-in-training, and then only sometimes.

In a number of instances, one or the other of us has successfully argued for retention of a patient at a given level, when the other thought that the level was too high. Retention at the higher level turned out to be beneficial to the patient in most cases. Where transfer from a Level Three group to a Level Two was mutually agreed upon, it was comforting to have thoroughly processed the proposal to transfer and to feel maximally assured that it was not motivated by counter-transference.

2   Clarification of transference issues in the group is greatly facilitated by the availability of separate parental transference objects (imagos). The patients do not have to shift one person into and out of mother and father roles, instead they are more likely to settle on one therapist as one parental imago and the other as the second, and to stick to that position. Further, the patient can easily project or misunderstand interactions between the therapists, an opportunity which provides clinical data of a kind never clearly available where only one therapist is involved in the treatment. The patient can do such things as attempt to take sides or to manipulate one therapist against the other in repetition of early familial situations. Several patients can witness the same event and report different and conflicting versions of it, e.g. 'they were fighting' – 'Oh no! They were manipulating us.'

In the case of strong transference reactions such as love or hate, the less cathected therapist can help the group or its members to work with their strong and threatening feelings. This relieves a particularly difficult therapeutic bind which can occur when help is needed in expressing hate and rage and such help is unacceptable from its transference object; where there is only one therapist such help may be temporarily unavailable because it is unacceptable, and important opportunities for growth are missed or delayed.

3   Fewer interruptions to the treatment process occur with co-
    therapists because the co-therapists can arrange to take vacation
    time separately, and are not likely to be sick at the same time. There
    are several benefits that accrue from such a situation: feelings
    about the absence of one parental object can be explored *in vivo*
    with the help of the group and the therapist who is present; the
    therapist can feel free to be sick or take needed time off knowing
    that the group is not left in the lurch at a bad moment, the thera-
    pist's income is not depleted by being sick so he does not attend
    sessions when he is too sick to be of use to the group and/or will
    only make his illness worse, leading to prolonged absence in the
    future or to guilt on the part of group members.
4   Failure of either therapist to understand the material in any given
    session is less likely to result in unnecessary frustration or pro-
    longed therapeutic stalemate, because it does not usually happen
    that both therapists are equally at sea; the one who recognizes
    what is going on can make the necessary interventions. This point
    raises the question of overlapping counter-transference blind
    spots; if such exist, the possibility is that neither will understand
    what the material means. Our personal experience to date indicates
    that the probability of such blind spots is more theoretical than
    empirical. This, however, is likely not to be the case with un-
    analyzed therapists.
5   Closely allied to point 4 is the advantage resulting from differences
    in underlying psychodynamics between co-therapists. For one
    therapist to resonate, for example, more closely with validity and
    the other with anality provides complementary understanding of
    different aspects of the group and its members; such complemen-
    tarity is invaluable both during the therapy session and in discussions
    afterwards.
6   It is generally easier to keep all the places in a group filled. This is
    because there are two therapists available to supply people who
    could fill a vacancy. A single therapist might be more tempted to
    rationalize the inclusion of a motivationally or diagnostically
    inappropriate patient because he had less of a pool of potential
    patients to choose from. Since groups have a proper, i.e. most
    productive, size, maintaining that size is important. However,
    proper group size is only useful if it includes members who can
    provide the necessary resources to the level of goal resolution
    appropriate to the particular group.
        An added advantage is that the co-therapist is available for a

second screening of a prospective group member, when necessary. Should there be a question concerning the person's appropriateness for a particular level of group functioning, for example, a screening interview by the other therapist would be warranted.

7   The potential two-edged sword represented by an alternative possibility of support versus competition amongst the co-therapists was cited above in the introduction to this chapter. This theme requires further development.

It is axiomatic in psychoanalytic psychotherapy that the emotional needs of the therapist must not depend upon the patient for gratification. However we may idealize psychotherapists and psychoanalysts, theorizing that the work and the fee should be its own reward and that the therapist's personal recognition of his own good work should be sufficient; this does not always appear to be so with many or most of the practitioners with whom we are acquainted. Nor is 'honest appreciation' and 'gratitude' by patients always honest and grateful; it may be manipulative and masking quite different attitudes. A competent co-therapist can provide realistic support; this takes the form of encouragement and appreciation of good work on the one hand, and help in the case of confusion or errors on the other. The co-therapist in the post-group processing session can act as a counterweight to false or defensive praise from patients that would otherwise tempt a therapist to believe he has done better work or is more insightful than he in fact is.

In the often very difficult times when prolonged or violent anger is directed at one therapist the other therapist's support in the form of objectivity and understanding is invaluable, and makes it much more possible to endure and accept the negative barrage without attempting to mollify the patients or to change their focus by means of a seemingly valid interpretation; tolerating such anger may be one of the hardest tasks an individual psychotherapist faces, particularly in these days when infantile aggression in many cases has replaced infantile sexuality as the major hidden and forbidden drive component within psychotherapy patients. To sum up: the ego of the therapist is protected against stress and is kept healthy by the presence of and relationship with a professional peer – this is an incalculable boon for the patients.

If, however, rivalry or conflict were present between co-therapists, the strain on the ego of each and the loss to the group members would be devastating. Without going into detail, it is sufficient to say that counter-transference on the part of one or both therapists would become unmanageable in time; this would repeat past experiences or inflict fresh traumas upon the group members instead of therapeutic progress.

There are two antidotes for such development. One is the quality of the relationship between the co-therapists, with emphasis on regular, session-by-session discussion (post-session processing) of the therapy as it progresses and including mutually sharing the subjective responses of the co-therapists to the group and to each other. *This must be done!* Time for this must be regularly scheduled and insisted upon whatever the inconvenience resulting from it may be, and the fee charged should be adequate to cover the time spent 'processing' so that no excuse can be made to avoid it.

Should real differences arise between co-therapists and they cannot be worked out through open communication, one or the other should leave the group as quickly as is compatible with general group working-through processes. Following that, a careful self-scrutiny by both co-therapists as to how they got themselves into such a situation is in order, quite probably including a trip back to the couch.

8   Closely related to point 7 is a second possible *folie-à-deux*. Inevitably therapists make errors of omission or commission because of ignorance or, more likely, counter-transference. This is where the co-therapist can be extremely helpful and where nothing exists in a single therapist group to replace this particular function of the co-therapist (this resource is not present in individual psychotherapy, either). The mistakes of one therapist can be noted and corrected by the other therapist in a co-therapy situation; if they result from ignorance, relevant theoretical knowledge can be supplied, if they are counter-transference manifestations, that too can be made clear, if a secure and non-threatening relationship exists. It is *not* the function of one co-therapist to perform therapy with the other, a tactful, empathic discussion should be enough to alert one co-therapist to the probable presence of counter-transference around certain issues or members – he will work it out himself or make arrangements to work it out with professional help other than that of his co-therapist.

The obverse of such helpful behavior would, of course, be criticism, justified or otherwise, of one co-therapist by the other. This will lead to defensive behavior in the form of unfruitful discussion of group process between co-therapists and loss of sensitivity on both parts while performing therapy. The 'third ear' cannot operate in the required way when one is expecting to be criticized by one's partner or if one is sitting there waiting for one's partner to foul up again. Conversely, nothing is more conducive to a good 'third ear' than the knowledge that if a mistake is made, or something is misperceived, a friend is there to set it right, and to help one in a non-punitive way to understand how and why it went wrong. An example of defensive behavior between co-therapists is given in chapter 9.

9   The interpersonal dimension is very difficult and unrewarding for many people today. This difficulty is often rooted in the early failure of adequate development in the sphere of object relations because congruence between need and environment (other persons) was lacking. The co-therapy group provides a unique opportunity for patients to experience a working relationship between adult figures which demonstrates congruence and support for the patient rather than competition for his love and manipulation of him. This new experience exerts a powerful therapeutic force at several levels: first, the patient sees and becomes part of a system in which people can work together for expression and gratification of individual needs without exploiting one another; further, the patient finds that there is much more satisfaction available for him personally in a situation where two mature adults can function on his behalf as a team. This contrasts with what he experienced in his own childhood where object relations were faulty or gratification was seen as connected to exploitation and manipulation either by the parents of one another or between parents and children. The range of potentially corrective transference phenomena and interpretation goes from symbiotic through oedipal levels of fixation.

We can best summarize the advantages of the co-therapy mode in this way. It creates, like any other group method, a system that serves as an input to a group of patients. That input, when it includes a consonant or valid relationship between co-therapists, is more powerful by a quantum jump than the best input provided in a therapy group working without a co-therapist. This opinion will, naturally, be objected to by many in the field; that will not make it less correct.

The following set of facts and opinions is likely to be even more objectionable to a greater number of group psychotherapists. Psychoanalysis teaches us that the more correct the interpretation, the louder the 'ouch' is likely to be. There *are* disadvantages to the psychotherapist in a co-therapy situation. More to the point, there are advantages to going it alone. The following is at least a partial list of those advantages.

1   The financial gain is greater; one can make twice as much money if one goes it alone. There seems to be a 'going rate' for group psychotherapy, as there is for individual psychotherapy, and one is likely to get patients to pay that rate whether a single therapist or a pair of therapists is to be conducting the treatment. And if one believes that this therapy is as good as, and especially if he can convince himself that it is better than, that performed by a pair of co-therapists, why should he halve his fee, or why shouldn't he charge his patients as much as they charge theirs? And so he does.

2   There is greater freedom in making all the practical arrangements at one's own discretion. Fee, time, place, and duration of sessions are clearly most convenient for the psychotherapist who can arrange them exactly to suit himself. Another person's schedule or wishes are never going to suit one as well as one's own. Co-therapists must accommodate to one another as well as to patients and single therapists do not have to accommodate to anyone but patients.

3   A single group psychotherapist can act out his counter-transference urges to the limits of his self-awareness. There is no other authoritative person in a position to scrutinize the behavior of the therapist and to call attention to questionable actions or interventions. There is no peer available with whom one must discuss doubts or second thoughts, and who also has access to the data. For there is no question that psychotherapists, despite their best intentions, will distort that data when counter-transference is in operation.

4   A special source of gratification is available to the single group therapist. Although it is only another form of counter-transference, it is more subtle and correspondingly more widespread than obvious forms of acting out as discussed above. We are referring to the gratification of the therapist's narcissism. He does not have to share the positive transference of the group members with anyone else. And, further, no one disagrees with him or tells him that he missed the point of some group behavior, thus wounding his self-esteem. It is true that patients may tell him unpleasant things but he can choose to dismiss such statements as projection, negative transference or whatever; this is not so easy to do with statements made by a respected peer.

Thus, the single group therapist can make more money, better arrange things for his or her own convenience, act out counter-transference urges with less check, and get a maximum of narcissistic gratification. The reader will not, however, have failed to notice by now that each of the advantages to the single psychotherapist is either of *no benefit* to the group members or represents clear *disadvantages* to them.

This brief chapter has described the advantages and disadvantages of the co-therapy method from the perspective of a pair of psycho-analytically trained co-therapists. The advantages listed include: ongoing consultation on diagnosis, psychodynamics, and group level appropriateness; opportunity for increased clarification and scope of transference phenomena as related to parental imagos, less interruption of ongoing group process by therapist absence, as well as greater opportunity to explore, on the spot, the dynamics of feelings about therapist absence; likelihood of more consistent and microscopic under-standing by the therapist of ongoing material from sessions; increased analytic power resulting from complementarity of therapist dynamics; larger pool of available and appropriate patients for each group; greater therapist effectiveness because of support from his co-therapist, an effective counterweight against counter-transference in each therapist is provided by the other; and the opportunity to observe and analyze reactions to interpersonal behaviors between parental figures.

The disadvantages of the co-therapy method listed include: financial loss to the therapist; decreased freedom for the therapist to make his own idiosyncratic arrangements, loss of possible counter-transference gratifications; and reduction of potential for narcissistic gratification for the therapist. It was noted that disadvantages to therapists practicing co-therapy do not necessarily represent disadvantages for their patients whereas, except for a possibly increased financial burden, advantages of the co-therapy method to the therapists are always advantageous to patients also.

Appendix 1
Phases of group development

The tables below summarize seven aspects of the phases of group development that are described by Herb Shepard and Warren Bennis. We are grateful to Dr Bennis and Dr Shepard for their generous support of our theoretical journey, and their permission to reprint their tables in the same form that they appeared in their article 'A theory of group development' (1956, pp. 428, 434). These summary tables provided the prototype for ours, which are presented at the end of chapter 5.

Table App. 1 **Phases of group development (after Bennis and Shepard)**
Phase I Dependence–power relations

	Sub-phase 1 *Dependence–submission*	Sub-phase 2 *Counterdependence*	Sub-phase 3 *Resolution*
1 Emotional modality	Dependence–flight	Counterdependence–flight. Off-target fighting among members. Distrust of staff member. Ambivalence	Pairing. Intense involvement in group task
2 Content themes	Discussion of interpersonal problems external to training group	Discussion of group organization; i.e. what degree of structuring devices is needed for 'effective' group behavior?	Discussion and definition of trainer role
3 Dominant roles (central persons)	Assertive, aggressive members with rich previous organizational or social science experience	Most assertive counter-dependent and dependent members. Withdrawal of *less* assertive independents and dependents	Assertive independents
4 Group structure	Organized mainly into multi-sub-groups based on members' past experiences	Two tight sub-cliques consisting of leaders and members, of counter-dependents and dependents	Group unifies in pursuit of goal and develops internal authority system

5 Group activity	Self-oriented behavior reminiscent of most new social gatherings	Search for consensus mechanism: voting, setting up chairmen, search for 'valid' content subjects	Group members take over leadership roles formerly perceived as held by trainer
6 Group movement facilitated by	Staff member abnegation of traditional role of structuring situation, setting up rules of fair play, regulation of participation	Disenthrallment with staff member coupled with absorption of uncertainty by most assertive counter-dependent and dependent individuals. Sub-groups form to ward off anxiety	Revolt by assertive independents (catalysts) who fuse sub-groups into unity by initiating and engineering trainer exit (barometric event)
7 Main defenses	Projection Denigration of authority		Group moves into Phase II

Table App. 1 (cont.)
Phase II Interdependence–personal relations

	Sub-phase 4 Enchantment	Sub-phase 5 Disenchantment	Sub-phase 6 Consensual validation
1 Emotional modality	Pairing–flight. Group becomes a respected icon beyond further analysis	Fight–flight. Anxiety reactions. Distrust and suspicion of various group members	Pairing, understanding, acceptance
2 Content themes	Discussion of 'group history', and generally salutary aspects of course, group, and membership	Revival of content themes used in sub-phase 1: What is a group? What are we doing here? What are the goals of the group? What do I have to give up – personally – to belong to this group? (How much intimacy and affection is required?) Invasion of privacy vs. 'group-giving'. Setting up proper codes of social behavior	Course grading system. Discussion and assessment of member roles
3 Dominant roles (central persons)	General distribution of participation for first time. Overpersonals have salience	Most assertive counterpersonal and overpersonal individuals, with counterpersonals especially salient	Assertive independents

4 Group structure	Solidarity, fusion. High degree of camaraderie and suggestibility. Le Bon's description of 'group mind' would apply here	Restructuring of membership into two competing pre-dominant sub-groups made up of individuals who share similar attitudes concerning degree of intimacy required in social interaction, i.e. the counterpersonal and over-personal groups. The personal individuals remain uncommitted but act according to needs of situation	Diminishing of ties based on personal orientation. Group structure now presumably appropriate to needs of situation based on predominately substantive rather than emotional orientations. Consensus significantly easier on important issues
5 Group activity	Laughter, joking, humor. Planning out-of-class activities such as parties. The institutionalization of happiness to be accomplished by 'fun' activities. High rate of interaction and participation	Disparagement of group in a variety of ways: high rate of absenteeism, tardiness, balkiness in initiating total group interaction, frequent statements concerning worthlessness of group, denial of importance of group. Occasional member asking for individual help finally rejected by the group	Communication to others of self-system of interpersonal relations; i.e. making conscious to self, and others aware of, conceptual system one uses to predict consequences of personal behavior. Acceptance of group on reality terms

Table App. 1 (cont.)

	Sub-phase 4 Enchantment	Sub-phase 5 Disenchantment	Sub-phase 6 Consensual validation
6 Group movement facilitated by	Independence and achievement attained by trainer-rejection and its concomitant, deriving consensually some effective means for authority and control. (Sub-phase 3 rebellion bridges gap between sub-phases 2 and 4)	Disenchantment of group as a result of *fantasied expectations of group life*. The perceived threat to self-esteem that further group involvement signifies creates schism of group according to amount of affection and intimacy desired. The counterpersonal and overpersonal assertive individuals alleviate source of anxiety by disparaging or abnegating further group involvement. Sub-groups form to ward off anxiety	The external realities, group termination and the prescribed need for a course grading system, comprise the barometric event. Led by the personal individuals, the group tests reality and reduces autistic convictions concerning group involvement
7 Main defenses	Denial, isolation, intellectualization, and alienation		

Appendix 2
The force field

The following paragraphs demonstrate how theoretical models that have been derived from one theory can be used as a bridge construct to another theory.

The example that we use is one of Lewin's field theory models (the force field) which when applied to systems analysis concepts permits an operational definition of an inferred group goal to be developed.

Consider the following: the 'level of equilibrium' and 'system goal' are terms that are used interchangeably in systems analysis. A thermostatic system that is set for an equilibrium of between $60°$ and $70°$ F can be said to have this as a temperature goal. If the setting were unknown, this 'goal' could be inferred from the manner in which the temperature was regulated in the room. This is the same method by which we 'infer' the goal of a group: when the group's behavior appears to be 'regulated' in the balance between flight and fight, for example, we can infer that this is the goal.

Lewin's force field model is defined as a field of force that is the resultant of driving and restraining forces. The direction that the forces are driving toward describe a goal direction. The point on the goal continuum at which the forces are balanced is called, by Lewin, the 'level of equilibrium', which in our language would be the goal that could be inferred for the period of time of this balance. Thus in Lewin's force field, the level of equilibrium can be stated as an inferred goal (sub-goal) related by driving forces to a directional goal. However, driving forces in one direction serve as restraining forces in the opposite direction. Therefore a goal can be assumed at either end of the continuum, as shown by the diagram. When the group-as-a-whole is viewed as a system, then the driving forces towards one goal (in this case an inferred goal of fight) will represent one set of role forces, and the driving forces towards the opposite goal (in this case an inferred goal of flight) will represent an opposing set of role forces. In this sense, the group system is defined as a function of interdependent roles. Driving forces can also be translated into communication output behaviors from the systems.

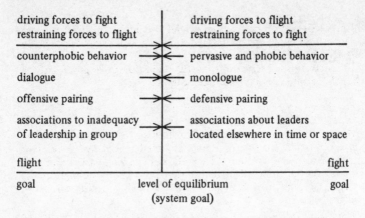

Figure A2.1 Adapted force field model showing driving forces to the goals of (a) flight and (b) fight, driving forces to flight serving as restraining forces to fight and vice versa; with the level of equilibrium representing the sub-goal which defines the inferred goal of the system at the time the field of force was described

The diagram represents the field of force that keeps the group caught in a balance at the level of equilibrium between moving toward or moving away from a problem experience. The rationale of placing fight and flight on a continuum of movement is Howard and Scott's theory of stress (1965) in which it is suggested that all human behavior can be explained in terms of problem-solving behavior that moves either toward or away from the problems that are inherent in the process of living. Conceptualizing the fight and flight modes in the group in this way permits an implicit 'as if' goal of fight and flight to be inferred at opposite ends of a continuum of movement, each one serving as a region of positive valence. Each force (arrow) thus represents two vectors, a driving force in relationship to the goal toward which it is pointing (fight for example) and a restraining force in relationship to the goal to which its companion, opposing arrow is pointing (flight for example). It is easiest to influence the direction of movement away from the level of equilibrium by weakening the restraining force than it is by strengthening the driving force. This is a particularly important fact as it applies to the process of psychotherapy because making conscious the pre-conscious or unconscious weakens the restraining force to ego control. Insight is thus a product of a change in the field of force.

The force field diagram has been developed from an actual episode in a training group, and the information was obtained from the participants as they analyzed their interaction. This same information could have been equally well inferred from direct observations of behavior. The usefulness of the force field lies in providing a way to describe group phenomenon so that they are linked to laws of change as well as to provide a conceptual model which the therapist can use as an objectified guide for his interventions, as well as a check on the accuracy of his perceptions.

Thus, organizing observations of the behavior in a group into a model, like the force field, permits the therapist to

1 Infer the group phase goal (flight or fight).
2 Use the model as a referent point for a decision as to whether the group is in fixation, regression or transition. The group would be judged in fixation if the force field depicted a repetitive, redundant state; in regression if the force field depicted an earlier and outmoded style of interaction; and in transition (from the flight phase to the fight phase) if individuals were actively working to change the group *status quo*.
3 Use the conclusions from his analysis of the force field to decide whether or not to intervene.
4 Use his knowledge of the 'laws' of the force field in order to prepare his intervention by choosing which restraining force to reduce.

It is, for example, easier to influence the direction of movement away from the level of equilibrium by weakening a resisting force than it is by strengthening a driving force. Thus, to help the group shift from the flight phase of development into the fight phase of development, the therapist would need to interpret the resistance to fight. He might, therefore, interpret the group support of monologue, and wonder aloud what it was about dialogue that the group was defending itself from.

If, on the other hand, the therapist decided that the group had not established sufficiently supportive pairing relationships to be able to work through the issues in the fight phase, he might interpret offensive pairing as a denial of the group's wish to have friends that they can turn to when they felt the need to be defended.

It is no accident that defining group laws support and/or explain the operation of other aspects of group phenomena. From knowledge of the force field it can be predicted that it is more efficient to facilitate group movement by reducing the restraining force than it is to attempt to increase the driving force. This makes sense from the point of view of the economics of energy. It requires more energy to increase the driving forces, and the energy required to increase the driving forces to the point that they overwhelm the restraining forces is exhausting and stressful work for the group and increases the overall tension in the system. This increased energy requirement, and its concomitant exhaustion and stress, serve as an additional restraining force. Thus the therapist who requires the group to increase the driving force as a method of facilitating group movement is like a facilitator who attempts to lighten Sisyphus' task by pushing with one hand and increasing the load with the other, instead of decreasing the slope of the hill.

Glossary

Achievement criteria, levels I, II and III See Summary Table, chapter 6, Three levels of group process.

Acting out The behavioral expression of emotional tension of a past intrapsychic conflict displaced onto the present situation in such a manner that aspects of the original tension-causing situation are reproduced symbolically.

Actual environment The past, present and future reality possibilities and probabilities for locomotion towards goals in the actual environmental territory.

Amplification A group phenomenon related to resonance and to the condenser phenomenon. The pool of associated ideas in the group is condensed into deep, primitive affect; the quantity and intensity of this affect is greatly increased as a function of the group.

Annihilation anxiety The unconscious expectation of being destroyed by the object, resulting from the projection of destructive wishes against the object.

'As if' goals Group goals that are inferred from group behavior. Synonymous with 'heuristic goals' which, when formulated, serve as hypotheses that explain group behavior more elegantly than the goals that are stated for or by the group.

Asch experiment An experiment which demonstrated the tendency of a person to distort perception under group pressure in conformity with the group's perceptions.

Authority as a developmental phase See Summary Table, chapter 5, Phases of group development

Authority issue See barometric event.

Barometric event Used by Bennis and Shepard in their theory of group development as a paradigm for the myth of the primal horde, as outlined by Freud, in which the rebellious followers band together, kill the leader and form a totemistic community (see Freud, 1957, p. 112).

Basic assumption group Bion's term for the 'as-if' group of dependency, flight-fight and pairing serving to defend the group against primitive anxiety.

Basic trust   The expectation that the mother will return and minister appropriately to the child according to its needs; the child's belief that there is thus a correspondence between the world and the child's needs.

Behavioral emphasis, levels I, II and III   See Summary Table, chapter 6, Three levels of group process.

Boundary   The definitional parameter of a system which differentiates between the inside and the outside of the system and is permeable.

Cohesiveness   See Summary Table, end of chapter 4, The constructs of group dynamics.

Communication   As above.

Communication behavior   Outputs from the group-as-a-whole system. Also see Summary Table, end of chapter 4, The constructs of group dynamics.

Condenser phenomenon   The sudden manifestation of deep and primitive wishes and affects, resulting from the pooling of related associations in a group.

Counterdependence as a developmental phase   See Summary Table, chapter 5, The phases of group development.

Counterdependents   Used in Bennis and Shepard's theory of group development to describe members who are counterdependently reactive to leadership. Modified to counterdependent role systems for the theory of the invisible group.

Counterpersonal as a developmental phase   See Summary Table, chapter 5, The phases of group development.

Counterpersonals   Used in Bennis and Shepard's theory of group development to describe members who have strong needs for interpersonal distance. Construct modified to counterpersonal role systems for the theory of invisible group.

Criteria for group viability, levels I, II and III   See Summary Table, chapter 6, Three levels of group process.

Deductive reasoning   Arguing from the general to the particular. Process by which theory or general law is connected to the observation of particular facts through an intermediate construct which is related to both theory and fact.

Dependence as a developmental phase   See Summary Table, chapter 5, The phases of group development.

Dependency group   See basic assumption group.

Dependents   Used in Bennis and Shepard's theory of group development to describe members who are dependently reactive to leadership. The construct is modified to the dependent role system for the theory of the invisible group.

Diagnostic guide, levels I, II and III   See Summary Table, chapter 6, Three levels of group process.

Disenchantment as a developmental phase   See Summary Table, chapter 5, The phases of group development

Displacement   A defense mechanism which consists of transferring an unconscious cathexis from its original object or situation to a more acceptable and less threatening object or situation; most systematically utilized in the analytic transference.

Dyad　Two persons (or systems) in relationship to each other.

Ego-autonomy　A term referring to the ego's biologically determined independence from the id in the performance of its own functions, and in having its own energies at its disposal for performing such functions.

Ego-syntonic pathology　Behaviors or ideas which, although acceptable to the ego, are maladaptive and are usually rationalized or split off; such behavior usually anchors behaviors and ideas acknowledged as pathological by the ego.

Enchantment as a developmental phase　See Summary Table, chapter 5, The phases of group development.

Entropy　In information theory and computer science, a measure of the informational content of a message evaluated as to its uncertainty. Used in theory of invisible group to mean communications outputs that are disorganized and disorganizing in that they convey 'noisy' information (messages that are ambiguous, redundant or contradictory).

Ethology　The study of animal behavior.

Fight as a developmental phase　See Summary Table, chapter 5, The phases of group development.

Flight as a developmental phase　As above.

Flight-fight group　Bion's term for one of the three basic assumption groups.

Folie-à-deux (à-trois, à-plusieurs)　An interaction between two (three, many) persons which satisfies the unconscious, pathological aims of both persons simultaneously, as when transference wishes of the patient are gratified by the analyst in satisfaction of his countertransference wishes.

Fusion　The state of a person who regressively loses the ability to recognize his separate existence and instead experiences psychic identity with another person; the psychotic loss of ego boundaries between the self and the mother accompanied by the cathexis of both with unneutralized energies.

Gestalt　Form, pattern, structure or configuration.

Goals　See Summary Table, end of chapter 4, The constructs of group dynamics.

Group-as-a-whole　The label given to a group when defined by inductive reasoning, and whose dynamics are explained as a qualitative function that is *different from* or *other than* the sum of its parts.

Group-as-a-whole system life space　gcb - f(G-A-W, GE); or group-as-a-whole communication behavior is a function of the group in interaction with the group environment, where the group environment is defined in terms of systems of group.

Group goals, levels I, II and III　See Summary Table, chapter 6, Three levels of group process.

Group-of-individuals　The label given to group when defined by inductive observation of the individuals in it, and whose dynamics are explained as a quantitative function that is *equal to* or *greater than* the sum of its parts.

Group-role system life space   rcb = f(R,G-A-W); group-role communication behavior is a function of the group-role in interaction with the group-as-a-whole environment.

Group structure, levels I, II and III   See Summary Table, chapter 6, Three levels of group process.

Group system cohesiveness   See Summary Table, end of chapter 4, The constructs of group dynamics.

Group system communication   As above.

Group system communcation behavior   As above.

Group system goals   As above.

Group system norms   As above.

Group system roles   As above.

Group system structure   As above.

Heuristic goals   See 'as if' goals.

Hot seat   Term applied to the process in a group in which one group member becomes the focus of group conformity pressure, frequently manifested aggressively.

Hypercathexis   Additional cathexis of already cathected ideas or situations, sometimes leading to consciousness, attention, or preparation for danger.

Imago   An unconscious, stereotypical set, based on a person's fantasies and distortions about a primary relationship experienced within the early familial environment; this set determines a person's reactions to others.

Independents   Used in Bennis and Shepard's theory of group development to describe members who are pro-active in relationship to work and unconflicted in their reactions to leadership. Not used in the theory of the invisible group.

Inductive reasoning   Arguing from the particular to the general. A reasoning process by which to arrive at general principles or laws by establishing propositions about the class of phenomena (i.e. group) on the basis of observations of a number of particular facts (i.e. human behavior).

Interdependence as a group phase   See Summary Table, chapter 5, The phases of group development.

Invisible group   A label given to the group that exists as a construct of deductive theory. Inferences from theory are applied as an application of the behavior of individuals and groups generally during a specific group event.

Invisible group, theory of the   Expression of group phenomena as a function of the input/output transactions between the systems person, member, role and group-as-a-whole.

Level I, II and III   See Summary Table, chapter 6, Three levels of group process.

Levels of group   As above.

Life space   Defined by Lewin as the person's (P) perception of his psychological environment (E), the knowledge of which makes it possible to predict his behavior (b); written as an equation: behavior is a function of the person in interaction with the environment, or b = f(P,E). Adapted in the theory of the invisible group to represent the life space of the systems person, member, role and group-as-a-whole, and to predict communication behavior as represented by inputs and outputs between systems.

Manic defense against depression   The hypercathexis of grandiose, pleasurable ideas, while splitting off or disavowing painful, sad feelings and the things and ideas associated with them.

Membership criteria, levels I, II and III   See Summary Table, chapter 6, Three levels of group process.

Member system cohesiveness   See Summary Table, end of chapter 4, The constructs of group dynamics.

Member system communication   As above.

Member system communication behavior   As above.

Member system goals   As above.

Member system life space   mcb = f(M, G); member communication behavior is a function of the member's irreality and reality perceptions of the group environment by irreality and reality inputs from the environment.

Member system norms   See Summary Table, end of chapter 4, The constructs of group dynamics.

Member system roles   As above.

Member system structure   As above.

Mirror phenomenon   Patients in a group are able to see various aspects of their social, psychological, and body images as reflected in other members. Use is made of projection, introjection, and identification in progressing towards a more realistic evaluation of one's self.

Narcissism   The investment of self and object representations with grandiose and exhibitionistic qualities and wishes; other people being experienced primarily as adjunctive sources of gratification.

Narcissistic transference   A transference characterized by a view of the analyst as an adjunct to or extension of the analysand, whose sole purpose is to gratify the grandiose and exhibitionistic wishes of the analysand.

Neg-entropic   Used in the theory of the invisible group to mean organized and organizing communication output (see entropy).

Noise   Defined in information theory as ambiguity, redundancy and contradiction in the communication channel which affects the transfer of information.

Norms   See Summary Table, end of chapter 4, The constructs of group dynamics.

Observing ego   That part of the psychic apparatus which retains its reality-testing function during psychotherapy or psychoanalysis, while the rest of the personality experiences regressive phenomena.

Obsessive-compulsive rationalization   Attempts at covering up the pathological character of obsessive thoughts and compulsive actions by providing logical or rational explanations for them.

Oedipal   Used in psychoanalytic theory as paradigm for conflicted attraction between child and parent of opposite sex, based on

the Greek myth of the foster child Oedipus who unwittingly killed
his father and married his mother and subsequently blinded himself;
thus fulfilling prophecy.

Operational objectives, levels I, II and III   See Summary Table, chapter
6, Three levels of group process.

Oral ambivalence   The coexistence of loving and destructive urges
toward the object arising during the sadistic, biting phase of oral
libidinal development.

Overpersonal as a developmental phase   See Summary Table, chapter
5, The phases of group development.

Overpersonals   Used in Bennis and Shepard's theory of group development to describe members who have strong needs for interpersonal
closeness. Construct modified to overpersonal role systems for the
theory of the invisible group.

Pairing group   Bion's term for one of the three basic assumption
groups.

Pathogenic introject   A bad object is brought into the psychic
apparatus by the process of introjection; the object is 'bad' because
it carries the projected, aggressive fantasies of the person who now
introjects it; its presence disrupts the adaptive functioning of the ego.

Perceptual discrimination style   The system's idiosyncratic style of
discriminating and integrating similarities and differences in the
organization of information. This, in turn,
1. Defines characteristics of the field of force which determine the
   organization of energy in relation to the system equilibrium;
2. Determines the characteristics of information output (communication behavior) in terms of reality and irreality information;
3. Influences boundary permeability through input-determining
   perceptual filter.

Person system cohesiveness   See Summary Table, end of chapter 4,
The constructs of group dynamics.

Person system communication   As above.

Person system communication behavior   As above.

Person system goals   As above.

Person-system life space   pcb = f(P,E); person communication
behavior is a function of the person in interaction with his psychological environment, defined by his reality and irreality information
store.

Person system norms   See Summary Table, end of chapter 4, The
constructs of group dynamics.

Person system roles   As above.

Person system structure   As above.

Person's life space   pcb = f(P,E). A person's communication behavior
is a function of the person in interaction with the psychological
(perceived) environment.

Phases of development, levels I, II and III   See Summary Table,
chapter 6, Three levels of group process.

Play-within-a-play   As in Shakespeare's *Hamlet* where the secondary
play symbolically enacts the major conflict in the primary. Used in

the theory of the invisible group as an example of the role system symbolically enacting the group-as-a-whole system conflict.

Power as a developmental phase   See Summary Table, chapter 5, Phases of group development.

Projective identification   An unconscious attempt to evoke one's own feelings, fantasies, and other psychic contents in the object in order to create an identification.

Rebellion as a developmental phase   See Summary Table, chapter 5, Phases of group development.

Resonance   The tendency in a group for each member to reverberate in response to any group event at whatever level his own fixation points and dynamics dictate; e.g. ambivalence will be experienced passively or actively, at a phallic and/or oral level, depending on each individual member's set.

Role system communication   See Summary Table, end of chapter 4, The constructs of group dynamics.

Role system communication behavior   As above.

Role system cohesiveness   As above.

Role system goals   As above.

Role system norms   As above.

Role system roles   As above.

Role system structure   As above.

Roles   As above.

Sadism   A fundamental component of instinctual life in which the instinctual aim is to enjoy the suffering or humiliation of other people.

Scapegoat   From the symbolic ritual of loading the 'goat' with society's sins and driving it into the desert leaving society blameless. Used in the theory of the invisible group to represent a group-as-a-whole conflict resolution strategy in which the conflict-producing aspect of the group role of goat (container of the group conflict) is then disowned in a group attack.

Splitting   An early defensive organization of the ego resulting in the coexistence of two contradictory attitudes which do not influence each other but instead alternate.

Structure   See Summary Table, end of chapter 4, The constructs of group dynamics.

Symbiosis as a developmental phase   See Summary Table, end of Chapter 5, Phases of group development.

Symptoms of fixation, levels I, II and III   See Summary Table, chapter 6, Three levels of group process.

System life space $cb = f(S,E)$ – where S = system; E = system environment which comprises the sub-systems, systems and supra-systems with which the defined system is in potential input/output relationship.

Systems in interaction   Systems are in interaction when neither system's boundary is permeable to the other.

Systems in transaction: dependent/independent   The dependent system in transaction has a boundary permeable to an independent system whose boundaries are impermeable to it.

Systems in transaction: interdependent Systems in interdependent transaction have boundaries permeable to each other.

T-group Training group originally formed in an academic setting with the purpose of teaching the dynamics of group that occur under the conditions of a power vacuum that is created by the leader's refraining from behaving as expected.

Theory of stress (Howard and Scott) Used in the theory of the invisible group to define all human behavior as problem-solving behavior that can be characterized in terms of fight, flight, freeze or work in relationship to a problem.

Theory of the invisible group Inductive description of group as a set of hierarchically and isomorphically related systems called person, member, role and group. Each one of these can be defined by the system life space which depicts the probable path to goal and thus predicts probable behavior of the system that the life space is representing.

Therapist positive/negative reinforcement behaviors, levels I, II and II See Summary Table, chapter 6, Three levels of group process.

Transactions Systems are in dependent transactions where one system's boundary is permeable to the other but the other is impermeable to it. Interdependent systems transactions are when both systems have boundaries that are permeable to each other's input.

Triad Three persons (or systems) in relationship to each other.

Visible group The observable group members and their behavior present during a group event which can be described, and the dynamics of which can be defined through the process of inductive reasoning.

Work as a developmental phase See Summary Table, chapter 5, The phases of group development.

Work group Bion's term for the reality-oriented, problem-solving aspect of the group process.

Working-through The process of interpreting and reinterpreting the material in psychotherapy, as the patient experiences and re-experiences his conflicts in all their different ramifications, levels, and areas; considered to be absolutely essential for structural change.

Recommended reading

General systems theory

Bertalanffy, L. von (1968), *General Systems Theory: Foundations, Development, Applications,* revised edn, George Brazillier, New York.

Ruben, B., and King, J. Y. (eds) (1975), *General Systems Theory in Human Communication,* Harden Book Co., Rochelle Park, NJ.

Group dynamics: general

Cartwright, D., and Zander, A. (eds) (1960), *Group Dynamics, Research and Theory,* 2nd edn, Row, Peterson & Co., Elmsford, New York.

Hare, P. A. (1962), *Handbook of Group Research,* Macmillan, New York.

Whitely, J. S., and Gordon, J. (1979), *Group Approaches in Psychiatry,* Routledge & Kegan Paul, London.

Group psychotherapy

Bion, W. R. (1959), *Experiences in Groups,* Tavistock, London.

Foulkes, S. H. (1975), *Group Analytic Psychotherapy, Method and Principles,* Gordon & Breech, London.

Psychoanalysis

Brenner, C. (1976), *Psychoanalytic Technique and Psychic Conflict,* International Universities Press, New York.

Hartmann, H. (1958), *Ego Psychology and the Problem of Adaptation,* International Universities Press, New York.

Jacobson, E. (1964), *The Self and the Object World,* International Universities Press, New York.

Kohut, H. (1977), *The Restoration of the Self,* International Universities Press, New York.

Laplanche, J., and Pontalis, J.-B. (1973), *The Language of Psychoanalysis,* W. W. Norton, New York.

Mahler, M. S. (1968), *On Human Symbiosis and the Vicissitudes of Individuation,* International Universities Press, New York.

Sandler, J., Dare, C., and Holder, A. (1973), *The Patient and the Analyst,* International Universities Press, New York.

Strachey, J. (ed.) (1966), *The Standard Edition of the Complete Psychological Works of Sigmund Freud,* The Hogarth Press and the Institute of Psycho-Analysis, London.

General background reading

Bennis, W. G., and Shepard, H. A. (1956), 'A theory of group development', *Human Relations,* vol. 9, no. 4, Nov.: 415–37.

Festinger, L. (1957), *A Theory of Cognitive Dissonance,* Rowe, Peterson & Co., Evanston, Ill.

Howard, A., and Scott, R. A. (1965), 'A proposed framework for the analysis of stress in the human organism', *Journal of Applied Behavioral Science,* 10: 141–60.

Lewin, K. (1951a), *Field Theory in Social Science,* Harper & Row, New York.

Watzlawick, P. (1976), *How Real is Real? Communication, Disinformation, Confusion,* Random House, New York.

Bibliography

Agazarian, Y. M. (1969), 'The agency agent of change, systems analysis approach' in Goldberg, M. H., and Swinton, J. R. (eds), *Blindness Research, The Expanding Frontier*, Pennsylvania State University Press, University Park and London.

Aristotle (1947), *Analytica Posteriora* (complete) in McKeon, N. (ed.), *Introduction to Aristotle*, Modern Library, New York.

Asch, F. E. (1951), 'Effects of group pressure upon the modification and distortion of judgement in groups, leadership and men' in Guetzkow, H. (ed.), *Group Leadership and Men*, Carnegie Press, Pittsburgh.

Ashby, W. R. (1965), *An Introduction to Cybernetics*, Wiley, New York.

Bateson, G., *et al.* (1956), 'Towards a theory of schizophrenia', *Journal of Behavior Science*, 1:251-6.

Bennis, W. G., and Shepard, H. A. (1956), 'A theory of group development', *Human Relations*, 9:415-37, No. 4, November.

Berne, E. (1964), *Games People Play*, Grove Press, New York.

Bertalanffy, L. von (1968), *General Systems Theory: Foundations, Development, Applications*, revised edn, George Braziller, New York.

Bertalanffy, L. von (1969), 'General systems theory and psychiatry, an overview' in Gray, W. *et al.* (eds), *General Systems Theory and Psychiatry*, Little Brown, Boston, ch. 2, part 1, pp. 33-50.

Bion, W. R. (1959), *Experiences in Groups*, Tavistock, London.

Bion, W. R. (1962), *Learning from Experience*, Heinemann, London.

Birdwhistle, R. L. (1960), 'Kinesics in communication' in Carpenter, E., and McLuhan, M. (eds), *Explorations in Communication*, Beacon Press, Boston.

Brenner, C. (1976), *Psychoanalytic Technique and Psychic Conflict*, International Universities Press, New York.

Carpenter, E., and McLuhan, M. (eds) (1960), *Explorations in Communication*, Beacon Press, Boston.

Cartwright, D. A. (ed.) (1951), *Field Theory in Social Science*, Harper & Row, New York.

Cartwright, D., and Zander, A. (eds) (1960), *Group Dynamics, Research and Theory*, 2nd edn, Row, Peterson & Co., Elmsford, New York.

Cherry, C. (1961), *On Human Communication,* Science Edition, New York.

Coch, L., and French Jr, R. P. (1948), 'Overcoming resistance to change', *Human Relations,* 1:512–42.

Dobzhansky, J. (1962), *The Evolution of the Human Species,* Yale University Press, New Haven and London.

Durkin, H. (1978), Unpublished Lecture Number One.

Festinger, L. (1957), *A Theory of Cognitive Dissonance,* Rowe, Peterson & Co., Evanston, Ill.

Festinger, L., and Aronson, E. (1960), 'The arousal and reduction of dissonance in social context' in Cartwright, D., and Zander, A. (eds), *Group Dynamics, Research and Theory,* 2nd edn, Rowe, Peterson & Co., Elmsford, New York.

Fine, R. (1973), *The Development of Freud's Thought,* Jason Aronson, New York.

Foulkes, S. H. (1965), *Therapeutic Group Analysis,* International Universities Press, New York.

Foulkes, S. H. (1975), *Group Analytic Psychotherapy, Method and Principles,* Gordon & Breech, London.

Foulkes, S. H., and Anthony, E. J. (1957, 2nd edn, 1965), *Group Psychotherapy, The Psychoanalytic Approach,* Penguin, Harmondsworth, Middlesex.

Foulkes, S. H., and Anthony, E. J. (1973), *Group Psychotherapy: The Psychoanalytic Approach,* 2nd edn, Penguin, Harmondsworth, Middlesex.

Freud, S. (1910), *The Future Prospects of Psycho-Analytic Therapy,* collected papers, II, 285; standard edn, XI, 144–5.

Freud, S. (1957), *Group Psychology and the Analysis of the Ego* (trans. and ed., J. Strachey), Hogarth Press and Institute of Psycho-Analysis, London. Written in 1921.

Gibb, J. R. (1956), *Factors Producing Defensive Behavior Within Groups,* Group Process Laboratory, University of Colorado, Boulder, Colo., August.

Giovacchini, P. L. (1975), *Tactics and Techniques in Psychoanalytic Therapy, vol. II, Countertransference,* Jason Aronson, New York.

Hare, P. A. (1962), *Handbook of Group Research,* Macmillan, New York.

Hartmann, H. (1958), *Ego Psychology and the Problem of Adaptation,* International Universities Press, New York.

Howard, A., and Scott, R. A. (1965), 'A proposed framework for the analysis of stress in the human organism', *Journal of Applied Behavioral Science,* 10:141–60.

Jacobs, T. (1973), 'Posture, gesture, and movement in the analyst: Cues to interpretation and countertransference', *Journal of the American Psychoanalytic Association,* 2:77–92.

Jacobson, E. (1964), *The Self and the Object World,* International Universities Press, New York.

Khan, R. M. (1973), 'The role of illusion in the analytic space and process', *The Annual of Psychoanalysis,* 1:231–46.

Kohut, H. (1971), *The Analysis of the Self.* International Universities Press, New York.

Kohut, H. (1977), *The Restoration of the Self,* International Universities Press, New York.

Korzybski, A. (1948), *Science and Sanity: An Introduction to Non-Aristotelian Systems and General Semantics,* 3rd edn, International Non-Aristotelian Library, distr. Institute of General Semantics, Lakeville, Conn.

Langs, R. (1978), *The Listening Process,* Jason Aronson, New York.

Laplanche, J., and Pontalis, J.-B. (1973), *The Language of Psycho-analysis,* W. W. Norton, New York.

Lewin, K. (1948), *Resolving Social Conflicts,* Harper & Row, New York.

Lewin, K. (1951a), *Field Theory in Social Science,* Harper & Row, New York.

Lewin, K. (1951b), *Frontier in Group Dynamics,* Harper & Row, New York.

Lewin, K., Lippitt, R., and White, R. (1939), 'Patterns of aggressive behavior in experimentally created "social climate" ', *Journal of Psychology,* 10:271-99.

Mahler, M. S. (1968), *On Human Symbiosis and the Vicissitudes of Individuation,* International Universities Press, New York.

Malan, D. H., Balfour, F. H. D., Hood, V. G., and Shooter, A. M. N. (1976), 'Group psychotherapy: A long-term follow-up study', *Archives of General Psychiatry,* 33:1303-15.

Manos, N. (1979), 'An outpatient psychotherapy group in Greece', *International Journal of Group Psychotherapy,* XXIX, 2, April, p. 253.

Menninger, K., and Holzman, P. (1973), *Theory of Psychoanalytic Technique,* Basic Books, New York.

Miller, J. G. (1961), *Information Input Overload, Self-Organizing Systems,* Washington Press, Washington, DC.

Perloff, M. B. (1967), 'Advances in analytic group therapy' in Marmor, J. (ed.), *Frontiers of Psychoanalysis,* Basic Books, New York.

Pines, M. (ed.) (in press), *The Evolution of Group Analysis,* Routledge & Kegan Paul, London.

Reik, J. (1948), *Listening with the Third Ear,* Grove Press, New York.

Ruben, B., and King, J. Y. (eds) (1975), *General Systems Theory in Human Communication,* Harden Book Co., Rochelle Park, NJ.

Ruesch, J., and Bateson, G. (1951), *Communication: The Social Matrix of Psychiatry,* W. W. Norton, New York.

Sandler, J., Dare, C., and Holder, A. (1973), *The Patient and the Analyst,* International Universities Press, New York.

Scheff, T. J. (1963), 'The role of the mentally ill and the dynamics of mental disorder', *Sociometry,* 26:426-35.

Schutz, W. C. (1958), *FIRO: A three-dimensional Theory of Inter-personal Behavior,* Holt, Rinehart & Winston, New York.

Schutz, W. C. (1978), *FIRO: Awareness Scales Manual,* Consulting Psychologists Press, Palo Alto.

Shannon, C. E., and Weaver, W. (1964), *The Mathematical Theory of Communication,* University of Illinois Press, Urbana, Ill.

Simon, A., and Agazarian, Y. (1967), *S.A.V.I., Sequential Analysis of Verbal Interaction,* Research for Better Schools, Philadelphia.

Strachey, J. (ed.) (1966), *The Standard Edition of the Complete Psychological Works of Sigmund Freud,* The Hogarth Press and the Institute of Psycho-Analysis, London.

Watzlawick, P. (1976), *How Real is Real? Communication, Disinformation, Confusion,* Random House, New York.

Watzlawick, P., Beavin, J. H., and Jackson, D. D. (1967), *Pragmatics of Human Communication, a Study of Interactional Patterns, Pathologies and Paradoxes,* W. W. Norton, New York.

Weinberg, H. L. (1973), *Levels of Knowing and Existence: Studies in General Semantics,* Institute of General Semantics, Lakeville, Conn.

Whitely, J. S., and Gordon, J. (1979), *Group Approaches in Psychiatry,* Routledge & Kegan Paul, London.

Wiener, N. (1961), *Cybernetics,* 2nd edn, Wiley, New York.

Yalom, I. D. (1970), *The Theory and Practice of Group Psychotherapy,* Basic Books, New York.

Yovits, A. (1962), *Self Organizing Systems,* Spartan Books, Washington.

Index